W9-ACI-717

BY JOHN DOUGLAS
AND MARK OLSHAKER

Mindhunter: Inside the FBI's Elite Serial Crimes Unit

Unabomber: On the Trail of America's
Most-Wanted Serial Killer

Journey into Darkness

Obsession

The Anatomy of Motive

Broken Wings

The Cases That Haunt Us

BY JOHN DOUGLAS

The Abduction of Etan Patz

Man Down

Sexual Homicide: Patterns and Motives
(with Robert K. Ressler and Ann W. Burgess)

Crime Classification Manual
(with Ann W. Burgess, Allen G. Burgess,
and Robert K. Ressler)

John Douglas's Guide to Careers in the FBI

BY STEPHEN SINGULAR

Talked to Death: The Life and Murder of Alan Berg

A Killing in the Family

A Season on the Reservation
(with Kareem Abdul-Jabbar)

JOHN DOUGLAS
with STEPHEN SINGULAR

A TRUE STORY OF
SEX AND DEATH
ON THE INTERNET

ANYONE YOU
WANT ME TO BE

A LISA DREW BOOK

POCKET STAR BOOKS
New York   London   Toronto   Sydney

A Pocket Star Book published by
POCKET BOOKS, a division of Simon & Schuster, Inc.
1230 Avenue of the Americas, New York, NY 10020

Copyright © 2003 by John Douglas with Stephen Singular

Originally published in hardcover in 2003 by Scribner

All rights reserved, including the right to reproduce
this book or portions thereof in any form whatsoever.
For information address Scribner, 1230 Avenue
of the Americas, New York, NY 10020

ISBN: 0-7434-4880-4

First Pocket Books paperback edition June 2004

10   9   8   7   6   5   4   3   2   1

POCKET STAR BOOKS and colophon are registered
trademarks of Simon & Schuster, Inc.

Cover design and illustration by James Wang

Manufactured in the United States of America

For information regarding special discounts for bulk purchases,
please contact Simon & Schuster Special Sales at
-800-456-6798 or business@simonandschuster.com.

CONTENTS

INTRODUCTION

by John Douglas

By the mid-1980s, I'd been employed by the FBI for more than a decade and had helped create the Behavioral Science Unit at Quantico, Virginia. Using FBI profiling techniques, our unit had been pursuing serial killers from coast to coast and assisting law enforcement in identifying some of the most dangerous criminals in the United States. As we'd gained success and built a national reputation, police departments across the country had sought our help in solving difficult cases. I was consumed with this job and had few colleagues to delegate responsibilities to. More and more people wanted the FBI's help, and how could I turn down requests from those hunting serial killers? How could I not help families that had been victimized by the worst of crimes? When could I learn to say no? The answer to the last question came in 1983, when I went into a coma and barely escaped death. This brush with mortality caused me to lower my workload and to consider retirement. In 1995, I walked away from the job I loved.

I left the Bureau but didn't lose any of my desire to educate the public about protecting themselves from extremely dangerous people. I wrote about my FBI career in *Mindhunter*, which gave laypeople access to information and techniques used by the federal government to locate and catch serial murderers. I spoke on college campuses about how to keep yourself from becoming a victim. After hearing my presentation, listeners often came up to me and shared their own experiences with violent crime. When shaking their hands or looking into their eyes, I could tell that they'd been raped or robbed or deeply hurt by others. They were "silent victims," too ashamed or embarrassed to step forward and talk to law enforcement about what had been done to them. They were afraid of being victimized again—this time by the judicial system. I believe that criminals should be punished to the fullest extent of the law, but I could not fault these people for not wanting to testify because of the fear they lived with every day. Nothing was more satisfying to me than telling people how to protect themselves from predators.

I believed that law enforcement was making progress in the war on crime—until something happened that no one could have predicted. In the midnineties, the Internet arrived, and along with its great contribution to our society in so many areas, it began generating an entirely new criminal realm. The Wild, Wild West had returned, but this time it didn't look like cowboys and Indians or lawmen and gunslingers shooting at each other on the American frontier. Things had become much more complicated. The new outlaws were sitting at keyboards typing—and defrauding, robbing, manipulating, and seducing people all over the world, and in some cases, ending their lives. After watching the dramatic spread of on-line crime, I realized that the same techniques and insights we'd discovered at the FBI could now be applied in cyberspace.

Criminals had found a new hunting ground, and instead of preying on a handful of people as they might have done in the past, these on-line predators could contact and manipulate tens or hundreds or even thousands of victims at a time. Instead of cruising the streets for potential victims, they were cruising the information highway. The possibilities were infinite and law enforcement was having trouble even figuring out how to use this new technology, let alone how to find and stop the perpetrators. There often weren't enough qualified people tracking on-line criminals, and cyber-investigations were highly complicated. If police departments had had more resources in place a few years ago, the story you are about to read might not have unfolded in the same way with the same number of victims.

In 2000, my coauthor, Stephen Singular, told me that he'd been following the John Robinson case in suburban Kansas City. I began reading about the case and talking to some of those involved in the Robinson investigation. The more I read, the more intrigued I became. This was the first known example of a serial killer using the Internet to find his victims, seduce them with his charm and the promise of a better life, lure them to his turf, and kill them. It was a deeply compelling example of how the Net could be abused by the most dangerous people in our society. It showed how someone with an extensive criminal background could transfer his predatory skills into the high-tech world—and just how vulnerable people can be in cyberspace. All of my previous work about serial killers seemed to have led me in the direction of this story. I suddenly had a new mission: to tell the public that the same dangers it had needed to be aware of in the regular world, it now had to be aware of in the on-line realm. You absolutely could not take for granted that people were who they said they were in cyberspace. Once you logged on to the Internet and began exchanging e-mails, you needed to be smarter and more vigilant than ever.

The John Robinson story, which is an amazing tale in itself, needed to be shared with those looking for romance and sex on-line. It was the best window I'd yet found into the new emotional and criminal reality that high technology had created. New machines had created new crimes—and new law enforcement tools. Robinson made history on the Net, and so did those who caught him.

The purpose of this book is educational—and it's intended to be a warning. The on-line world has changed the nature of the awareness required to prevent yourself from being victimized. In the off-line world, you can pick up on the physical signals coming from people who could do you harm. You can use your intuition, your survival instincts, your senses, and your common sense to know when trouble is near. In cyberspace, you're cut off from your senses and some of your instincts. You're often dealing with a fantasyland that is unlike anything that preceded it. You don't see the whole person at the other end of your e-mail but interact with a stranger who is only showing a small and highly selective portion of himself or herself. When you operate in such a place, you need to be keenly attuned to who you are and what you're doing, as well as what possible predators are doing. Had the women in these pages been more discerning about such things, they might be alive today.

More than anything else, the arrival of the Internet inside private residences triggered the need for a new level of thought regarding this magnificent technological tool. The essence of that thought was simple: "Be conscious of what your computer is capable of and whom it can connect you to. It has effectively invited the entire world into your home, but is everyone welcome?"

In other words, you needed to become your own profiler of human behavior. You needed not only to understand the drives of the people the Net had hooked you up to—their desires and their real motivations—but just as importantly, you needed to understand yourself. What were your own weaknesses and vulnerabilities? What were your most secret longings? Where and how could you be manipulated? What were you afraid of? What kind of flattery were you most susceptible to? How did you see yourself? How did you want others to see you? What did you feel you were lacking that only another person could provide? Where were your emotional buttons and how easily could they be pushed? What parts of yourself did you have control over and which parts were you willing to let someone else control?

Several of these questions might have been casual, but not all of them were. As the following story demonstrates, some held the power of life and death.

PREFACE

In March 2000, the phone rang in Steve Haymes's office and the voice on the line was urgent. Somebody needed to talk to him right now. Haymes was a parole officer in Liberty, Missouri, a suburb northeast of Kansas City, and in a sense he'd been expecting this call for fifteen years. He'd also been dreading it. The caller was part of a newly created task force put together by the police department in Lenexa, a suburb of Kansas City, Kansas. The Kansas-Missouri border runs through the heart of Kansas City and Haymes worked only a handful of miles from the Lenexa station. As soon as he answered the phone, the parole officer knew the matter was serious.

"The task force said they wanted to speak to me about someone," he recalls. "They didn't tell me who but said they needed to meet with me immediately. They came out here to Liberty that same day and asked me if the name John Robinson meant anything to me. I said, 'Absolutely, and I've got a file here on him about yea thick.'"

"Yea" translated into roughly twelve to fourteen inches high. The file contained, among other things, the names of several local women who'd been missing for about a decade and a half.

Haymes welcomed the men into his office at the Missouri Board of Probation and Parole in a one-story beige building set behind a gas station and mini-mart. They began asking him questions and he began dredging up disturbing memories. The officer's hair was a little grayer than it had been back in 1985, when he'd first looked into Robinson's background, but he was still trim and his blue eyes conveyed intelligence and sensitivity. It was those eyes that had put him in this job throughout the past quarter century. In college, Haymes had studied criminal justice and had wanted to pursue a career in law enforcement, but faulty eyesight had kept him from becoming a policeman. He'd found work overseeing those on parole. Behind his small mustache, soft voice, and polite manner was an intensity and tenacity that in the mid-1980s had led him into the most frustrating investigation of his life.

"I'd maintained Robinson's file for all those years between 1985 and 2000," he says. "Normally, after a couple of years, some of that information would be in archives or destroyed, but fifteen years later his entire file was sitting in my desk. It had never gotten far from me."

When he brought the file out for the detectives on the task force, they were amazed at its size and complexity. Haymes himself was surprised to hear about the new allegations against Robinson, especially those involving the Internet. Yet, when he thought about it, he realized that the con man had always used the latest technology for his new schemes. That was part of his pattern, his evolution through the criminal justice system during the past thirty-five years. Until now, Haymes had been the only person who'd closely examined that pattern or paid close attention to Robinson. No one else had woven together the whole tapestry of his past or penetrated the surface of his personality. No one else had seen the full range of his activities, some of which almost defied belief, or where they might be leading. No one else had looked deeply at Robinson's roots or tried to uncover the source of his behavior or extremely unusual psychology. Nobody but Haymes had imagined what law enforcement was actually confronting.

Early in 1985, the slightly built parole officer had undertaken this mission alone—and in March 2000 he was still haunted by it. He was about to become a lot more haunted.

Hard Choices
& Missed Opportunities

I

n 1919, Al Capone had first arrived in Chicago from Brooklyn. He'd been sent there by Mafia boss Johnny Torrio, who wanted him to take over the rackets in the Windy City. The following year Prohibition was instituted across the United States, and Capone seized this opportunity to turn illicit booze into an empire. His home base was Cicero, a western suburb of Chicago, and prostitution rings, gambling, and bootleg-liquor operations were run from his headquarters in the Hawthorne Arms Hotel on Twenty-second Street. If Cicero had long been known for its buying and selling of police and politicians, the action inside the Hawthorne Arms solidified its reputation for Mob corruption. At the same time, clean cops were aggressively starting to pursue Capone and his gang. Five years after coming to Chicago, Capone got into a gun battle with the authorities on Cicero Avenue, which left his brother Frank dead.

John Robinson's father, Henry, was eight when the violence erupted. The image of Frank Capone getting killed in the neighborhood—and then Al Capone repaying the favor the next year by dumping the corpse of Assistant State's Attorney General William H. McSwiggin on a Cicero street corner—was extremely vivid in the memories of local people. They often talked about the bloodshed and spoke with awe of Capone's headquarters, with its armed guards, metal windows, and impenetrable doors. Stories of the gangster and his crew were handed down from one Cicero generation to the next, part of a living oral history. On December 27, 1943, John Robinson entered a world where tales of legendary gangsters were common to every young boy.

In this neighborhood, having power and using it in illegal ways commanded respect. The streets were full of anecdotes about famous criminals who'd made up their own rules and lived by their own laws. Some locals admired those who could beat the system and make good money doing it, and a few old-timers regarded Capone as a hero. John Robinson heard these stories and absorbed them into his makeup, into his ideas about what was good and what was evil. He would not grow up to be a large boy or a strong one. He would not impress others with his physical prowess or good looks. As a youngster and later as an adult, he looked soft and round, friendly and harmless. If he was going to have power, he would have to find creative ways of getting it and using it. Al Capone had once said that you could go a lot further in life with a kind word and a gun than with just a kind word. Robinson only absorbed half of this adage—he would use kind words and smiles throughout his life to get what he wanted, but guns were not part of his routine. He didn't need them in his line of work.

He grew up with four siblings: an older brother, Henry Jr., whom he did not like at all; a younger brother, Donald, of whom he was quite fond; and two sisters, JoAnn and Mary Ellen. He was much closer to JoAnn than to Mary Ellen (this swinging back and forth between intense personal likes and dislikes would mark him for life). The

Robinson family lived in a well-kept but modest home at 4916 West Thirty-second Street. They drew little attention to themselves, and decades later, after Robinson became infamous, nobody in the neighborhood could even recall the people who'd once lived at this address. John's father, Henry, worked as a machinist for Western Electric. When sober, he was a steady presence in the family, hardworking and law-abiding, totally unlike the gangsters from Cicero's colorful past. From time to time, according to Robinson's prison records, the older man went on bad drinking binges that disrupted everything. Despite this, his middle son had warm memories of him.

John did not feel that way about his mother, Alberta, who held the family together and kept the kids in line. When one of them misbehaved, she meted out the discipline and punishment. Five decades later, Robinson's wife would testify to her coldness to John. Alberta demanded that her children be clean and neat, and she pushed them to better themselves. John seemed to respond to this prodding and was the most promising and ambitious of all the Robinson kids, the most eager to break out of their constraining blue-collar environment.

By thirteen, he'd channeled some of that ambition into becoming an Eagle Scout and was a senior patrol leader of Boy Scout Troop 259, sponsored by the Holy Name Society of Mary Queen of Heaven Roman Catholic Church in Chicago. A picture from that time shows a round-faced boy in his well-pressed Scout uniform; he's offering a cherubic smile to the camera and giving a patriotic three-fingered salute. He'd recently been accepted into downtown Chicago's renowned Quigley Preparatory Seminary for boys who were interested in becoming priests. He'd already told a number of people that he would eventually go to work in service to the Vatican.

A few weeks after making Eagle Scout, Robinson and 120 other Boy Scouts traveled to London to give a royal command performance for the newly crowned Queen Elizabeth II. Robinson, dressed in a bright red outfit, led all the others out onto the Palladium stage, becoming one of the first Americans to sing for Her Majesty and the youngest of his countrymen to appear at this acclaimed venue. The event made the front page of the *Chicago Tribune,* in an article headlined "Chicago Boy Scout Leads Troop to Sing for Queen." His troop put on what they called "The Gang Show," and after singing for the monarch, the boys gathered backstage to look at the celebrities who were also there to perform. When Judy Garland moved past him, Robinson boldly pursued her and caught up with the movie star, reaching out and shaking her hand.

"We Americans gotta stick together," he told her.

"You're right," she said, laughing and kissing him on the cheek.

Another actress, the British singer Gracie Fields, hugged Robinson and told him, "You're a mighty handsome youngster."

The kid from Cicero loved the attention and being in the spotlight, but he soon returned to the seminary and quietly resumed his studies, still thinking of becoming a priest. He was a good student but not a great one. He wouldn't be remembered there for his academic success but for his shrewdness: he always seemed to be thinking about what he would say or do next. He appeared to be calculating the effect he had on others and often acted as if he were smarter than everyone else. Yet he didn't leave behind a negative image at the school. He graduated from Quigley at seventeen, not having distinguished himself at all.

Rumors had begun to surround Robinson suggesting that he was involved in a lot of things besides pursuing a religious education. Growing up in Cicero, he'd been exposed not only to stories of legendary gangsters but to people with ongoing connections to the Mob. He'd watched his father trudge off to the smokestacks at Western Electric each day and watched the older man labor tirelessly to support a family on a workingman's wages. He'd watched his father seek escape from the grind in alcohol. By late adolescence Robinson knew that there were other, faster ways to turn a buck. His first exposure to crime came through meeting low-level underworld characters he did favors or legwork for, in exchange for money. By the close of his teenage years, his life had already become more complicated and entangled than it would have been on the narrow path toward the priesthood.

In 1961, he attended Cicero's Morton Junior College, and in later years he would claim to have become a fully trained medical X-ray technician there. He would also brag about receiving more medical training at West Suburban Hospital in Oak Park, Illinois. With these limited credentials, he was able to land a job in the X-ray department of a Chicago hospital. His career was launched, but it was not a career in medicine.

In 1964, Robinson met an attractive young blonde named Nancy Jo Lynch and she was soon pregnant. They rushed into matrimony in a Catholic ceremony and he went back to work at the hospital. The young couple were starting a marital dance that would last through every imaginable kind of turmoil—and survive into the next millennium. From the beginning, they were locked together by mutual need, a need so deep that apparently nothing could break it. Robinson had avoided legal trouble, but almost as soon he got married, this changed. His living expenses were increasing and he was under pressure to take care of his wife and his about-to-arrive child. He didn't respond to this by working harder or more hours. Before long, he was accused of stealing money from his employer.

Robinson's marrying a pregnant woman had been an embarrassment to his family, but this was worse. The young man whose life had seemed so promising just a few years earlier, when he'd earned the title of Eagle Scout and sung for the queen of England, was on a downward spiral, but maybe he could learn from his mistakes and not repeat them. When confronted by his bosses with the suspicion that he'd embezzled from the hospital, he asked for their help, begged for another chance. If they would not tell the police about his transgressions, he would pay them back everything he'd taken. They agreed to this arrangement and he was not charged with a crime. What he'd learned from his mistakes was that he could get away with doing illegal things—even when he'd been caught doing them.

II

Following his troubles at the Chicago hospital, Robinson decided to restart his career in another location, a couple of states to the west. He and Nancy relocated to Kansas City, where the couple began raising a family that would eventually include four children: John Jr., Kimberly, and twins Christopher and Christine. By touting his medical training, Robinson found a job performing pediatric X-rays at Children's Mercy Hospital and X-rays on adults at General Hospital, later known as Truman Medical Center. He'd shown his new employers letters of recommendation that he said came from Morton College and other documents stating that he was a medical lab technologist, a nuclear medical technologist, and a radiographic technologist. Robinson was quite good at talking about this kind of work and seemed knowledgeable. His colleagues thought he was outgoing and friendly, and initially many of them liked him—until they saw him perform his duties. He was clumsy with babies and pediatric patients. He spoke to infants as if they were grown-ups and handled them awkwardly. He could barely take an X ray or read the results, but still . . . this was the pediatric health care field and he was dealing with infants and small kids. This wasn't the sort of work one would be doing unless one was trained and competent, wasn't the sort of job that anyone told lies about. Maybe he was just nervous because this was a new job in a new hospital and a new city. Maybe his performance would improve with time and experience.

Neither Missouri nor Kansas required that X-ray technicians be licensed, so when Robinson had told his employers about his extensive medical training, they believed him. The American Registry of Radiologic Technologists, however, had no paperwork showing that he'd ever been certified in any of the areas he'd claimed to be. No records backed up his insistence that he'd received training at Chicago's West Suburban Hospital. At Children's Mercy Hospital, he'd covered the walls of his office with official-looking documents detailing his credentials (nobody at the facility realized that all of them had been forged from a boxful of blank certificates; whenever he needed a new degree or other qualification, he simply pulled one from the box and wrote on it whatever he wanted to). If no one had yet caught on to his scam, among his colleagues he was building a reputation as something of a wild man, a night owl who left his wife at home with their young son, John Jr., while he roamed the Kansas City nightclubs or tried to start up affairs with female coworkers. He seemed obsessed with human sexuality. He had a taste, people were saying, for one of the most notorious spots in K.C., the Jewel Box, a club that featured male transvestites. He was curious about the violent side of sex, a subject that was absolutely hushed up in the Midwest in the 1960s. That curiosity was not being satisfied inside his marriage, so he went looking outside of it. Between his glaring incompetence on the job and his extracurricular activities, his time at Children's Mercy was running out. When management fired him, he began searching for another position in the medical field.

Robinson was soon hired as a lab technician and office manager at Fountain Plaza X-Ray, a thriving business owned by Dr. Wallace Graham, President Harry Truman's personal physician. Dr. Graham, like many others, was quickly impressed with how Robinson presented himself, but the physician was an easy mark. President Truman himself had once warned Dr. Graham that while he was diligent and gifted in his work, he was naive about the darker side of human nature. In 1946, the president wrote a letter to Graham's father, lauding the physician but adding that he "is entirely too accommodating . . . the young doctor will work himself to death if he lets all the chiselers take advantage of him."

At his new job, Robinson once again tacked up a handful of medical certificates on his wall, proudly displaying them to all visitors. He also tried to seduce female patients in the X-ray lab and immediately saw an opportunity to exploit Dr. Graham. By late 1966, the office was losing so much money that it couldn't afford to give its employees Christmas bonuses, but nobody could figure out where all the missing funds had gone. Reports were surfacing about Robinson's bungling performance as a medical technician; one doctor complained that in his haste to complete a project, the young man had poured a urine sample down a sink. A few months later, a coworker alleged that Robinson was embezzling. He was not only using Dr. Graham's signature stamp on checks, but after he'd x-rayed patients, he asked them to pay him cash on the spot instead of making out a check to the office. Some people complied. Robinson was nothing if not brazen—stories were circulating through the office that he'd made love to a couple of colleagues and had seduced a patient, engaging her sympathy by telling her that his wife was terminally ill.

Those running Fountain Plaza X-Ray estimated that over $100,000 and perhaps as much as $300,000 was missing from their business. Dr. Graham also noticed that Robinson had taken an office chair that did not belong to him. When confronted with these accusations, Robinson tried to talk his way out of them by saying that he hadn't stolen anything but was only transferring money from one account to another. When that explanation failed, he offered to pay back all the funds he'd stolen. Dr. Graham would not hear of that and called in the Kansas police. Robinson was arrested and led away from the medical building in handcuffs. In August 1969, he was prosecuted and found guilty of "stealing by means of deceit," but remarkably, he served no time, receiving a sentence of three years probation.

In most jurisdictions there is a significant gap between time served for physically harming a human being and the leniency shown to those who engage in monetary or white-collar crime. Robinson's criminal career would underline this gap again and again. His first run-in with the law had resulted in little more than public shame and humiliation, but as he would repeatedly demonstrate in the years ahead, he could not be humiliated into changing his behavior. Each time he went to court, his wife, who now had two small children at home, would come to his aid. She would testify on his behalf as a character witness and praise his virtues as a husband and father. She would do whatever she could to bring him home. This pattern—of him committing offenses and her rallying to his side—would grow deeper and stranger in the years and decades ahead. It would stretch the definition of love far beyond what most people would consider the snapping point.

In some ways, Robinson worked in reverse from the

many criminals who have trouble establishing long-standing human relationships. He stayed married and kept expanding his family and his traditional roles as father, husband, and provider, but domestic stability did not settle him down. It appeared to bring out his wildness and his desire to break the law and to generate money any way he could. The more conventional one part of his life became, the more he explored the darker side of himself and others. The more his wife tried to help him, the more he violated the codes of marriage. He seemed to need the stability of marriage in order to give free rein to his deviancy. Once he took on adult responsibilities, he began searching the landscape for vulnerabilities in people and in the places that employed him. He was now under pressure to support his wife and children, and like most people, he constantly needed more income. He was never interested in working steadfastly for others, in getting raises and promotions and in gradually moving ahead. All that took far too much time. Routines were boring and pay increases lay in the distant future. He was lazy and ambitious at the same time. He enjoyed looking for weaknesses and hunting for criminal opportunities, using his natural intelligence and cunning to observe things carefully and to find areas to exploit.

Getting caught stealing from Dr. Graham didn't deter Robinson, but only made him more determined to get better at being a thief. On probation, he worked as the manager of a television rental company. When the owner learned that Robinson was lifting merchandise, he was fired but not arrested or prosecuted. He went back on the street looking for another chance—eager to convince someone new that he was something he was not.

III

In 1969, Robinson became a systems analyst for Mobil Oil, the best job he'd had thus far. His pleasant appearance and glib manner had once more helped him land the position. No one at Mobil had bothered to look into his background or discover that he was still on probation. His own probation officers were so impressed with his new employment that they believed he'd put his past behind him. While he was working at Mobil, the Missouri Board of Probation and Parole wrote a letter stating that Robinson "does not appear to be an individual who is basically inclined towards criminal activities and is motivated towards achieving middle class values."

A second officer, this one a female, offered the opinion that Robinson was "responding extremely well to probation." She encouraged him "to advance as far as possible with Mobil Oil."

His advancement was soon cut short when he was accused of stealing 6,200 postage stamps from the corporation, worth just under $400. He was fired and charged with theft but ended up paying restitution and again avoiding jail. Because his record in Kansas City was lengthening, he and Nancy made plans to leave the area. In 1970, the Robinsons moved back to Chicago. John took a job as an insurance salesman with a company known as R. B. Jones;

he made such a good impression on those interviewing him for this position that no one at the firm thought about running a background check on him (most businesses would normally only do that for those who raised suspicions). Robinson was good at selling insurance policies and had found something he could be successful doing, despite his having violated his parole in Kansas by coming to Illinois. But after working there only a few months, he began stealing from his employer, embezzling $5,586 before he was caught and fired. Once more the police were brought in, but Robinson avoided jail by making another restitution payment, and the charges against him were dismissed. With no prospects in front of him in Chicago, and a hopeless record as a corporate employee, he began thinking of a new career direction: he wanted to form his own business. He had more connections in the Kansas-Missouri region than in Illinois, so perhaps he should resettle in Kansas City. This decision was made easier when a Chicago court told a Kansas circuit court that he'd just broken the law in Illinois. Robinson was ordered back to the Kansas City area and his probation was extended for three more years. The family headed west again and settled in Raytown, Missouri, where he opened a medical consulting firm called Professional Services Association, Inc.

In 1971, as he was trying to establish the company, he was arrested for a parole violation and sent to jail. A Missouri probation officer named Gordon Morris studied Robinson's recent history of con games and small-time thefts, concluding that he needed some time behind bars. In Gordon's view, such punishment would serve as a "strong motivation for a complete reversal" in Robinson's behavior and could only help this chronic offender. In spite of the strong recommendation, the inmate was released after only several weeks. Back on the street, Robinson's criminal instincts immediately took over, and he created an investment scam designed to steal $30,000 from a retired schoolteacher named Evalee McKnight. His repeated arrests had done nothing to stop him from devising more scams.

An unsettling dance was taking place between Robinson and law enforcement. He kept breaking the law and the system kept giving this white-collar offender second and third and fourth chances. Many people believe that career criminals can be rehabilitated, but the evidence doesn't support that. Robinson perfectly fit the profile of someone who could not be motivated or forced to change. You can't rehabilitate a mind that was never "habilitated" or socialized in the first place. You can't force repeat offenders to feel the pain their actions cause the victims. You can't instill empathy in people who don't have this quality. You can't cure ingrained cruelty or greed. These people rarely get better in their psychological health after going into counseling, but only become worse and more sophisticated in their deviancy. They're often quite intelligent and quickly learn the buzz words of psychotherapy and the kinds of behavior that are effective in front of prison therapists or other officials. They know how to present themselves as if they've been rehabilitated—they know how to talk convincingly. Yet they are constantly becoming more mission-oriented and their mission is not to redeem themselves but to hone their skills. They don't study the real techniques of healing or of helping themselves; they study their own past errors when committing crimes so they can get better at their work and further their careers, just as any other professional does. And they get more daring.

One day in the early 1970s, Robinson was running Professional Services Association when he asked his secretary, Charlotte Bowersock, to prepare some letters for prospective clients. The letters stated that the Board of Regents of the University of Missouri–Kansas City "had voted [Robinson] the full rights and privileges of professor" at the School of Dentistry. The secretary, a naive young woman who needed this $7-an-hour job, mailed out the letters even though they were filled with lies. For one thing, UMKC had no Board of Regents. If that claim weren't bold enough, the dental school dean's signature had been forged on the letters. This scam was imaginative but went nowhere, unlike another one that Robinson had recently launched.

He'd presented himself to the University of Kansas Medical School as a financial consultant for its Family Practice Department. His new business suits, his smooth manner, his ability to speak well, and his general sense of appearing competent had impressed the physicians. Everyone he met at the medical school liked him, so Jack Walker, the department chairman, hired him, believing Robinson to be "an expert as a physicians' professional consultant," he once told the *Kansas City Star*. Walker was also the mayor of the respectable Kansas City suburb of Overland Park. He may have been taken in by the man's people skills, but he wasn't so impressed when he began hearing stories from the doctors in Orthopedic Surgery about how the new consultant was handling that department's money. A few months into the job, Robinson was let go after being suspected of theft.

Then he approached John Hartlein, the executive director for Marion Laboratories, a well-known pharmaceutical company in Kansas, and asked the director to invest in PSA. When Hartlein declined the offer, Robinson fabricated a letter from Marion Labs to himself, suggesting that it wanted to acquire PSA. Robinson sent the fake letter out to potential investors and added Hartlein's signature at the bottom. The letter also referred to the founder of Marion Labs, Ewing M. Kauffman, at that time the owner of the Kansas City Royals baseball team. Baseball was highly popular in Kansas City, and Kauffman was one of the metropolitan area's most prominent citizens. The letter read:

Dear Mr. Robinson,

At Mr. Kaufman's request, I have received the material you submitted on November 15, 1973. It is the decision of the executive committee that we continue discussions toward making Professional Services Association, Inc., a wholly owned subsidiary of Marion Laboratories, Inc.

We will begin discussions for your training manuals at $364,000. Of course, you will be a necessary part of our overall plan, if we can reach an agreement in the near future.

If you have any questions, please do not hesitate to contact me.

Yours very truly,
S/John E. Hartlin
John E. Hartlein
Group Executive

Robinson misspelled Hartlein's name the first time he used it and misspelled Kauffman's name as well, but those were minor problems compared to what was coming. Some of those who got the letter were quite familiar with both Marion Labs and Ewing Kauffman. Mac Cahal, a Prairie Village businessman, received the forgery and took it seriously, committing $2,500 to PSA before deciding that he should phone Kauffman to talk about this investment. The call unleashed outrage.

"Ewing," Cahal told the *Kansas City Star* some time later, "hit the ceiling."

Cahal contacted the Securities and Exchange Commission, which sent forth investigators to look into Mr. Robinson and Professional Services Association. Two years later, a Missouri federal grand jury returned a four-count indictment against him for false representation, securities fraud, and mail fraud. Six months after that, Robinson pled out to charges of interstate securities fraud. Three more weeks passed before U.S. district judge John W. Oliver levied a $2,500 fine against the defendant and extended his probation for another three years. Beyond that he received no further punishment. In the last half dozen years, he'd gotten two similar sentences but spent only weeks behind bars.

By pleading no contest to the most recent charges, Robinson was not held liable for money he'd taken from PSA investors; he didn't have to pay any of it back. In upcoming years, one of the most puzzling questions surrounding Robinson was where he got the money that allowed him not just to support a wife and four children, but to become upwardly mobile and to constantly improve his lifestyle. He never worked at any job for long, and his legal bills were ever present. One part of the answer was that while he made restitution on many of his thefts, law enforcement personnel have speculated that he never gave back all the money he stole from various businesses (he may, for example, have taken as much as a quarter million dollars from Dr. Graham and Fountain Plaza X-Ray and ended up pocketing most of it). Another suggestion is that by pleading guilty in 1976 to the PSA rap, he may have stashed away thousands of dollars that he'd collected from unsuspecting contributors to this business. Also, he occasionally presented himself to people as a money manager who was eager to help them grow their portfolios. He was as convincing in this role as he was in so many others.

"We can only guess how much money he took from people who were too ashamed to come forward to the police and report it," says one officer. "The problem is that when this happens to someone, they tend not to want to pursue the charges in court or to confess their own role. When you've been taken by a con man, you don't want to look foolish to the whole world."

IV

Until now, the Robinsons had been living on the Missouri side of the border, but in July 1977 they relocated to an upscale neighborhood across the state line in Kansas, in the town of Stanley. Using money he'd put away and a breezy, confident manner with the local financiers, Robinson was able to buy a $125,000 nine-room home that sat on three handsome acres in an area known as Pleasant Valley Farms. Stanley was in Johnson County, which was on its way, as people moved out from Kansas City to this rural landscape, to becoming one of the wealthiest suburban areas in the United States. In earlier centuries, Native Americans had lived here and left behind their Shawnee names. The wife of an Indian chief had been called Lenexa—today a large town in Johnson County. The county seat is Olathe, which is Shawnee for "beautiful." Johnson County was steadily growing, but Pleasant Valley Farms was removed from most of the population. The Robinson property, with its ranch-style design and its fashionable wooden shingles, was surrounded by elm and maple groves. It had a horse stable, a corral, a riding path, and a pond filled with fish. Robinson worked hard to fit in with the country gentry around him. He was often seen out in the yard tending his lawn or building a fence or making something for his children to play on.

At Pleasant Valley Farms, people knew Robinson as a devoted father and scoutmaster. Like his dad, John Jr. was well on his way to becoming an Eagle Scout. Robinson was very visible in the community, teaching Sunday school as an elder in the local Presbyterian church (although he'd been raised a Catholic); at Christmas, he dressed up like Santa Claus and gave treats to all the kids. As president of a group of volleyball officials, he assigned referees to games at area schools and was regarded as a good official himself. The license plate on his new Fiat read REFEREE. He'd also stepped forward and served as the "unofficial caretaker" at Pleasant Valley Farms, cleaning up the neighborhood pond and horse trails. He took over the Pleasant Valley Homeowners Association and even went so far as to haul a neighbor into court for failing to use wood shake shingles to reroof her house after it was hit by lightning. In Stanley, he was scaling the ladder of social responsibility and respectability. He bought a couple of horses so he could join the local equine groups. People at Pleasant Valley Farms knew nothing about his criminal past or brief periods in jail.

The move from Missouri to Kansas perfectly symbolized Robinson's rising fortunes. The Kansas side of the border, if you were living in Johnson County, was a more prestigious address, although some Missourians might argue the point. The 1,200-mile Santa Fe Trail had gone through the heart of Johnson County and helped make Kansas City a prosperous town. The patch of land connecting Kansas and Missouri had seen a lot of rivalry and a lot of American history—much of it bloody. Back in 1838, the federal government had forced a tribe of Potawatomi to leave their home in Indiana, and their route west became known as the Trail of Death. After sixty-one days of hardship and thirty-nine fatalities, their journey ended just to the south of Johnson County. Prior to the Civil War, the antislavery leader John Brown had roamed this part of Kansas spreading his message of freeing blacks from white ownership. In 1859, he was seized at Harpers Ferry in what is now West Virginia and executed.

Kansas was a free state and Missouri was not. Raiders from both sides crossed the border, burned property, and killed their fellow citizens. In Linn County (where John Robinson would eventually buy a farm), a pro-slavery leader named Charles Hamilton and his followers lined up eleven Free State citizens and shot them dead. In October 1864, the largest cavalry battle west of the Mississippi River also took place in Linn County; once the carnage ended, Americans began using the phrase "Bleeding Kansas." In 1892, the infamous Dalton gang was shot to death not far from Linn County, in the village of Coffeyville, after they were caught robbing a bank. Frank and Jesse James, the Ma Barker gang, and Pretty Boy Floyd terrorized the region as well. And in the mid–twentieth century, two of the world's best-known killers, Perry Smith and Dick Hickock, had started out on their murderous trek to western Kansas from the latter's home in Olathe. Their savage killing of all four members of the Clutter family was immortalized in Truman Capote's *In Cold Blood*. The Kansas side of the border had produced legendary lawmen as well, including Wild Bill Hickok and Buffalo Bill Cody.

Nearly a century and a half after the Civil War had ended, the old rivalry between Missouri and Kansas lived on in their politics, their sports competitions, and their views of one another across the state line, which ran through the center of Kansas City. The athletic teams at Kansas University in Lawrence were named the Jayhawks, after the pro-abolitionist Jayhawkers during the War Between the States, while the teams at Missouri University in Columbia were called the Tigers, after a home guard unit in the Civil War. In his own peculiar way, John Robinson would eventually rekindle the rivalry that had always existed along the border, but this time it would erupt inside the legal system. The residue of the Civil War still lingered around this landscape, and it didn't take much to set loose the old bad blood.

At Pleasant Valley Farms, Robinson introduced his newest business venture. Hydro-Gro, Inc., was a company based on the principle of hydroponics, a way of growing vegetables indoors within a nutrient-rich environment. He created a sixty-four-page booklet entitled *Fun with Home Hobby Hydroponics* and promoted the enterprise by boasting, "If It Grows, It Grows Better Hydroponically." He also promoted himself. As you read this booklet, he hoped that you would "form an acquaintance with John Robinson as a sensitive and stimulating human being. John Robinson's lifetime goal in hydroponics is as far reaching as his imagination." The book described water-based home-gardening products that allowed families to grow tomatoes, cucumbers, and other vegetables "in a minimum space, in the corner of your home." The literature featured a photograph of Robinson's five-year-old twins, Christopher and Christine, wearing their GROW YOUR OWN T-shirts and smiling into the camera. The Hydro-Gro literature claimed that Robinson was one of America's hydroponics pioneers and a "sought after lecturer, consultant and author."

Not everyone who knew Robinson at Pleasant Valley Farms remembered him as a sensitive human being. Some neighbors felt that he was condescending and abrupt when they queried him about the business or refused to invest in it. Others heard Robinson screaming at his family members inside their spacious home, with its two large stone fireplaces and well-kept grounds, or noticed him barking orders at his wife and kids. Still others heard stories about how Robinson raised his hand to his wife, and people could see for themselves that he fed his horses so little they seemed in danger of starving.

Those who decided to invest in Hydro-Gro came away from the experience with a very different view of Robinson from the one he promoted in the company literature. Nancy Rickard first met him after her father, Brooks, put up $25,000 for the new business. Nancy's mother, Beth, was dying of cancer and her father was under pressure to pay the mounting bills; he thought Hydro-Gro could bail him out. Robinson won over Nancy Rickard by hiring her to illustrate his how-to gardening booklet. The Rickards didn't see any return on their investment. In fact, they lost every penny of the $25,000. No one knows how many other investors suffered similar losses.

One thing in Robinson's promotional literature was accurate. He did have a "far reaching" imagination. This was evident when he tried to use Hydro-Gro in a grand publicity scheme designed to help finance his business. On December 8, 1977, the *Kansas City Times* carried an article stating that John Robinson, the president of an innovative hydroponics company, had been named the Man of the Year. The honor was bestowed on him for employing disabled people and was presented at a luncheon sponsored by a local sheltered-workshop association. The previous year he'd been a consultant at Kansas City's Blue Valley Sheltered Workshop. When Robert G. O'Bryant, the president of the workshop, resigned, Robinson was elected to take his place. From this position, he'd sent out a letter to Kansas City mayor Charles Wheeler on behalf of the Kansas City Area Association of Sheltered Workshops. The letter asked His Honor to attend a luncheon where awards would be presented to those who'd most generously helped these workshops.

"We would like," the official-looking document read, "to invite you or a representative from your office to be present for a small keynote speech."

Robinson wanted the mayor to be there so he could personally hand out the Kansas City Area Association of Sheltered Workshops' Man of the Year award.

Within two weeks, the mayor's office had gotten another letter that appeared to be signed by former Blue Valley Sheltered Workshop director Paul Reiff, who was described as the chairman of the Business Recognition Luncheon. This letter mentioned Mildred Quinnett, the mayor's secretary, and said that Wheeler had approved "a proclamation and commendation or a combination of the two" for the upcoming event. After sending out this letter, Robinson, to make certain that everything was on track for the luncheon, called Quinnett and impersonated Reiff. The trick worked. Robinson was scheduled to receive the proclamation from the mayor at City Hall on December 5, 1977, and two days later the luncheon went off as planned. State senator Mary Gant presented Robinson with a Man of the Year plaque and praised him in a speech that had been written by the honoree himself. He'd also put together a six-page press release about his accomplishments, which he distributed to the media. He claimed to have been a medical consultant for more than 165 clinics or other facilities; the press release quoted numerous medical people about his achievements, all of whom would later deny saying these things.

Nancy Robinson and her four children, along with about fifty local businessmen, came to the event. They all watched as her husband stood up and acted surprised to receive the plaque, then graciously thanked everyone for honoring him in this unexpected way. The *Kansas City Times* covered the story and its headline stated, "Group for Disabled Honors Area Man." As soon as the article went into print, the phones started ringing at the *Times* with howls of indignation from those who'd seemingly supported Robinson for this award.

The paper quickly discovered that the "honoree" had created the plaque himself, had done the writing promoting himself as a friend of the handicapped, and was behind the entire luncheon and the proclamation from the mayor. Robinson had fabricated everything. The mayor's office, after learning what had happened, was extremely embarrassed, and the group that had "given" Robinson the award demanded that he cease all contact with them. The *Kansas City Times* ran a scalding story on Robinson, entitled "Man-of-the-Year Ploy Backfires on 'Honoree.'" It exposed both his shameless exploitation of the sheltered workshops and his extensive criminal background. It was the first time Robinson had received any widespread publicity that began to hint at who he really was.

"I thought, this guy is bad news," Paul Reiff later told the *Kansas City Times*. "If he'll use an organization that's trying to help the disabled to his personal advantage, he'll stop at nothing."

Yet most people, including those in law enforcement, still thought of him as nothing more than a small-time con man, a chiseler.

V

In the past few years, Robinson had progressed from petty theft to conjuring up a false identity to stealing stamps to involving the Kansas City mayor's office in a relentlessly self-serving scam. The Man of the Year scheme had been foiled, but Robinson was starting to tap into other groups where he might find potential victims among the weak and the ill. Like others whom he would come to resemble, Robinson was drawn to jobs that involved counseling or the ministry or medically related work. Tex Watson of the Charles Manson family, for example, became a jailhouse minister. So did David Berkowitz, the "Son of Sam" killer in New York. When Berkowitz appeared on CNN's *Larry King Live,* he held a Bible in his hand throughout the interview, determined to show that even behind bars, he'd found a way to exert power and control over others. Robinson didn't gravitate to the medical profession or to helping the disabled because he wanted to aid his fellow citizens. His real career, which was still taking shape, perhaps even in his own mind, was locating groups of potential victims who were vulnerable or drawn to fantasy or dependent on others.

By the late 1970s, one person who'd been dependent on Robinson for the past decade and a half had apparently had about enough of him. His wife had turned into a chain-smoker whom people described as increasingly nervous and distressed. Nancy now clearly understood that she was living with a repeat offender who showed no signs of going straight. He'd embarrassed the whole family during the Man of the Year fiasco and seemed incapable of holding a job or staying out of legal trouble. He was unfaithful and this habit would only get worse as he got older. In the decades ahead, Nancy would be reduced to conducting surveillance on her husband, following him around in her car to see whom he was meeting and where. She would gather the details, confront him head-on, threaten to end their marriage, and even throw him out of the house, but his exile never lasted. The children always wanted him to come home, so she let him back in. He was capable of things that no one had yet imagined, but he seemed incapable of one thing: giving up his wife or family.

Nancy could see that her husband's penchant for trouble was escalating, and she was worried for her own future and her kids' welfare. If she knew that John was unfaithful, she did not know what seedy corners of Kansas City his curiosity had led him into. Nor did she know that he was becoming interested in the subculture of sadomasochistic sex. If all that wasn't enough, her neighbors were starting to talk about John because he made explicit comments to women at Pleasant Valley Farms. The Robinson children were chagrined at school because their father had gotten a reputation for getting arrested and creating humiliating public scenes. By 1980, after much inner debate and procrastination, Nancy was thinking of filing for divorce, but she waited a little longer, hoping things might improve.

Her body told her they wouldn't. Her eyes were growing more strained, her posture more stooped. She bent forward when she walked, as if she were pulling a heavy weight. Her face was losing some of its early prettiness, as worry set into pockets of her skin. This small, slightly built woman, with bright blond hair that swept around one side of her face, looked weathered and worn, but she did not file for a divorce or break up the family. She endured. She smoked and suffered along, deciding to stay with Robinson and to accommodate his bad moods and occasional outbursts, directed at her and others. She was the peacekeeper inside the home, the rock for her children, a steady presence in a situation that was at best unpredictable.

In time, she would take standing by your man to an entirely new level.

In 1979, Robinson was released from federal probation with a glowing recommendation from his probation officer, Ronald L. Ferguson. In his report, Ferguson wrote that he hoped Robinson "will continue to reap the rewards of good citizenship. . . ."

He began collecting those rewards by taking a job as the employee relations manager at Guy's Foods in Liberty, Missouri. The firm, which manufactured potato chips and other foods, had just been sold and was transitioning to new ownership. Typically, no one there had taken the time to look into Robinson's background; because of his apparent competence and warm personality, he'd quickly been hired. Guy's liked the way he handled people and his intelligence. Robinson seemed a natural at the position. He was being given another opportunity to have a legitimate career and might have progressed well at this solid and successful company, but that wasn't his goal. He merely used the facade of his personality while searching for the weak links at Guy's.

He began an affair with a secretary and launched another round of thefts inside the business. In one, he fabricated nonexistent Guy's employees and then paid them with money that went into his own pocket. In another, he deposited a $6,000 company check in an account that he created to look like a Guy's corporate account. He used some of these funds to rent an apartment in the Johnson County suburb of Olathe, where he had sexual escapades with female coworkers. Within a few months, tens of thousands of dollars were missing from the company. His more pressing problem was that his secretary had fallen for him and now told him that he had a clear-cut choice: he could either leave his wife and marry her—or she was going to the police with what she knew about his stealing from Guy's. When he wouldn't meet her demands, she made good on her threat. Nancy Robinson now knew for certain that her husband was not only a crook but had been cheating on her at the office.

At the end of 1980, Robinson was fired from Guy's and charged with felony theft. His former employer also hit him with a civil lawsuit asking for him to return what he'd stolen. He eventually settled the civil suit by agreeing to pay the company $50,000 in restitution (he paid Guy's $41,000 over the next four years). On the criminal side, he pled guilty to stealing a $6,000 check, but instead of facing the maximum seven years for this felony conviction, he was given only sixty days of "shock time" in the Clay County Jail. In addition to the sixty days, he got five years probation in Missouri.

After this last debacle, the idea of divorce again surfaced for Nancy Robinson. Many of her friends and acquaintances were openly encouraging her to take this step, but before following through on their advice, she and Robinson went into marriage counseling. Once again, they stayed together, for better and for worse.

Robinson soon opened another business, called Equi-Plus, which offered his management consulting services to the public and hoped to bring new products to the marketplace. One of those products was designed to provide the consumer a better way of storing bull sperm. He rented a suite in Overland Park and hung out an Equi-Plus sign. Before long, his phone started to ring. A local outfit named Back Care Systems conducted corporate seminars on treating employees' back pain on the job. The company approached Equi-Plus and asked Robinson to create a marketing plan for them. He undertook this mission and started sending them invoices that seemed very high—if not downright suspect. Unlike many other corporations in the past, Back Care Systems began gathering information on Robinson's history and his current activities. The company took its findings to the Johnson County district attorney's office, where prosecutors began yet another investigation into John Robinson. He sought legal advice and a lawyer told him that the best strategy for countering the authorities was to have sworn affidavits from customers about the soundness of his business. He came up with these documents by forging them.

The most significant aspect of Equi-Plus was not its success or failure, but something Robinson encountered while creating it. Two of his neighbors and potential Equi-Plus clients at Pleasant Valley Farms, Bob and Scott Davis, introduced him to the world of computers. In the early eighties, personal computers were quite rare, and the average person was barely aware of the technological revolution that was just a few years away. The Davises showed him what was on the high-tech horizon, and Robinson was intrigued by these new possibilities. He'd always found innovative ways to employ machines in his criminal adventures. He'd had his secretary use a typewriter to generate fake letters and he'd forged other documents by using Wite-Out and Xerox copiers. That seemed like amateur stuff compared to what he might be able to do with a word processor or more sophisticated technology. Everything could be utilized to expand his repertoire as a con man.

By mid-1984, he'd posed as so many different things to so many different people that he decided to try something new. He met a local woman named Mildred Amadi who desired to end her marriage to a Nigerian man and convinced her that he was an attorney who could represent her in divorce proceedings (he'd recently been telling other listeners that he'd raised the funds for Sylvester Stallone's latest hit movie, *First Blood*). As part of his arrangement with Amadi, she gave him her marriage license and birth certificate, as well as the title to her automobile. In the months ahead, she would complain to the authorities that she wasn't sure what Robinson had done with her legal documents and he never did help her get a divorce.

Until now the scams he'd run were designed to make money. They hurt people and were clearly illegal but had not yet taken a darker turn. They were just con games, but that was about to change because, like other serial criminals, Robinson was a work in progress, someone who was constantly evolving toward greater risks and new rewards. It was as though he kept pushing himself to see what he was capable of or if he had any limits at all.

VI

He now created yet another company in Overland Park, this one called Equi-II, which he described as providing consulting services to medical, agricultural, and charitable ventures. He also leased a duplex at 8110 Troost Avenue in Kansas City, Missouri, in a run-down neighborhood with a white population on one side of Troost and a black population on the other. Legal investigators, who were by now constantly paying attention to Robinson for one reason or another, believed that he'd hired an experienced prostitute to take charge of this Troost address and had opened a profitable bordello there. The word on some of the tougher Kansas City streets was that if you were drawn to rough sex, or to sadomasochistic practices, you could find it here. Robinson himself had reportedly been engaged in such pursuits for years before deciding to turn these interests into a source of revenue. There were also rumors of cocaine as another income stream.

In 1984, he hired an attractive nineteen-year-old woman named Paula Godfrey to work at Equi-II as a sales representative. The year before, the dark-haired Godfrey had graduated from Olathe North High School, where she'd been an honor student as a junior and a senior, as well as a talented figure skater. She was active in Senior Rowdies, an offshoot of the pep club, and contributed to a literary magazine called *Mindburst*. To improve her skating, she rose at 4 A.M. and practiced at a local rink called the King Louie Ice Château. She tried out for a professional skating job with the Walt Disney World on Ice Show, but illness hurt her performance and she began searching for work with a future.

When she met Robinson, she thought she'd found a solid company run by a good businessman. He told her that he wanted to enroll her and several other women in a clerical skills training program in San Antonio. Robinson would pay all of her expenses and provide her the work experience she was looking for. The two of them chose a date for her trip to Texas, and Robinson came to pick her up at her parents' home. As far as her family knew, they were headed to the Kansas City airport.

Her father, Bill Godfrey, expected a call from his daughter that evening or within the next few days, but it never came and the Godfreys got worried. Bill was so upset that he flew to San Antonio to track down Paula. He learned that she'd never checked into the hotel where she'd said she would be staying. He returned to Kansas City and went looking for Robinson, confronting him at his Equi-II office. Robinson was unflappable and told the man nothing useful. Godfrey said that if he didn't hear from his daughter in the next three days, there would be serious trouble. Almost immediately a handwritten note, postmarked Kansas City, appeared in the Godfreys' mailbox. It had apparently been sent from Paula and informed her parents that she was all right.

The letter said that she was grateful to Robinson for his help and she didn't want to see her family. It contained profanities, which was unusual for the young woman, was typed badly, and was signed, "Love Ya, Paula." Her father didn't recognize the signature and the grammar was unfamiliar. There was no reasonable explanation for her wanting to stop seeing her family. The Godfreys contacted the authorities to report that their daughter had vanished, but when the police went to Robinson and asked about the young woman, he said he couldn't help them out. He knew nothing about Paula Godfrey. He was just a businessman.

Her parents turned over the note to the Overland Park police, who examined it and concluded that it was real and their daughter was fine. They prepared to close the investigation. Only one probation officer was leery of Robinson's connection to Godfrey, but with the appearance of the letter, there wasn't much he could do.

"As the girl was of age and there was no evidence of wrongdoing," he wrote in a file, "Overland Park terminated their [missing-person] investigation."

The Godfreys themselves were maddened by this decision, but without the help of the local police they could do little on their own. So the investigation died.

Years later, another letter seemingly written by Paula would turn up. This one was found by Irv Blattner, a business connection of Robinson's who was also an ex-con. In the second letter, "Paula" was depicted as an angry acquaintance of Robinson's who'd stolen his money and his car before leaving the area. If the first letter had appeared out of character for her, the second one was even more so; it sounded nothing like the former ice-skater.

In the early 1990s, Blattner died of cancer. Before passing, he told a relative three things: John Robinson was extremely dangerous, the relative should contact federal agents if something happened to him, and Robinson was directly involved in the disappearance of Paula Godfrey. The cancer victim had saved the old letters as evidence in case he met an untimely or violent death.

No one ever discovered what happened to Paula Godfrey. Years later, however, reports surfaced about how in the mideighties Robinson had become connected to the cult of the International Council of Masters (ICM), a secretive sadomasochistic group with members all over the world. His taste for the exotic had apparently driven him toward those who shared his desires. The ICM cult had been born in London in 1921, when half a dozen professional men initiated a club to satisfy their deepest sexual longings, which ran in the direction of the Marquis de Sade's. The men had a common bond: they all wanted to be the dominant partner, or "master," of submissive women, known as slaves. One got into the club only after the founding members had determined that the initiate shared their tastes and could keep quiet about the cult. The ICM developed a communal dungeon, and each member contributed his own ideas and equipment for the purposes of sexual torture or rape. The masters wore purple, hooded robes and the slaves white robes with metal handcuffs joined to chains. The masters untied the slaves' robes in front of a group and made the women stand naked before everyone. The slaves were "trained" to do whatever was demanded of them, and the women were traded back and forth among the men. The men joined the cult of their own volition, but that wasn't necessarily true of all the women.

The ICM's first-ever meeting was held in a London basement warehouse on Friday, May 13, 1921. The cult eventually spread across Europe and opened dungeons in America. It was constantly looking for new recruits, and when Robinson learned of the group, he apparently decided to become a member. His superiors graded him on his ability to bring in new slaves, and over time he was so successful at this that he reputedly rose to the top of the local branch. His name inside the organization was Slavemaster. The young women he introduced to the other members wore leashes around their necks and other paraphernalia, and they did exactly as they were told—or faced the consequences. Anyone trying to escape the ICM was subject to violence. No one knows how many of the young women Robinson met in the eighties may have ended up as slaves in this group.

While exploring new sexual territory, he was building income from his various businesses. He constantly needed cash to keep up with all the expenses of his Pleasant Valley Farms home and his family of six. It took a lot of money to maintain appearances in the suburban community and to stay active in the town, the school, and the local church. It took a lot of money—and energy—to live one life in the town of Stanley and another down on Troost Avenue in Kansas City or as a member of the ICM. It took a lot of juggling of identities and multitasking and what, in psychological terms, was sometimes known as compartmentalization.

Robinson had an extraordinary ability to break up his personality and behavior into different pieces and to place them into radically different boxes; then he would pull out from one box or another whatever was needed for a particular occasion. He could be anyone he or someone else wanted him to be. If the role was refereeing a soccer game, he was convincing at that. If it was finding new slaves for the cult, he seemed to be successful at that too. According to some people, he was, despite all this philandering and criminal activities, a good father, just as he would one day be perceived as a good grandfather. He was able to separate the various aspects of his life and never let them touch each other—or let one undermine the other. It was as if he were not just one man, but half a dozen or more. He wasn't living just one life, but six or seven. And everything he did gave him new experiences and ideas for things he wanted to try in the future.

In the mideighties, he took his wife and children on an extended vacation to Europe. They visited several countries, and when he returned home, Robinson spoke enthusiastically about how much he'd enjoyed his trip abroad and all the sights they'd seen. While overseas, he was generating novel plans for using travel in a new financial scam, but it would take him another decade or so to perfect it. In the meantime, he'd found other unimaginable ways of making money.

One Man's Struggle

VII

In late 1984, Stephen Haymes was a district supervisor with the Missouri Board of Parole and Probation. Haymes had dealt with many criminals and knew well the difficulties of predicting their behavior. Some people changed in prison and straightened out their life. Others never did and always remained incorrigible. Until now, no one within the legal system had paid much attention to Robinson. He was regarded as just another crook with a penchant for small-time financial schemes (although a few of them had gone far beyond the penny-ante stuff of pinching stamps). Through his law enforcement sources in both Missouri and Kansas, Haymes had become aware of Robinson's involvement with Paula Godfrey and his potential role in her disappearance. But at that time the parolee was being supervised by a probation officer in Olathe, on the Kansas side of the border, and the Godfrey investigation had never really led anywhere. Still, Haymes had not forgotten about the man. When his phone rang on December 18, 1984, he got an alarming reminder about Robinson.

The call was from Ann Smith, who worked at Birthright, a local nonprofit group that counseled young, single mothers-to-be who didn't want abortions but desired to keep and support their children. Smith told Haymes that Robinson had called Birthright a few days before and told her that he and fifteen other suburban business leaders had started a philanthropic organization called Kansas City Outreach. It was offering a six-month program designed to provide job training, housing, and other assistance to unwed mothers. Each mother would live in an Olathe duplex and receive $800 a month plus expenses. Robinson said that he was on the board of a local bank and a member of the First Presbyterian Church of Stanley. He claimed that such prominent corporations as Xerox and IBM would be funding his group. He also said that he was working closely with Catholic Charities and provided names and agencies to back up this claim. It seemed to Ann Smith that he was knowledgeable in this area and had answers for everything. He wanted both Birthright and the Truman Medical Center to refer possible candidates to him, because he and his fellow businessmen wanted to give something back to the community.

During the Christmas holidays, the center informed Robinson that it had some African-American women with infants who were in need of assistance, but he wasn't interested in them. Whenever the center contacted him about available babies, he asked if the mother was black or white. This question set off a tremor or two inside the center because it was well known in social service circles that healthy white infants brought a higher price in the black-market adoption trade than African-American children. Since most of the mothers at Truman were black, Robinson didn't offer to help any of them.

When Haymes got the call from Ann Smith, he contacted a local judge, John Hutcherson, to inform him about Robinson's recent activities. Like Haymes, the judge was alarmed and told the officer to look into Robinson's background and learn whatever he could about his current work with unwed mothers. Haymes began digging into

Robinson's past and doing legwork on the case, but this took time and the holidays stretched everything out and days were falling off the calendar—while Haymes tried to figure out what to do next. He kept busy looking into Robinson's extensive criminal record and attempting to digest the last twenty years of the man's life. Robinson stayed busy too, searching for a white mother and child. Haymes was beginning to pursue the man more aggressively than anyone before him ever had, and to penetrate Robinson's facade, but the probation officer was just one beat behind Robinson's latest con game.

The Truman Medical Center had led Robinson to nineteen-year-old Lisa Stasi, a pretty, dark-haired young woman with a hard-luck story that had lately gotten harder. Her father had died during her childhood in Alabama and one of her brothers had killed himself. Lisa had grown up wanting stability and a family of her own. Her friends described her as lonely, vulnerable, and gullible but also determined to improve her circumstances. In 1983, she moved to Kansas City, and after meeting a young sailor named Carl Stasi, she appeared to have found what she was looking for. Lisa was soon pregnant, and in August 1984 the couple were married in Huntsville, Alabama. The following month she gave birth, but the arrival of the baby, a girl named Tiffany, did not bring peace to the household. The infant set off conflict that ended with Carl reenlisting in the navy and leaving the area, while Lisa entered Hope House, a battered women's shelter in Independence, Missouri. She was living at Hope House when a social worker named Cathy Stackpole told her that a generous Kansas City businessman wanted to help her and her daughter. Lisa was deeply relieved and delighted.

In early January 1985, when Robinson first met with

her, he promised to give Lisa an $800-a-month silk-screening job in Texas. If that didn't work out, he could assist her in getting her high school diploma in Kansas City or enroll her in another training program outside of Chicago. One way or another, he would get her out of the situation she was in. He did not present himself to her as John Robinson but as "John Osbourne," an Overland Park entrepreneur who ran a company called Equi-II. He'd been quite successful, he told her, and now he had a strong desire to do good works; there was no better way than assisting young mothers in need. It was also important to him that the mothers and their children not be separated, as they might be in other social service programs. That was why he'd started Kansas City Outreach and come to her aid.

After taking Lisa and the baby away from Truman Medical Center, Robinson did not move them into an Olathe duplex that he'd talked about, but installed them, along with two other young women, at a Rodeway Inn in Overland Park, near his Equi-II office. While Lisa stayed there, he promised her that he was finalizing travel plans for her and the baby. He had the young mother sign four blank pieces of stationery and provide him with the names and addresses of several of her relatives. He said that he needed these in order to keep them informed of where she was once she'd left Kansas City for Chicago.

On January 9, Lisa and Tiffany visited her sister-in-law, Kathy Klinginsmith, who was Carl Stasi's oldest sister. When the pair arrived at the Klinginsmiths', a blizzard was raging outside, so Lisa parked her old Toyota in front of their house and ran inside clutching the baby. She told Kathy that she'd met a benevolent Overland Park businessman who was going to help her finish high school and find a job in the Chicago area. Kathy was taken aback, but didn't know whether to intervene. Maybe this was a good development, a big step up from Hope House. When Lisa went to the phone and dialed the Rodeway Inn to check her messages, she learned that John Osbourne had been frantically looking for her at the motel. He'd panicked and begun calling around town trying to locate her. He now phoned her at the Klinginsmiths' and said he was coming to get her and the baby right now—despite the snowstorm that was covering the metropolitan area.

After hanging up, Lisa told Kathy that she wasn't sure if she should go with him. Kathy's concerns were quickly turning into fear. When Robinson reached the Klinginsmiths' address, he didn't park in front of it, but left his car down the block and out of sight, then walked through the blizzard to their home. Stepping inside, he didn't say a word to Kathy or acknowledge her in any way. He seemed absolutely focused on removing Lisa and the baby from the home. His behavior struck Kathy as abnormal and she sensed danger—it wasn't just Robinson's expression that was menacing. He stood five feet nine inches, weighed two hundred pounds, and was physically imposing to someone smaller than himself. He may have been fleshy and soft around the middle, but the glare in his eyes was anything but soft. It was disturbing and frightening. One day Klinginsmith would identify this expression as evil.

She tried to talk Lisa out of going, but Robinson insisted. Kathy was no match for the man's forcefulness. Against her sister-in-law's advice, the young mother walked out of the house with Tiffany held next to her, all three of them disappearing into the snowstorm. As Klinginsmith watched them go, she had a terrible feeling that she would never see Lisa or the baby again. The feeling was so powerful that she called her husband and said that something was badly wrong, that they had to take action now.

Robinson drove the mother and child back to the Rodeway Inn and checked them into Room 131. Lisa tried to phone her sister-in-law and then her mother-in-law, Betty Stasi, but could only contact Betty. During their conversation, Lisa cried and attempted to explain to the woman that she'd been forced to sign four pieces of paper or she would lose Tiffany. It was Betty herself, she'd been led to believe, who'd wanted her to do this and it was Betty who was trying to separate her from her daughter. Her mother-in-law told her this was totally false and cautioned her not to sign anything else.

"I've got to go," Lisa said into the phone. "Here they are."

She hung up, but her last three words stayed with Betty. She couldn't stop thinking about them because of the fear in Lisa's voice and because the words implied that more than one person had come into the room to take Lisa and Tiffany away. How many people were working with this strange man who had assumed control of Lisa's life? Where was he taking Lisa and Tiffany? Why had the young mother been asked to sign four pieces of paper? Betty was now as worried about Lisa and Tiffany as Kathy Klinginsmith was.

The next day the Klinginsmiths contacted the Overland Park Police Department, as well as the FBI. The police went to the Rodeway Inn, but Lisa and Tiffany had checked out. Their bill had been paid not by John Osbourne, who'd checked them into the room, but by John Robinson with an Equi-II corporate credit card. After Kathy Klinginsmith learned this, her husband, David, drove to the Equi-II address at Ninety-eighth Street and Metcalf Avenue. Robinson was there alone and David confronted him with questions about Lisa and Tiffany. Robinson acted put upon at first, indignant that anyone would think he had done anything wrong. Then he suddenly transformed himself—his eyes focusing and growing hard, his muscles stiffening, and anger taking over his entire body. He no longer looked soft. He flew into a rage and pushed the man out of his office.

David Klinginsmith was shaken up. He would soon tell the police about receiving a strange phone message from someone named "Father Martin." This was apparently a priest from the local City Union Mission, who indicated to David that Lisa and Tiffany were all right. When David tried to follow up on the message and talk with Father Martin, there was no one by that name to be found. And no one seemed to know what had become of Lisa and Tiffany Stasi.

Robinson had taken the baby girl to his home in Stanley and handed the child over to his wife, who was surprised that her husband was in custody of an infant. Nancy Robinson, who'd raised four kids of her own, was also surprised by Tiffany's condition. The baby smelled bad, had dirt under her fingernails, and needed diapers and food. She had arrived at the house with nothing. Nancy bathed her and then went out into a snowstorm and got supplies for the child. As she was taking care of the infant, John explained to her that the baby had come from a private adoption agency and that he'd had to pay $4,000 for her. He'd apparently somehow gotten the adoption papers from the office of an Olathe attorney named Doug Wood, who would one day become a Johnson County commissioner. Robinson told his wife that Don and Helen Robinson, his younger brother and sister-in-law from Chicago, would be flying in the next day to adopt the baby.

The Chicago couple had been married about a decade and had no children of their own. Helen had taken fertility drugs to become pregnant, but this hadn't worked. For some time, the couple had been looking for a way to adopt. At a 1983 family reunion, Don had told his brother that he'd been pursuing this goal by working with Catholic Charities and a Lutheran agency, but he'd had no luck. Adoption fees were high and the wait was several years. He'd asked John if he knew any attorneys who handled adoptions or if he knew any single women who might want to give up their child to a good family. John said that he was willing to help and was aware of a lawyer who specialized in this area. Although the older brother had been in and out of jail on numerous charges, Don didn't seem to have many qualms about enlisting his aid in finding a baby. The younger Robinson sibling was soon on the phone with an attorney who used the name Doug Wood, and Wood was eager to offer his services for an adoption.

In the spring of 1984, John told Don to send him a check made out to Equi-II in the amount of $2,500. The money was to be disbursed to several people and a baby would be available in October of that year. Don and Helen were overjoyed by this news and began preparing for the infant's arrival. They created a nursery in their home and made plans to furnish it with a crib, baby toys, and clothes. When October came, John explained that some things had changed and the baby wasn't yet available. The Robinsons were disappointed but willing to be patient and see what developed. Three months later John called them and said that he'd found a baby but the infant was Italian and had medical problems and big feet. He advised that they pass, so they did. A few days later he phoned again and asked the couple to fly to Kansas at once. On the morning of January 10, they landed in Kansas City and were met by John at the airport. He told them how he'd dealt with lawyers and judges to arrange the adoption, and he provided them with notarized court documents and a birth certificate. After driving them to his office in Overland Park, John had them sign a "Petition for Adoption," and Don gave him a second check for $3,000.

John told them a tragic story about how the child had come to him: the baby's mother had committed suicide and left behind in a shelter this beautiful infant named Tiffany, who needed parents and a good home. Don and Helen were ecstatic as they rode with John back to his home and were thrilled to see the child outfitted in a tiny new dress. They renamed her Heather Tiffany and took pictures of the baby with her new relatives, including the Robinson children. In one photograph Heather is sitting near a rocking horse and on the lap of a proud-looking John Robinson. He wears a festive yellow sweater and a patriarchal smile, looking pleased to be the head of this clan. The following day Helen and Don and their new daughter returned home to Chicago.

In July 1985, John Robinson mailed his brother adoption documents bearing the signatures of Johnson County lawyers Doug Wood and Ronald Wood and Magistrate Judge Michael Farley. Judge Farley was a small-claims-court judge who did not handle adoptions. Doug Wood and Ronald Wood, who were unrelated, would one day testify that they never did any adoption work for Robinson or anyone else in his family. All three signatures had been forged. A woman named Evi Greshem was listed as the notary public on the adoption papers. She'd never been a notary public, but in 1985 she was Robinson's mistress and had engaged in sadomasochistic practices with him—at approximately the same time he was believed to be in the International Council of Masters. Greshem had also signed some blank pieces of paper because he'd asked her to.

VIII

While the Robinsons celebrated with pictures and congratulations, the Klinginsmith family had grown frantic with worry for Lisa and her baby. They weren't the only ones with grave suspicions about what had become of the mother and child. Birthright's Ann Smith had called Stanley's First Presbyterian Church to confirm Robinson's membership there and his connection to the Kansas City Outreach program. The church knew Robinson but had never heard of this adoption program. She then contacted the Olathe bank whose board Robinson claimed to sit on. They knew nothing at all about the man. This prompted Smith to call the Missouri Board of Probation and Parole, where she reached Stephen Haymes and told him about Robinson. Haymes went to work talking with local social workers.

"When I first pulled Robinson's file," says Haymes, "and took a look at what we had, I knew that he was a con man, a slick character. My immediate curiosity was, 'What's in it for him?' And I figured it was not something good. But what it was I didn't know and I spent a lot of time trying to figure out just that question.

"When I'm supervising a probationer or parolee, I'm trying to understand, 'Who is this person and what kind of danger do they represent to the public? Is it physical danger or theft?' I took a look at Robinson and knew that he was involved in a number of criminal activities going back to the 1969 conviction for theft from Dr. Graham and then theft in Chicago from a company he was working for there. I knew he was a classic con man and you don't see really good con men very often. We deal with a lot of pretty poor-quality criminals who do things very impulsively or under the influence of drugs or alcohol. A very sophisticated criminal we don't see that often, not those who set up businesses, some legitimate and some phony, and then manipulate things and steal by setting up limited partnerships or things like that.

"What really got my attention in 1984 was the initial call from Birthright that said he was trying to do something very suspicious with a young girl and a baby. This doesn't fit with him. It doesn't fit with a good con man because they go around the block to avoid hurting people because they're smart enough to know the penalties when people get hurt are much more significant."

Haymes tried to make personal contact with Robinson but wasn't successful. He then sent a letter to Robinson telling him to show up at his probation office on January 17, 1985. Robinson, who'd been busy with Lisa and Tiffany Stasi and with Don and Helen Robinson, ignored the letter. Haymes fired off a second one, sent by registered mail, demanding that Robinson appear at his office a week later, on January 24. Haymes also called the local field office of the FBI and asked if they knew of any baby-selling operations in Kansas City. The FBI responded by saying that they were aware of John Robinson and some of his activities but weren't currently investigating him, and they didn't know of any baby-selling rings in the area.

On January 24, Robinson came to Haymes's modest

North Kansas City office in an upbeat, bouncy mood, as he usually was when first presenting himself to people. He seemed confident and cheerful. Haymes had prepared for the meeting by laying out on his desk Robinson's extensive criminal file, so the visitor could see his past staring him right in the face. Robinson appeared unflappable, indifferent to the file. He was talkative, well-dressed, and forthcoming with certain information. When asked about Lisa and Tiffany, he acknowledged that he and five of his business connections were trying to help the unfortunate in the community and had approached both Birthright and Truman Medical Center looking for mothers with infants. Haymes questioned him about the apartment at 8110 Troost Avenue, which the officer believed he was running as a house of prostitution. Robinson said that he was currently offering living space to two young women there, and Haymes could drop by the address and talk with them himself.

The meeting was charged because Haymes sensed that he wasn't being told the truth yet he wasn't sure what the truth was. When he asked Robinson what he was receiving in return for all the good deeds he claimed to be doing, Robinson smiled and replied that he was getting the satisfaction of helping people worse off than himself. This was gratifying to someone of his nature. The answer only made the officer more edgy and frustrated.

"Robinson had a lot of excuses about where Lisa and Tiffany were and what had happened to them," Haymes says. "He'd set up some phony information out there trying to say that they were okay. With me, he was just indignant that—gosh, here he was trying to be nice and help people and he just couldn't believe that people would accuse him of doing something. But people were disappearing: Paula Godfrey and then Lisa and Tiffany. Some of what had happened with Paula—the letters and things like that—would also happen with Lisa. I believed that he was going from stealing to harming people now, but we still had pretty much nothing but dead ends on these cases."

Following the meeting, Haymes spoke to the Truman Medical Center, which had referred two other young women to Robinson, and was told they were doing fine under his supervision. But the center was aware that a third young woman whom it had sent to Robinson, Lisa Stasi, had lately vanished. Both the Truman Medical Center and the Overland Park Police Department had been looking for her but with no results.

When Haymes contacted the Overland Park Police Department about Stasi, he was told that they didn't believe a crime had been committed because there was no evidence suggesting this. The department did acknowledge that Paula Godfrey, who'd worked with Robinson in 1984, had also disappeared. The police explained that they hadn't pursued this case because of a letter her family had received, apparently written by Godfrey herself, stating that she was okay.

Haymes's suspicions deepened when he spoke with Stasi's relatives and others, learning that they'd just received typed letters supposedly from Lisa. One was addressed to Cathy Stackpole, the Hope House social worker. It contained punctuation errors and read in part:

Dear Cathy:

I want to thank you for all your help. I have decided to get away from this area and try and make a good life for me and Tiffany. . . . I borrowed some money from a friend and Tiffany and I are leaving Kansas City. The people you

referred me to were really nice and helped me with every-
thing. I am very greatful for everyones help. . . .

I will be fine. I know what I want and I am going to go
after it. Again thanks for your help and Hope House and
thanks for telling me about outreach. Everyone has been so
helpful I owe you a great deal.

(her signature)

Another letter was addressed to her mother-in-law, Betty
Stasi, and it read in part:

Betty
Thank you for all your help I do really appreciate it! I
have decided to leave Kansas City and try to make a new
life for myself and Tiffany. . . . She deserves a real mother
who works and takes care of her. The people at Hope
House and Outreach were really helpful, but I just
couldn't keep taking charity from them. I feel that I have to
get out on my own and prove than I can handle it
myself. . . . Marty [Lisa's brother] wanted me to go to
Alabama to take care of aunt Evelyn but I just can't. She is
so opinionated and hard to get along with right now I just
can't deal with her. Marty and I fought about it and I
know he will try to force me to go to Alabama. I am just
not going there.

I will let you know from time to time how I am and
what I am doing. Tell Carl that I will write him and let
him know where he can get in touch with me.

(her signature)

Despite this letter's personal details, Haymes doubted its
authenticity. So did Lisa's relatives. They told him that
Lisa didn't talk this way or know how to type.

On January 30, 1985, police officer Larry Dixon went to Robinson's business address and confronted him about Stasi. Robinson calmly told Dixon that a man named Bill had recently come to his office and said that he, Lisa, and Tiffany were all moving to Colorado to start a new life. This was the same story Betty Stasi had earlier heard and relayed to her son, Carl, concerning Lisa's whereabouts. After learning this, Carl Stasi, like the police, stopped trying to track down Lisa and Tiffany.

Stephen Haymes, however, did not stop looking for the mother and child or stop searching for what role Robinson may have played in their disappearance. The officer was dogged in his efforts but was also surrounded by persistent and troubling questions. Was Robinson as innocent as he portrayed himself to be? Or had he evolved from a con man into a homicidal predator who'd now killed at least two young women? Was he working alone or with a partner? What had Lisa's last words to Betty meant, when she'd said, "Here they are"? If Robinson was a killer and working by himself, how had he gotten rid of Stasi so quickly, in the middle of a terrible snowstorm, while taking care of a baby at the same time? Both the ground and the nearby rivers and lakes would surely have been frozen.

No bodies had shown up and there was no physical evidence of two murders. There was no evidence of any kind linking the man to the missing women—so how could Haymes persuade a judge that Robinson was dangerous or that his probation should be revoked?

IX

With all these questions in play, Haymes got together with Karen Gaddis and Sharon Jackson Turner, two social workers at the Truman Medical Center's Obstetrics Department who'd been involved with Lisa and Tiffany being handed over to Robinson. Haymes listened with dismay and then shock as they described how the man had presented himself to them and how he'd managed to gain custody of the mother and daughter. It was becoming clear to the officer that trusting people everywhere had been no match for the skills and cunning of John Robinson. Scamming a doctor was one thing. So was bilking potential investors out of a few thousand dollars. But talking seasoned professionals into letting him gain control of a vulnerable young mother and her child was something else altogether. Robinson had more skills than Haymes had realized. He was astounded at how quickly and easily the man had fooled the social workers.

He contacted Robinson to set up another visit. When they got together, Robinson told him that he had some new and useful information: a local woman had recently informed him that Stasi was back in Kansas City and had done some baby-sitting for her. If the police could track down the woman, they could probably find Lisa.

Haymes doubted this report and began calling Robinson

at odd hours and asking him unsettling questions, hoping to catch him off guard, but the probationer seemed to have an answer for everything. At the end of January, the officer dropped by Equi-II to see what the operation looked like. He noticed the array of medical diplomas on the walls and the document that said Equi-II belonged to the Kansas City Chamber of Commerce (it didn't, as Haymes soon found out). Robinson bragged about his Kansas City Outreach program and showed the visitor the extensive literature he'd created for Equi-II, which he described as a consulting firm with an emphasis on limited partnerships for cattle investors. Robinson talked with conviction, passion, and knowledge about Equi-II; he acted exactly like a successful financial consultant and would have convinced most people. The probation officer listened carefully, absorbing the information with a growing sense of incredulity and discomfort. He'd never seen anyone labor harder at building an image with elaborate stories and paperwork. Haymes kept looking for a scintilla of shame or a hint of guilt, but there was none. The officer had never encountered anybody like John Robinson. It was as if the man weren't merely playing a role, but believed everything he was saying—as if he became another person when he was talking.

While Robinson's crimes and the way he perpetrated them were groundbreaking in the study of serial killers, his overall personality was not unique. Robinson possesses the characteristics of a classic "antisocial personality." This disorder has nothing to do with having or not having the ability to socialize. Many antisocials are good at presenting themselves to others. They have superficial charm, above average intelligence, and the ability to masquerade. They are also emotionally stunted, unreliable, and insincere. Robinson fit all of these characteristics and then some. One thing he did not have was mental illness. He knew right from wrong and knew the consequences of his heinous acts on others.

In retrospect, Robinson reminded me of other killers whom I'd interviewed or studied. When you speak with these individuals, they have an answer for everything. Unless you thoroughly study their case, they can fool you. They'll tell you what they think you want to hear and project the blame on others. During one such interview, a convicted rapist told me that he hadn't raped anyone. He said, "The victim wasn't wearing any panties and was looking to have sex, so I obliged." Because Robinson had such superficial charm, he was able to easily manipulate his victims, his family, and early on the law enforcement community. We make the mistake of treating people like Robinson the way we expect to be treated. This doesn't work because what separates us from him is a conscience. Robinson had no conscience or remorse. He and others like him know and understand they are lying, but they don't get flushed in the face, shift their body, wet their dry lips, or look away when they lie. They'll look you right in the eye and tell you what good people they are and that they must be believed.

"The common criminals we deal with may lie," says Haymes, "but they're not very good at it. They'll tell you, 'I wasn't at the bar last night and I haven't been drinking,' when they reek of alcohol. It's pretty easy to break that lie down, and usually, when most people are cornered with a lie, they will come around and confess. He would never do that. No matter how tight you had him boxed in, he would just spin off and start a whole new set of lies. We would spend hours or days proving those were all lies and then we would have another set of lies to deal with. His inability to tell the truth, even when the truth might have done him better, was what struck me.

"Plus his demeanor was quite different from the average person we deal with. He was older and more refined as far as his education and skills. He always wore a coat and tie, soft-spoken, with a round, kind of boyish face. Nothing set him off easily as a criminal to the average person who had contact with him. He didn't meet the stereotype of the guy with tattoos."

Haymes soon paid another visit to Equi-II, this time with a second probation officer named Bill Neely. Both men questioned Robinson at length about Lisa and Tiffany, and he explained to them how a man named Bill had been waiting for the mother and daughter when he'd transported them to the Rodeway Inn during a snowstorm about a month earlier. The pair had left with Bill and that was the last he'd seen of them. When Haymes and Neely went to the Rodeway Inn to check out this story, the motel clerk recollected that Lisa and Tiffany had left the premises the final time with Robinson.

Haymes contacted the local FBI office and spoke to veteran Special Agent Thomas Lavin and his younger partner, Special Agent Jeffrey Dancer, about the two vanished women (Godfrey and Stasi) and the missing baby. Haymes not only wanted the FBI's expertise, but there were other legal issues as well. The Missouri-Kansas border ran right through Kansas City, and that made everything in this complicated set of circumstances even more complicated. Robinson used the old criminal trick of moving quickly between jurisdictions, something that other serial killers, such as Ted Bundy, had once done.

"Robinson was jumping back and forth across state

lines, which was frustrating to local law enforcement," says Haymes. "State lines are a pretty big barrier for local city police. Robinson lived in Kansas but had this supposed charitable apartment in Missouri. He was soliciting babies from organizations in Missouri and Kansas. Lisa Stasi was from northeast Kansas City, Missouri, but she technically disappeared out of Overland Park, which is in Kansas. So that creates all sorts of problems.

"I would not be surprised that Robinson didn't decide that the more he jumped around, the more difficult it would be. I don't know how much he intentionally chose these locations, but it was effective in making things more difficult for us."

The FBI agents did some legwork on Robinson and quickly discovered his activities on many criminal fronts. They also connected him with the ex-convict Irvin Blattner, who may have helped Robinson with several moneymaking scams. The U.S. Secret Service was investigating both men for forging a signature on a government check. While Haymes and the FBI were trying to construct a case against the pair, the district attorney's office in Johnson County was working on a parallel investigation into Equi-II and the apparently fraudulent role Robinson had played in posing as a divorce lawyer for Mildred Amadi. Law enforcement was moving in on Robinson from every side and his arrest seemed imminent, but the closer they got, the more resourceful he became.

One lead the police ran down was a Cora Holmes, who'd met Robinson through a stripper friend of hers. Holmes was looking for work and had called the man to see if he could employ her in any capacity. He explained to her that the cops were harassing him about a missing person and he needed her help. Holmes then lied to the police by telling them that Lisa had recently spent the night at her house and had made plans to go to Arkansas with a man named Bill Summers. While Holmes was misleading the local detectives, Special Agent Lavin and Overland Park detective Cindy Scott contacted the woman whom Robinson claimed had hired Stasi as a baby-sitter. Under their grilling, she admitted that she too had lied for Robinson because she owed him $900 and had posed nude for him in the past. He had pictures of her that she didn't want shown around, so she'd gone along with his plan.

The FBI now created a sting operation, using one of their agents to go undercover as a prostitute. Her job was to have lunch with Robinson, while wearing a wire, and to tape their conversation. During the meal, he told her that he ran a business employing call girls. His clientele consisted mostly of professional men—doctors, lawyers, and judges—and the work paid extremely well. If the agent was willing to fly to Dallas or Denver for a weekend encounter, she could earn as much as $3,000, but there were conditions. She would not only have sex with the men but engage in sadomasochistic practices. The S&M routines, he explained to the agent in disguise, usually involved a dominant partner and a submissive one, with the former pursuing pleasure through bondage or various ways of inflicting pain on the submissive. The dominant might spank, tie up, or whip the other person. The agent expressed her willingness to work with Robinson, but the FBI quickly backed off from the scheme because they realized just how serious he was and were afraid she might get hurt.

The FBI felt that Robinson was so dangerous that

they advised the Truman Medical Center to get the two young women out of his Troost Avenue apartment at once. The center complied.

Despite law enforcement's fears, making a case against Robinson was proving to be challenging. Both local and federal agencies, including the Secret Service, kept looking for ways to ensnare him, and in mid-March 1985, they got their first break. Irv Blattner turned against his old partner, signing a statement for the Secret Service that connected Robinson to numerous financial crimes. The next day, at a few minutes before noon on March 21, 1985, when Robinson showed up at Haymes's office for a probation meeting, he was arrested. As Haymes transported him to the Clay County Jail, Robinson told the officer that Tiffany and Lisa had been located and were doing just fine. After being booked, Robinson posted a $50,000 bond and was released within a few hours. He was back on the street and back in the business he was learning to master: finding novel ways of doing to others whatever his imagination could conceive of, while finding other ways of avoiding prison. Nothing quite matched the perverse joy of beating anyone out of anything he could.

"The con game was everything to him," Haymes says. "He just loved the game."

A day after Robinson's arrest, Haymes learned to his extreme concern that Robinson had not merely been trying to lure young mothers and children away from Hope House, but had been working the same scam at another Kansas City maternity home, known as the White House. To Haymes's knowledge, the man had not been successful in getting any kids out of the White House—so far.

On March 26, Robinson and his attorney, Bruce Houdek, came to Haymes's office to address the matter of Robinson's parole violation on three separate counts. Haymes was reviewing the probationer's recent behavior and putting together a report for Judge John Hutcherson.

"Robinson is continuing to involve himself in criminal activity," Haymes wrote in the report. "Robinson has been involved in criminal activity for over fifteen years and, to date, has managed to obtain probation when caught, but never required to serve a significant period of incarceration."

This seemed finally, after years of Robinson's avoiding any harsh punishment, about to change. The case against him was about to get much stronger, but Robinson was a far more creative and elusive adversary than anyone had yet understood.

X

In 1984, twenty-one-year-old Theresa Williams had come to Kansas City from Boise, Idaho. She'd worked around town at a Kmart and a self-service laundry before meeting Robinson at a McDonald's, where he initiated a conversation with her by telling the pretty young woman how much he could improve both her present and future life. His pitch worked and she soon became his lover, moving into the empty Troost apartment and performing sexual favors for men who paid for her services. In return, Robinson took care of her bills and supplied her with marijuana. Several things about him made Williams uncomfortable, but she was being provided for and didn't say too much. One was the gun he carried in a shoulder holster—in violation of his probation. Another was that he seemed to have a penchant for violence, including sexual violence, but this didn't prevent her from sleeping with or posing nude for him.

The longer she stayed with him, the more demanding Robinson became. On the evening of April 30, 1985, he had her don a sexy dress, paid her $1,200, and instructed her to leave the Troost Avenue apartment and wait in a nearby park for a limousine. When the car arrived, she jumped in and the driver blindfolded her and took her to another part of Kansas City. The car stopped at a mansion and the blindfold was removed. She was escorted inside, where a distinguished-looking, gray-haired man in his sixties accompanied her down to his basement. The man, known to her only as the Judge, had built a dungeon on the bottom floor of his home, designed for sadomasochism and various forms of sexual torture. After Williams stripped, he placed her on a device resembling a medieval rack and began to tighten the controls. Williams was experienced in the underground world of Eros and something of an adventurer herself, but this was more than she'd bargained for. This wasn't pleasurable but crossing the line into terror.

As she lay stretched out on the rack and he slowly increased the pressure, the pain overwhelmed her and she screamed out to be released. He wound the device tighter and the pain grew more intense, until she thought she might lose consciousness. She screamed again, louder this time, begging him to stop, until the Judge finally relented and took her off the rack. Shaken and hurting, she left the dungeon, was reblindfolded, taken out of the house, put in the car, and driven back to Troost Avenue, where she had to confront an enraged Robinson. He was upset because she'd failed to perform as she was supposed to. The Judge was not satisfied and that reflected badly on Robinson. Word of all this would get around town and that was not good for business. Williams endured Robinson's contempt and was forced to give him back the $1,200. Their relationship was becoming more volatile by the day.

While Robinson conducted these activities in Kansas City, he was still living with his wife and younger children in the suburb of Stanley. He was still playing a visible role in his community as an elder at the First Presbyterian Church, still attending his son's soccer games and serving as a referee. He was still generally being perceived as a good neighbor at Pleasant Valley Farms. People in Stanley knew him as a God-worshiping member of the congregation, a devoted father, a husband who provided well for his family, and a social asset. They had no reason to imagine that he was anything other than these things or to suspect that he had another life altogether when he left the suburbs and drove into the city. They had no concept of his real identity, no concept of his growing skills as a predator.

There are two important areas of concern and consideration for serial killers. The first is finding or selecting a victim. As time went on, Robinson had no problem in that area. Potential victims were everywhere, especially in later years when he began to use the Internet. The second concern and consideration is how and where are you going to dispose of a victim once you get what you want. Some killers openly display their victims by dumping or posing them in an area where they will easily be found. Robinson did not have that mind-set. He was smart enough to realize that if he used that modus operandi, he could possibly be linked to his victims. He always wanted the victims' families to believe that their loved one had met "Mr. Right" and moved somewhere to "live happily ever after."

By hiding or getting rid of the bodies, he was able to avoid detection for years, if not decades. He was reminiscent of John Gacy, who killed thirty-three people, burying many of them in the crawl space in his own house. It wasn't until he got sloppy in his MO that law enforcement started investigating him.

I personally believe Robinson knew that law enforcement lacked a method to link him as a potential suspect.

In the past, he'd fallen into the cracks of the legal system, so why not perpetrate more serious crimes and do this in multiple jurisdictions? He believed he was smarter than police and invincible. In some respects, he was correct. Why was he able to commit these crimes many times over? Because in the minds of victims, potential victims, community leaders, charitable organizations, and law enforcement, John Robinson didn't fit the profile. He was too old, too short, too nice, and so on. That is where we make mistakes—when we begin to think that serial predators like Robinson will look different from the rest of us. That is what makes them so disarming and they know it.

These individuals do their best to find ways to fit into society. For example, the following events took place during the height of Gacy's and Bundy's crime sprees. John Gacy had his photograph taken with then president Jimmy Carter's wife, Rosalynn. Ted Bundy worked in a rape crisis center, was politically active in the state of Washington, and later enrolled in law school. When I conduct interviews of serial killers and other sexual predators, I look closely into the eyes of these men. To the untrained, the look appears sincere and genuine. What I subsequently do is to imagine what look was on their face when they were perpetrating their heinous crimes. I ask myself, What did the victims see before they died? The look would have been pure evil. It was a look that could change in a microsecond. A look that these individuals keep to themselves when they are being investigated, interviewed, and treated during their so-called rehabilitation. But once they're alone and on the hunt, that look returns.

★   ★   ★

One morning in May 1985, Robinson got in his car and headed for 8110 Troost Avenue. He let himself into a third-floor unit of the apartment complex, where Theresa Williams was sleeping. Quietly entering the bedroom, he walked up to her and grabbed her by the hair. He hoisted her up by its roots, threw her over his knee, and spanked her hard, telling her that she'd been bad and needed to learn a lesson. Despite Williams's growing fear of Robinson and despite what she believed he was capable of, his behavior both hurt and shocked her. Yet it paled compared to what he did next.

He tossed her onto the floor, stood over her, and extracted the revolver that he kept concealed in his shoulder holster. As she watched the man and the gun come down toward her, she began to beg and to yell for her life.

Placing the barrel to her head, he said, "If you don't shut up, I'll blow your brains out."

He pulled the trigger—it clicked because there was no cartridge in the chamber.

Williams looked up at him, terrified, sobbing on the floor. Robinson removed the gun from her face and lowered it down below her shoulders, her waist, and her stomach, penetrating her vagina with the barrel and again threatening to kill her. Her screams turned into hysteria as she wailed for him to spare her life. Robinson stared at her, lying helpless beneath him. Then he slowly reholstered the gun, turned, and walked out of the apartment.

He soon came back with a new plan, a way for Theresa to help him out of his latest legal jam. He needed to find a way to destroy the credibility of Irv Blattner, who'd recently turned against Robinson and was trying to get his probation revoked. Robinson asked Williams to enter into a diary some words that he dictated to her—words indicating that Blattner was going to kill her. The purpose of this exercise was twofold. If Theresa disappeared for good, as Paula Godfrey and Lisa Stasi lately had, it would look as if Blattner had murdered her. Second, if Blattner testified against Robinson on his probation status, Robinson could use the diary to portray his adversary as someone who could never be trusted because he had homicidal intentions. In return for her assistance with this plot, Robinson promised to take Williams to the Bahamas on June 15. That was also, according to Robinson's orders, supposed to be the day the diary came to an end.

On June 7, Steve Haymes and the two FBI agents he'd been working with, Thomas Lavin and Jeffrey Dancer, showed up unannounced at the Troost Avenue apartment and talked with Williams. The police startled her, but she was more terrified of Robinson than she was of them. At first she lied to the men about her involvement with Robinson, telling them that she was employed at Equi-II in data processing. They listened carefully to her story and then told her some things she didn't know. They believed that two young women who'd worked for Robinson had vanished and perhaps been murdered. They also believed he might be planning something like that with her. As Williams absorbed what they were saying, she broke down and described the gun incident, mentioning Robinson's plans to take her to the Bahamas. She explained how he'd put all her things in storage, and that the last day of her life in the fake diary was June 15, only a week away.

She told them how Robinson had ordered her to write down sentences meant to sound like hers but intended to discredit Irv Blattner. And Robinson had created instructions for his lawyer to get the diary and some of her property out of a safe-deposit box.

After hearing this, Haymes and the agents took immediate action. Within hours, they'd moved her out of the apartment and to another part of Kansas City. Because of her allegations that Robinson had given her marijuana, had illegally carried a gun, and had sexually assaulted her, Haymes felt confident that he could get Robinson's probation revoked and have him locked up for the next seven years. With a witness to some of his crimes in police custody, it appeared certain that his days of freedom were about to end.

When he learned that the authorities had taken Williams from the Troost apartment (in their haste to transfer her to another location, they'd accidentally taken the landlord's television), Robinson exploded into more anger and more activity. He frantically began hunting the Kansas City area for her, looking everywhere he thought she might have gone. The FBI was aware of his movements and kept the young woman hidden by transferring her to three different addresses in the next three weeks. Robinson intensified his search by hiring a private detective to run her down, a former police officer with the Johnson County Sheriff's Department named Charles Lane. It wasn't Lane who ultimately found Williams but Robinson himself, after spotting her parked car. Lane then contacted the landlady where Williams was staying and confirmed she was there. During one of Lane's attempts to talk with Theresa, Special Agents Lavin and Dancer arrived and broke up the conversation. They were so alarmed that Robinson's private detective had found her that they quickly got money and a plane ticket from the probation service and hurried her out of town, this time relocating her in another state. This move may have saved her life, but it would complicate everything and ultimately cost the authorities in their efforts to put Robinson behind bars.

When the two agents and Haymes appeared at the probation hearing in a Clay County courtroom, they were more than reluctant to talk about Robinson's chief accuser or to reveal where Williams had gone.

Robinson's lawyer, Bruce Houdek, fired back that these tactics were unfair and outside the law. There was "no rational reason," Houdek told the court in a motion, why the state of Missouri and the FBI agents could not produce Theresa Williams so she could give a sworn deposition on the case. Without her appearance, he argued, Robinson's probation should not be revoked. Clay County circuit judge John Hutcherson disagreed, also feeling that the young woman could well be in danger and did not have to be physically present to make her accusations known. In late July, Robinson went before the court and was told that he'd violated his probation on three counts. It now seemed a given that he was going to jail for an extended period, but he was unwilling to give up.

He tried to convince the judge that his stellar civic life should keep him out of prison. He enlisted a private organization called the National Center on Institutions and Alternatives to create a handsome booklet that outlined for Judge Hutcherson his many volunteer efforts and his reputation in his community as "an honest and generous person." The report mentioned Robinson's work as a Sunday-school teacher and a church elder in Stanley, adding that "Mr. Robinson and his wife have always been involved in community activities."

The brochure cited his work as an Eagle Scout and as a cubmaster and a scoutmaster in the 1970s. It did not mention that in a statement put out by the Boy Scouts of America in the early eighties, the organization declared that John Robinson had been ousted as a cubmaster in December 1981 after he pled guilty to stealing from Guy's Foods.

"Thereafter," the statement read, "his registration in the Boy Scouts of America expired and was never renewed."

In one last desperate attempt to help himself, he forged yet another letter, this one from a "Linda White," which outlined how Robinson and his children had brought food and clothes to her home last Christmas Eve. White was supposedly an out-of-work pregnant mother of three kids, who'd already decided to give away the infant she'd delivered a few weeks after the holidays. Because of Robinson's great warmth and giving spirit, she'd changed her mind and kept the baby.

The judge was not persuaded by either "Linda White" or her heartfelt letter. In late August 1985, he revoked Robinson's probation and sentenced him to seven years in a Missouri prison. Before the sentencing could begin, Robinson was freed on a quarter million dollars' bail and quickly set about filing an appeal. Throughout the appeal period, he was ordered to report to Officer Haymes daily and to call him on the weekends. Haymes was more dogged than ever in his tracking of Robinson, never letting him far from his sight or his telephone.

"I was the bulldog that wouldn't let go," he says. "After the revocation in 1985, the FBI closed their file on Robinson at that point, but I kept showing up and haunting him."

But haunting wasn't enough. To his shock and then to his pervasive dismay, Haymes soon learned that his efforts were not enough to put the man away. During the appeal process, Robinson argued that he'd been denied his constitutional right to confront his accuser, because Theresa Williams had never shown up in the Clay County courtroom. In May 1986, a Missouri appellate court threw out Judge Hutcherson's ruling and sided with Robinson.

In the opinion of Judge David J. Dixon of the Missouri Court of Appeals' Western District, "There cannot be the least doubt that the actions of the probation service and the FBI agents denied petitioner due process of law."

Robinson was free to go, free to do what he did best. Haymes could only imagine—or perhaps he couldn't imagine—what the man might do next.

XI

Robinson resumed working at Equi-II, and in August 1985, only days after Judge Hutcherson had initially revoked his probation, he appeared on the cover of *Farm Journal,* a national agricultural magazine. He was pictured standing in the middle of a cow pasture, wearing a dapper sport coat and tie, smiling out at the world. He is happy, calm, and confident, and he would use this favorable publicity to promote Equi-II as a successful consulting firm that advised ranchers on the tax benefits of limited partnerships. In print, he came across as an expert in both finance and farming.

"For every dollar the limited partner invests," Robinson said, "he gets $2 to $4 in tax write-offs, along with a return of 25 percent to 50 percent on his investment over the life of the partnership."

As he'd done earlier when fleecing Harry Truman's physician and then scamming Ewing Kauffman's corporate office, Robinson again crossed the path of another prominent local figure. The *Farm Journal* article on limited partnerships quoted Sam Brownback, a Kansas State University agricultural law professor who would go on to become a U.S. senator from Kansas. Robinson used this periodical to speak optimistically about the future of partnerships for cattle ranchers looking for solid investment strategies. One man who actually got involved with Robinson in the limited partnership business, Bob Lowrey of Norwich, Kansas, lost $10,000. So did his associate, Bill Mills. Steve Haymes's fears were being realized: Robinson was only getting better at his ability to work con games. Yet he had made mistakes in the past that were about to ensnare him.

For months, Johnson County (Kansas) officials had been investigating Robinson's connection to Back Care Systems, which in 1982 had hired Equi-Plus to market its seminars. Robinson had promised to deliver a number of services to the company—promises that were unfulfilled—but he'd sent them invoices for his work. Early in 1986, while he was appealing his probation revocation in Missouri, Robinson went to trial on the Kansas side of the border over these financial practices. In late January, a jury found him guilty of submitting $3,600 worth of false billing. Because the defendant had been investigated for so many crimes in recent years, Assistant District Attorney Steve Obermeier asked Johnson County district judge Herbert W. Walton to apply the Habitual Criminal Act when deciding Robinson's sentence. Judge Walton followed this suggestion and ordered him to spend five to fourteen years in prison and to pay a fine of $5,000.

Before the sentence could begin, Johnson County filed still more charges against Robinson, this time for stealing $50,000 when acting as a middleman in a condominium sale in Page, Arizona. Robinson had allegedly collected $150,000 from a Kansas buyer but passed along only $100,000 to the seller. This was a sizable score compared to some of his earlier ones, but he needed more income than ever before. In addition to his ever-mounting legal bills, his family had continued living on their four-acre estate at Pleasant Valley Farms and two of his children were in college, while the twins were still in high school. With the conviction in the Back Care Systems case, Robinson's wife now realized that her husband's days of avoiding prison were coming to a close. He was about to be convicted on the middleman theft charges in Arizona as well, and he now faced a total of six to nineteen years behind bars. His crime spree appeared to be over and his income could obviously not be maintained while he was in prison. Without his ongoing money scams, his family would not be able to stay at Pleasant Valley Farms. Nancy was about to put the house up for sale and start looking for work. Her children could not escape the reality of their father's criminal past. His activities had not only harmed countless people outside of his family but profoundly affected those inside it as well, both economically and emotionally.

While these events were unfolding, the Kansas City–based *Business Journal* wrote a scathing exposé of Robinson that outlined his almost twenty-year-long criminal record. Through interviews and other research, the publication uncovered Robinson's trail as a phenomenally good chameleon.

"Apparently," wrote the *Journal*'s Delbert Schafer, "Robinson has developed a convincing manner of gaining the confidence of business people over the years. He has the ability to ferret out information and then use it to tell the listener exactly what he wants to hear."

After a couple of years of investigating the con man, Steve Haymes had noticed that whenever Robinson received some really bad publicity like this, the probation officer's phone started to ring with calls from strangers. These people had also encountered Robinson and some of his "investment strategies" in years past. Until now, they hadn't been able to bring themselves to tell the authorities what had happened.

"When someone kicks in your front door and burglarizes you," says Haymes, "you're always going to call the police. But when someone tricks you out of money, the police sometimes don't get called. There are certainly indications that there were some neighbors [of Robinson's] whom he was able to convince to give him money that was soon gone and to my knowledge this was never reported to the police. There was some embarrassment on the part of the victims. Probably in some of Robinson's business dealings, he just wore people down. He was good at wearing people down. He would come up with receipts and excuses and eventually people would just say, 'I give up.'

"Looking at most criminals I've dealt with over the years, you say, 'How did they get there?' and it's a fairly easy path to follow back. They didn't have a lot of guidance or bad guidance or perhaps they fell in with the wrong people or got involved in drugs or alcohol, and at least you have some idea of how they got where they are. With Robinson, it's not very clear-cut. He had many opportunities as a young person. His siblings did well. His parents, as far as I know, were good people and worked hard. So I don't know what made him make that turn.

"It was fairly late, well into his twenties, before the crimes started showing up. I think there were some dysfunctions in him that just continued to grow. The sex thing grew over the years, and other things, but what turned him to go the easy route?"

Pondering his own question, Haymes shakes his head. Then he shakes it again, still haunted by his inability to answer it.

XII

Before finally entering prison for an extended stay, Robinson was linked to one more event that went far beyond a financial scam or wearing down his creditors. In January 1987, Catherine Clampitt had left Wichita Falls, Texas, to start a new life up north. Because of substance abuse problems, she'd had difficulty raising her young son, Ryan, so he'd stayed behind with her parents in the Lone Star State. She moved in with her brother, Robert Bales, who lived in a Kansas City suburb, and soon began looking for work. The Korean-born Clampitt had been adopted by the Bales family and had grown up with a reputation that split off in two different directions. One depicted her as being quite intelligent and the other as possessing a wild streak. Everyone who knew and cared about her saw this split and wanted to help her manage it. Her brother, anxious to see her settled in a job, began scheduling interviews for her with businesses in the area, but she was willful and took steps of her own after spotting an ad that Robinson had placed in a community paper. A company called Equi-II was offering a well-paying position that involved travel and other benefits: her employer would even provide her with new clothes tailored to the image of his business. She called the number and got an appointment with

Robinson, who quickly hired her. As soon as she started the job, she began spending much less time at her brother's home, but it was unclear where she was staying. She was either traveling out of state or spending time at local hotels or someplace else. . . . For days and nights in a row, her brother was not certain what had become of her.

When she didn't show up for a week, he called the police. He also phoned Robinson's office, but Catherine's employer was unresponsive to his questions. Bales decided to stake out the Equi-II address and asked law enforcement to help him investigate. Once again, the police took the limited steps they'd taken before when someone who'd been working for Robinson had vanished without a trace; they interviewed him about the missing woman but concluded that there simply wasn't enough evidence to connect the man to the disappearance. This perception on the part of the authorities was as maddening for Bales as it had been earlier for Paula Godfrey's family and for Lisa Stasi's relatives, but the cops lacked the evidence to pursue Robinson as a suspect.

Catherine Clampitt would never be heard from or seen again.

Robinson was about to be incarcerated for several years, but that would only open up new opportunities for when he was once again free. Behind bars he would go much further into the technological realm of computers that he'd been introduced to in the early eighties, and this would ultimately show him new doorways into crime. He would use the training he received in prison not to rehabilitate himself but to widen his repertoire for contacting, charming, exploiting, and seducing those who met him. He was discovering a technology worthy of his imagination and skills.

He was middle-aged but his energy and stamina showed no signs of flagging. He was, in fact, just finding himself and his career. If he represented the harmful side of creativity, he was almost endlessly productive in uncovering new ways to fool and exploit. He had an astounding capacity for juggling, and in recent years he'd handled numerous relationships while running several business fronts and staying deeply involved in both family and local affairs. When he wasn't working for the neighborhood association, he was an activist in the local S&M underground, a part of the International Council of Masters, an entrepreneur, a forger, a fraud, a baby seller, and a pimp who kept two or three prostitutes busy working for him around the clock. He may have looked pudgy and out of shape, but he had incredible drive and determination when pursuing women of all ages and backgrounds, or when chasing new business schemes back and forth across the state lines of Missouri and Kansas. There were barely enough hours in a day to do all that he wanted to do, but in prison he would have plenty of time to think and to plan—to decide what he wanted to do after being released from his cell. He had time to explore his own ever-expanding identity. It seemed to have no borders or boundaries at all.

If some men were capable of deep sexual aggression and violence, the vast majority of them, especially when they were husbands and fathers, held these things in check. They denied the darker impulses, got them out in other ways, kept them buried inside. They learned how to manage their demons, held back their propensity for evil. They were committed to decency, even when it was a daily struggle. Society demanded that they not act out every urge, and they went along with these civilizing influences. They did it to be less of a threat to women and to try to have a beneficial effect on children. They did it to avoid trouble or unnecessary conflict. They did it to live their own version of the "common good." They fought these inner battles with themselves and usually won.

For Robinson the battle did not exist. At some point in adulthood, he had decided to express every part of himself—including the savage—just because he could. His world was not either/or. It was both/and. His ability to be different people in different situations was exceptional. Serial killers are often known for their massive deceptions, but he'd taken this game to new depths. He was unusual in his ability to play both the domestic and the predator's role to this degree. He could be both a doting father and someone who kept hiring young women who disappeared. He could be both a soccer referee and someone who ran a bordello or hired women out for S&M encounters in basement dungeons. He could be both a churchgoing husband and someone who sold an infant to his brother. He could stretch every boundary until someone made him stop—and that someone was not his wife or children. Their normality seemed to feed his need for the abnormal. Their support seemed crucial to his aberrant behavior. The flip side of his violence was his deep domesticity. This was an interactive dance that nothing could alter and that no prison psychiatrist would ever penetrate. Perhaps his rage was fed by his many emotional and financial responsibilities, his profound need for his family.

Robinson always had a loving home to return to, no matter where he'd been or what he'd done. In April 1986, Nancy was interviewed by the police and given the chance to describe the man she'd married more than two decades earlier. She said that she and John had grown closer since his recent legal troubles, and she described him as a good provider, a good husband, and a loving father. They had a good relationship, she said, but one could only imagine the kind of pressure she was under to help him shorten his time behind bars.

Also in 1986, Dirk Taiff, a presentence investigator, studied Robinson and wrote, "The defendant displays much anger and frustration regarding his legal problems, accepts minimal responsibility for his actions and attempts to portray himself as a hard-working, dedicated family man."

The investigator had talked to Steve Haymes about Robinson. By now Haymes had been examining the man's background since early 1985 and drawing his own conclusions. He wrote to Taiff, "In almost eleven years of work as a probation and parole officer, this officer has never seen an individual as criminally-oriented as John E. Robinson . . . It's this officer's belief that Robinson is a dangerous individual who has put forth no effort to rehabilitate himself through three prior probations in the state of Missouri."

A week after the inmate entered the Kansas State Penitentiary in Hutchinson, the *Kansas City Star* printed a two-page story headlined, "Kansas Prison Awaiting a Convincing Talker." Robinson was described as "a thief, a charmer, a skilled conversationalist and a crafty con artist who should have been locked away years ago. Only now, eighteen years after his first conviction, is the Johnson County businessman seeing the scales of justice crash down, ending a compulsion for white-collar crime that some authorities say they think may have had a darker side."

Not long after Robinson went to prison, his wife found a nursing job and early in 1988 she cashed out the four-acre estate and took a much cheaper apartment in Stanley. The family was facing hard times and widespread shame, as John would not only be locked up for years to come, but had generated terrible press for all of them. His criminal career had grown large enough that it could no longer be hidden from public view. His wife and children carried on, putting their lives together as best they could, not turning against their husband or father, always willing to grant him another opportunity and to take him back. Nancy was holding them all together.

XIII

Robinson began serving his sentence on May 16, 1987, and during the next four years, he would be regarded as an excellent inmate at the Hutchinson Correctional Facility. He was placed in South Unit along with 160 other medium-security inmates, and almost the first thing he did after arriving at the prison was to start complaining about severe chest pains. He went to the institution's doctor and asked for medication, receiving daily prescriptions of Tenormin and nitroglycerin. He apparently took the medicine but continued his vocal worries about his health. When he wasn't consumed with his medical problems, he found time to work, and here, inside the state's penal system, he received his initial training in the world of computers. He was chosen for this duty because of his obvious intelligence, his passion for learning new things, and his desire to please the authorities. They in turn were happy to have someone so competent and willing to take their instructions.

Robinson was a quick study and soon became a standout at this job. He not only reorganized the computer maintenance office but also, after a few months, was able to write new software programs, a process that would save Kansas roughly $100,000 a year. He'd found something he was good at and something that had a positive effect on everyone. Robinson was much admired by the staff, and in 1989 his physical plant supervisor, Jim Jestes, wrote of the inmate and his innovations on the job, "Even when he leaves, this office should function well."

Robinson made a similarly good impression on the medical and mental health staffs. Like many serial criminals, he was excellent at adopting the language of psychiatry and making himself appear normal. He knew just what to say and how to say it, and his intelligence was useful in these circumstances. Being examined in prison was one more chance for him to do what criminals do best: play the game of conning others and then win. Unfortunately, this happens all too often inside penitentiaries.

On a recent visit to New Zealand, I was taken to a psychiatric hospital for the criminally insane. I was to give a presentation to staff psychologists and psychiatrists regarding my research and experience with the criminal mind. Upon entering the classroom, I observed about thirty to thirty-five mental health personnel, who sat with their arms crossed on their chests and uninterested looks on their faces. I turned to my publicist and whispered, "Why did you book me to speak to this group?"

Early in my career I saw similar looks when I spoke to task forces. I found that the best way to handle the situation was to directly address a "problem" rather than to ignore it. Speaking before the New Zealand audience, I asked them what was wrong, and someone said he didn't like the way I put down the mental health professionals in my books. I went on to tell them my personal beliefs and experiences with the criminal personality. I told them that to understand the criminal you must look at the crime. The crime is a reflection of the offender. Almost in unison they said that if they did look at the crime, it would prejudice them during the treatment. I asked them how they knew if the offender was telling the truth, and they said they were taught to detect deception in their training. I told them that they must be much better than me at detecting self-deception because if I only relied on self-reporting from the criminals, I would think that the convicts were all innocent or themselves victims. Not all mental health professionals exclude case information and materials during an assessment, but some do and this can have dire consequences.

Two respected doctors at the Hutchinson Correctional Facility, Supervising Psychiatrist George M. Penn, M.D., and the Kansas Department of Corrections' Director of Medical Services, Ky Hoang, M.D., put together a nine-page analysis of Robinson. Entitled "Report of Clinical and Medical Evaluation," this November 1990 document characterized him as a "model inmate who . . . has made the best of his incarceration. . . . He is a non-violent person and does not present a threat to society. . . . He is a devoted family man who has taught his children a strong value system."

While imprisoned, Robinson suffered a number of small strokes that caused a minor slackness on the right side of his face but did not affect his speaking ability. According to the report, "his verbal skills [were measured] in the high average range, performance skills in the very superior range."

In conclusion, the experts who examined him at the Hutchinson Correctional Facility wrote that Robinson's behavior while incarcerated had been "remarkable" and he had displayed "concrete signs of rehabilitation." He was "a docile, non-violent individual who does not pose a threat to society. It is unlikely that further incarceration will be of any benefit to either Mr. Robinson or society." They recommended his immediate release.

In January 1991, Kansas took this advice and paroled Robinson, much to the concern of one person who'd never stopped following the progress of inmate #45690 at Hutchinson or thinking about the women who'd vanished after coming into contact with this prisoner. Steve Haymes was not at all convinced that Robinson—despite what the medical and psychiatric personnel in Kansas had written about him—was a changed man. Back in 1986, he'd characterized Robinson as the most criminally oriented person he'd ever met. Nothing in the past five years had altered this view.

"There wasn't a month that went by," Haymes says, "that I didn't wonder about him, and about Lisa and Tiffany. For several years, around that wintertime that Lisa disappeared, I would contact her family to see if there had been any additional news or if they'd heard anything. They hadn't and I was somewhat haunted by this because I had never gotten any answers to the most important questions I had at that time."

Haymes had other, more pressing reasons for staying aware of Robinson's activities in Hutchinson, reasons that had become increasingly personal.

"He wrote a letter complaining about me after his parole was put off in Missouri," Haymes says. "He blamed me for all the bad things that had happened to him, saying that it was a personal vendetta on my part to harm him."

The inmate had let a number of people know that someone within the legal system had, as he put it back in 1986, "a hard-on for John Robinson." According to what Haymes had picked up from various sources inside and outside the walls of the penitentiary, Robinson's criticisms of him were turning more serious. He wondered if once Robinson was set free, he would come after Haymes or his wife or his two young children. That was just one more reason for Haymes to do everything possible to ensure that the prisoner stayed locked up for as long as possible. The officer worked hard to make certain that even though Robinson had been freed in Kansas, he still faced up to seven years of jail time for violating his probation in Missouri. Haymes's views were adopted by the authorities, and the day that Robinson was let out of prison in Hutchinson—January 23, 1991—he was transferred over the state line to Missouri and taken a hundred miles east of Kansas City, where he was checked into the Moberly Correctional Center for more psychiatric and medical tests. He claimed that his health had become so frail during his stay at Hutchinson that he should be able to walk out of the Missouri prison and go home to his family. One of Missouri's examining physicians, Dr. Fred King, agreed with Robinson's assessment and described the patient as a "very sick man." Dr. King went on to state that Robinson's medical condition "should be considered in any parole hearing he has." He soon wrote another opinion that Robinson's problems were "life-threatening" and he "should be released without delay."

When Steve Haymes learned of this recommendation, he was both frightened and livid, more determined than ever to take action to keep Robinson behind bars. He created his own report on how dangerous he believed the inmate to be and delivered his views at a parole hearing in April 1991.

The next month, while waiting to learn his fate at Moberly, Robinson penned a letter to the Clay County circuit judge in charge of his case and in effect pleaded for mercy and for his freedom.

"I taught my children to believe in the basic fairness of our system of justice," he wrote. "They know now that justice is just a word and that the concept of justice in America is something that can be manipulated and used as a weapon by those empowered to enforce the law."

Robinson singled out Stephen Haymes as his nemesis—saying that the probation officer had lied and bent the law to keep him in jail:

"I guess we all underestimated the power of Mr. Haymes from the probation and parole department and his ability to keep me incarcerated. Since 1986, this man has done everything within his power to keep me in prison and to assure that the hand fell heavy on me and my family."

Then Robinson made a direct appeal for clemency to the judge himself:

"I am not asking you to release me as I know that would be an improper request which the court could not consider. What I am asking is that the court enter an order to the Missouri Department of Corrections and the Missouri Parole Board to remove all the false and misleading information from my file, consider the information available from the Kansas Department of Corrections and all medical recommendations. Unless I can obtain an order from the court that directs the Board of Probation and Parole to use only factual information, I will never have an opportunity for a fair hearing. Since two courts have already ruled on this issue, the problem seems simple and should not pose any ethical questions.

"Without such an order, I will remain in prison. If lucky, I will live long enough to get out but there will be little left. My illnesses are degenerative and without proper rehabilitation, testing and long term treatment will continue to get worse. My physical impairments and right sided paralysis will not get better. Bruce [his lawyer], my family and I all realize that decisions made by the Clay County Court and the Missouri Parole Board amount to a sentence of death. Our only question, is this what is considered proportionate for my crime in Missouri?"

The Missouri Parole Board rejected Robinson's argument and ordered him incarcerated for two more years. He was shipped to the Western Missouri Correctional Center in Cameron, a new medium-security facility housing more than two thousand prisoners, most of them serving time for substance-abuse-related offenses. Cameron was less restrictive than either Hutchinson or Moberly and proved to be rich turf for Robinson to make new contacts and unleash new schemes. He continued complaining about his medical problems and met a physician at Cameron named Dr. William Bonner, who found him to be bright and talkative, but not very sick.

Then the inmate ran into Dr. Bonner's wife, Beverly, who worked in the prison's library. Robinson and Beverly, who was attractive, outgoing, and intelligent, soon discovered that they'd met each other twenty years earlier when both of them had been employed at Mobil Oil. Like many people, Bonner was taken with his charm, his ability to focus in and pay attention to her and to no one else, and his easy banter. He could speak fluidly about so many different subjects. He seemed so interested in things outside the prison walls. He'd had so many experiences as an entrepreneur and a global traveler. They struck up a friendship and he began working alongside her in the library and volunteering to upgrade its computer system.

Although her husband was employed in the same facility as Beverly, she and Robinson became romantically involved. He told her that he was innocent and had been wrongly imprisoned and would be getting out soon. He told her about his businesses in the Kansas City area and his plans for restarting them after his release. He shared his dreams for the future and hinted that she could be a part of them, if she was willing to make some changes in her life. Did she like the idea of traveling while making money and seeing more of the world?

Robinson not only wanted his freedom back, but the chance to recover his economic losses. His years behind bars had had a very detrimental effect on his finances and his family. His wife was now managing a mobile home park called Southfork in Belton, Missouri, a Kansas City suburb to the south. The park promoted a theme that reflected the huge TV hit *Dallas* from several years earlier. The streets were named after characters such as Sue Ellen (Avenue) and Cliff Barnes (Lane). Nancy and her two youngest children lived on Valeen Lane (named after J. R. Ewing's sister-in-law). While her husband was serving six consecutive years in Kansas and Missouri prisons, Nancy's workload and financial responsibilities had greatly increased, but her social position had dramatically declined. The spacious country estate had been replaced by a row of mobile homes.

When Robinson left prison in 1993, he needed money and was confronted with obvious difficulties in landing a job, let alone attracting new business partners or investors. His résumé was now littered with convictions and a long gap for incarceration. He could have taken this opportunity to fulfill the authorities' expectations for his reform and gone about the hard work of rebuilding his life in the traditional way. He might have found a job in the computer field, which he'd consistently become more knowledgeable about, a field he'd already excelled in. But he didn't do any of these things and had never intended to. Inside the prison, he'd molded himself to fit exactly what the medical and psychological staffs had been looking for. He understood their concepts and knew their lingo, knew how to appear healthy and well adjusted and harmless. He'd become just what they wanted him to be, fooling them as thoroughly as he'd fooled many of the young women he'd been linked with before he was jailed. He wasn't changing his core behaviors, but refining them to fit the new world of technology and criminal opportunities. It was the same pattern he'd been repeating since the mid-1960s.

"Before personal computers and word processing arrived," says Haymes, "the more common means of doing business was a typewriter. Robinson was the master at cut-and-paste in the typewriter era. In the eighties, he realized that he could take advantage of a word processor to produce a document that looked like it was printed without running the risk of looking like it was cut-and-pasted. When he was involved in his alleged charitable activities, he was producing these forms for different people and trying to con them. They gave legitimacy to what he was saying because of how they looked.

"Years later, when other things came to light about Robinson in 2000, it really struck me what a terror this guy is for something like the Internet because he takes to these technologies and uses them very well. There was a lot of indication in the eighties that he was involved in some networks with other people, but it was much more difficult to do those sorts of things back then because you had to do a lot of things mechanically or by telephone or in person.

With a computer, you don't have to do things face-to-face. I'd never really put together what a threat he could be over something like the Internet."

If Robinson was good with the new technology, he also had a gift for sensing the deepest needs and desires of women. He understood that for some of them the greatest need was to feel useful. If they felt they were genuinely helping others, they would do things they might not otherwise consider doing. This applied not only to impoverished and desperate women, like Lisa Stasi, but to solvent and competent women who were emotionally unfulfilled, like Beverly Bonner. By the early nineties, she'd been married twice and had two sons from her first union, but she still hadn't satisfied some of her longings for experience and adventure. Robinson picked up on those longings when he met Bonner in prison—and decided to exploit them. To restart his businesses, he needed an energetic and legitimate partner, and he'd found one in the library at the Western Missouri Correctional Center. After his release, he went back home to his wife and children, but Beverly made plans to split with her husband and join Robinson in Kansas City. In February 1994, she was divorced from Dr. Bonner and the plan went forward.

Robinson had told Beverly about his old company called Hydro-Gro, which had once sold indoor gardening kits, and with her assistance he began reinventing it. The papers of incorporation listed her as the Hydro-Gro president, yet they conspicuously failed to include the name John Robinson (in part because he was a convicted felon). In place of his name was that of "James Turner" as company secretary. This was Robinson's first known usage of that alias, but it would resurface when he became active on the Internet. After hooking up with Robinson, Bonner began calling her mother and talking with enthusiasm about her new business connections and the exciting opportunities that lay ahead. She mentioned Hydro-Gro but also spoke about going overseas and working in the perfume industry. At first, Bonner told her mother the real name of the man who'd become her partner, John Robinson, but later she called back to say that she'd mistakenly referred to him. His real name, she said, was Jim Redmond.

Bonner obviously knew that Robinson was a career criminal and had just spent six years in prison. She was aware that he was asking a former correctional facility employee to help conceal his identity to her own mother. She saw that he was still married and had not begun divorce proceedings—yet none of that seemed to matter. The forty-nine-year-old woman had left her husband for him and did not question the direction of their relationship. She'd begun signing blank pieces of paper at his request—letters that she would one day write, he explained to her, and send to her relatives once she'd gone overseas for her new job. And in fact, before too long these people did begin receiving letters telling them about her travels abroad for her company and how much fun she was having doing this work. The letters appeared to come from Europe and one of them accurately described a street in Amsterdam, which Robinson had visited with his family in the eighties. The letters kept coming and coming, the final one reaching her mother in early 1997 and carrying a Russian postmark. It claimed that Beverly was gradually making her way to China.

Bonner's friends received similar mail with foreign postmarks and detailed accounts of what was happening in distant countries. The forwarding address on the envelopes was a mailbox in a commercial mail center, called the Mail Room, in the Olathe, Kansas, Crossroads Shopping Center. Robinson had rented this space in Beverly's name, and since her divorce her ex-husband had diligently been mailing his thousand-dollar monthly settlement checks to this box. If Dr. Bonner thought it odd that he should be sending checks to a Kansas mailbox when his ex-wife was supposedly working abroad, he didn't ask many questions and kept sending them anyway, $1,000 a month for eighteen months. After all, the letters people had received from Beverly certainly looked authentic, because Robinson had located a service that not only concealed a letter's point of origination but for a modest fee would postmark an overseas address on the envelope.

Before Beverly went away, Robinson had driven out to a southeastern Kansas City suburb and rented a storage locker at Stor-Mor for Less in Raymore, Missouri. Nancy Robinson had previously rented a space here, but Robinson now said that he needed a larger one for the belongings of his sister, who was named Beverly. Once, when he was visiting Stor-Mor, an employee asked him about Beverly and he replied that he was keeping her furniture in the locker while she was abroad working for Hydro-Gro. He went on to say that his sister was having such a good time in Australia, she might not ever return.

On another occasion at Stor-Mor, he unloaded a large sealed metal barrel from the vehicle he was driving, which belonged to Beverly Bonner, and placed it in the storage unit. Then he locked the unit and drove away.

XIV

Starting in 1994, Beverly's friends and family never saw or heard from her again. The following year one of her sons died and she was glaringly absent from his funeral. People at the service asked a lot of questions about her, but nobody had any answers. Some assumed that she must still be traveling or working in Europe. Some thought she might have run off with a man to another part of the United States. Others wondered if she was dead, but if that was the case, where was the body? How could she have vanished so completely from so many lives? And she hadn't disappeared completely because several of those close to her were still receiving letters from her, weren't they? She must have been all right.

A few people surmised that her absence might have something to do with John Robinson and her new job, but no evidence directly linked him to Bonner. No one had gone to the police with their suspicions, so the authorities didn't know Beverly was missing—not even Steve Haymes.

He had other things to worry about.

"When Robinson was released on parole," says Haymes, "he was living in Missouri but in southern Jackson County, which wasn't an area that I supervised.

My only involvement at that point was that I asked to be notified when he got out because he had allegedly made some threats against me and I wanted to know when he was released.

"I had been told by someone that they thought he blamed me for all the bad things that had happened to him and they thought he could potentially harm me. When he was released, I made contact with the parole people who were going to supervise him and tried to put a bug in their ear, and I sent them some information about him because on the surface he seemed like such a compliant person. He'd do what you wanted him to do and say what you wanted him to say, but I wanted them to have an idea of what he was about. After that, I checked periodically on him."

Over his two decades of being a probation officer, Haymes had had only a handful of direct threats from those he'd supervised or sent back to prison and another handful of indirect threats. Nobody had ever attacked him.

"The ones you worry about the most," he says, "are the ones who don't threaten you. People are often pretty unhappy with you, but for most of the people we deal with, probation is a kind of game and they understand that. They made conscious decisions to break the rules so they usually don't hold you personally responsible when they get caught. That's part of the risk. The fact that I report them or put them in prison isn't held against me."

He instinctively felt that Robinson would not feel this way. When Haymes heard that the man had possibly been threatening him, he did not hesitate to take this seriously—and to change his behavior.

"I knew that we had people who were missing and had

disappeared in the 1980s," Haymes says, "so I became more cautious after he got out in the midnineties. I varied my driving routes to and from work. I made sure I wasn't being followed. I had small children and I made certain that my wife was aware of what Robinson looked like and what kind of vehicles he drove and to be aware of any suspicious vehicles in the neighborhood. I made sure the kids were watched a little more closely and that they played in the back but not the front yard. I knew he was capable of things and blamed me for things and that he didn't accept a lot of responsibility for putting himself in that situation. So my level of caution went up."

Most people's level of caution about Robinson was nowhere near Haymes's—nor had it even been awakened.

As a child, Debbie Faith was diagnosed with cerebral palsy, and from an early age she'd needed a motorized wheelchair to get around. Her mother, Sheila, took good care of her, and so did her father, John, until 1991, when he died of cancer. The mother and daughter had been living in southern California, but now they began moving from place to place in their search for better conditions. They survived on Social Security payments, which amounted to $1,016 a month, plus food stamps, but Sheila constantly needed more money for Debbie's medical care. She wore arm braces and was dependent on the wheelchair and a catheter. As she grew out of childhood, she would be diagnosed not as having cerebral palsy but the equally crippling illness known as spina bifida. Approaching her teenage years, she weighed more than two hundred pounds and her mother could only put her to bed by using a hoist and a lot of physical exertion.

In spite of her illness, Debbie had an upbeat spirit and a good sense of humor. Sometimes she acted as if she were hardly disabled at all—racing other people in wheelchairs at the mall and enjoying the thrill of beating them and exploding into laughter at her victory. She loved country-and-western music and, like many girls her age, had teenage fantasies about her teachers in Fullerton, California, and about the stars she watched on TV. She was known to call television psychics and ask them to predict her future. One told her that she might walk someday, an opinion that doctors had shared with her as well. Her pain had never defeated her or left her hopeless or bitter. She was determined to win her fight against the disease and had ambitions to become a physical education teacher. Debbie wanted to help others who needed it the most, including those in wheelchairs and the deaf.

After John Faith passed away, Sheila tried to overcome her loneliness by running personal ads or going into on-line chat rooms. She was looking for romance and for someone to share the huge financial and emotional responsibility of raising her daughter. In 1993, Sheila relocated the two of them from Orange County to Watsonville, just south of San Francisco, but the move was short-lived: Sheila had a way of hooking up with married men who weren't about to leave their wife. The Faiths were soon making plans to go to Pueblo, Colorado, where they had friends and some better prospects. When they'd gone east, Debbie maintained contact with several girls in California through the Internet, while her mother commenced a long-distance relationship with someone special she'd just met. They had perhaps run across one another on the Net, although the details of their meeting were vague. The man lived out in Kansas or Missouri, and according to the few tidbits that Sheila shared with her friends, he was a successful farmer named John.

John liked to brag about his land and the horses he owned, and he said that if the Faiths came out to his part of the country, he was pretty sure that he could get Debbie, now fifteen, to ride one of his gentler mounts. That would be a great accomplishment for someone in her position, but John was willing to do whatever was necessary to make it happen. He also promised to get her into an expensive school for the disabled. Sheila was impressed. It took a generous and thoughtful and sensitive man to make an offer like this; there weren't a lot of single men out there who wanted to be a part of a family and would help a child who needed this much assistance. John and Sheila began talking regularly on the phone, and he asked her a lot of questions about herself, about her own desires and where she wanted to live and how she was able to support herself and Debbie. Their relationship was quickly heating up. John wanted them to move out to the Midwest and take up his offer to help Debbie; if they did this, he'd pay for an extended ocean cruise. Before long, the forty-five-year-old Sheila was describing John to her friends as her "dream man," the one she'd been looking for since her husband had died.

In the spring of 1994, the Faiths decided to leave Colorado and loaded their old car with some of their belongings. They drove off east to meet Sheila's new companion, ready for a bold adventure. Debbie took her wheelchair and other possessions, but Sheila left nearly everything behind, including her clothes, furniture, and kitchen utensils. Their neighbors in Pueblo were astonished to awaken one morning and find their friends gone. They never saw or heard from the Faiths again.

Before disappearing, Sheila had told her neighbors to keep track of her mail, which included Debbie's $1,016-a-month disability check, but no more mail arrived at the Faiths' Pueblo residence. After Sheila and Debbie vanished, their ex-neighbors learned that their letters were being forwarded to a Kansas address. They were going to the Mail Room in Olathe, the very same address that was receiving Beverly Bonner's mail and her monthly divorce-settlement checks from her ex-husband. The mailbox was rented in the name of James Turner, and the owner of this business would later say that a man matching the description of John Robinson had been picking up the Faith checks at that location ever since 1994. He picked up 152 of them, worth a total of more than $80,000.

Not long after the Faiths vanished from Pueblo, Sheila's brother, William Howell, started getting letters that purportedly came from his sister. They were typed and carried her signature at the bottom, telling him that she and Debbie were doing just fine.

A Most Seductive Web

XV

In the animal kingdom, predators seek out the weak and the infirm, usually isolating them from the herd before making the kill. They hunt with great skill and efficiency so that they or their offspring or their pack will have enough to eat. They choose their prey carefully and strike when the victim may not be paying attention. They learn how to get close enough to the food so that it can't escape.

Now that he was out of prison and back on the street, Robinson began searching for vulnerable people and found them everywhere. For years he'd been meeting women through fake charitable organizations, hustling them on the streets of Kansas City, offering them jobs and travel opportunities, picking them up in restaurants or connecting with them through personal ads in the print media. In the mid-1990s, his hunting ground was about to expand exponentially, and everything he'd learned about luring victims and exploiting their weaknesses was now going to be attached to the most powerful technology of the last decade of the twentieth century: the Internet and its World Wide Web.

Computers were first built in the 1940s following World War II, but only a few major corporations and government agencies used the original data-processing machines because they were so bulky and expensive. By the 1960s, the U.S. Defense Department's Advanced Research Projects Agency (ARPA) had begun designing a network that, in the case of war, would allow the military to continue to issue orders to the armed forces. Experts at the Rand Corporation had studied this problem and concluded that during an attack the main communication centers—telephone switching offices, broadcast stations, military and government buildings—would be among the first targets destroyed. Researchers felt that the best way to prevent such a disaster was through a computer network located in more than one place. Their strategy was implemented when the military built a system called ARPAnet.

In 1970, the network began with connections between four western universities: Stanford, the University of California branches at Los Angeles and San Diego, and the University of Utah. ARPAnet worked well but soon evolved into something quite different from what the early planners had had in mind. The systems' creators had imagined that the four universities would employ ARPAnet to communicate about professional matters and not much else. It hadn't occurred to them that civilians at the schools would start logging on to the computers and talking directly with one another by exchanging typewritten messages or that this system would be used for *personal* purposes, sometimes very personal purposes. No one had quite envisioned that this might be a whole new way to communicate your private thoughts. By 1972, people on ARPAnet were firing electronic mail back and forth and using a program called FTP (File Transfer Protocol) to transfer files between computers. Instead of making phone calls or dropping letters into mailboxes—this old and

incredibly slow method of communication would con-
temptuously be dubbed "snail mail" by those on-line—
they just sent instant messages across the system. To link all
the available networks together—to create an "internet," so
to speak—a common protocol was necessary. Technicians
invented one known as TCP/IP, and in 1983, TCP/IP was
up and running. The Internet had been born.

The growth of the Net was slow at first because most
Americans did not yet own personal computers. As this
gradually began to change in the late eighties and then
more rapidly in the 1990s, the service spread across the
nation and overseas, becoming an international network
connecting millions of computers and multimillions of
human beings. The Net was labeled the "information
superhighway" because it carried more data and moved it
faster than any previous device in human history. By the
midnineties, some 30 to 40 million Americans were going
on-line at least once a week and accessing the World Wide
Web—the system that allowed computer users to present
and retrieve information over the Internet. People who
would otherwise never have met one another were now
connecting in cyberspace and regularly communicating.
And as the ARPAnet founders had discovered more than
two decades before, much of the communication was
intensely personal.

By the midnineties, something radically novel had arrived
on the global stage, bringing with it a whole new world
unlike anything that had previously existed. This world
contained hidden realms within hidden realms, and each
had its own language, its own rules and on-line etiquette
(called Netiquette), its own secrets and subtle pathways
into even more hidden realms. A person sitting in front of

a computer screen in, for example, Chicago could instantaneously and simultaneously talk to individuals throughout that city and America and across the earth. The old concepts of geographical boundaries, borders, and limitations were gone. The walls were down. People were no longer doing things at the speed of physically moving objects from one place to another, but were trading their thoughts, their emotions, their images, their angers, their fears, and their deepest desires and fantasies at the speed of light. The human imagination seemed to be freed from the constraints and the conceptions of the past. When you went on-line, you could go anywhere you wanted to go that had an Internet connection, and you could be anyone you wanted to be. The world had suddenly been wired for new forms of communication—and personal interaction.

The Net was both a vast research tool into every possible subject and a gateway to information that most people could not begin to imagine. It provided services as varied as how to adopt a child from the United States or a foreign country to how to trade stocks or collect coins to how to stalk an unsuspecting person. If it offered the greatest collective library on the planet, it also provided the opportunity for frustrated couples to "adopt" nonexistent children in scams that cost people thousands of dollars and broke their hearts. The Net featured everything from pie recipes to bomb-making techniques and other information used by terrorists, both domestic and foreign. Since the mideighties, America's radical right had been linked through computer networks, and by the turn of the new millennium, international terrorists like Osama bin Laden and the Al Qaeda network were joined to their followers via e-mail and zip files. The Internet had an endless capacity for doing good as well as evil. It held humanitarian sites that donated food to people in starving countries every time you logged on to these Web pages, but it had other sites dedicated to promoting pedophilia involving three- and four-year-old children.

The Net had organized "cyber-gangs" that roamed the darkest recesses of the Web—gangs so technologically proficient that they could "reach in" to your computer and swipe your password, your home address, and your telephone number. They could steal your financial records and sabotage the files on your hard drive, destroying everything you'd created and stored. But as soon as these underground gangs were found to be operating in the on-line world, software companies began building "firewalls" to keep them out. Each time one of these firewalls—which shut down certain computer portals that allow in information—was cracked by a hacker, still newer barriers were generated to become even more impenetrable. It was a game with one set of technology masters taking on the other, with the side of crime prevention sometimes winning and sometimes taking a loss. Everything about the Internet was a competition to expand the notion of what was possible in the unexplored domains of cyberspace.

The Net meant new ways to do business, new ways to hunt for research material, and new ways to meet potential mates or partners. Every form of communication had become electronic, and both "E-business" and "E-romance" Web sites were everywhere. On-line personal ads and chat rooms became the new bars and singles' clubs—with one huge difference. Instead of having access to a few people in a physical setting, you could now access unlimited would-be partners worldwide. In years past, when people met, interacted with, and assessed each other in person, eye contact, body language, and appearance all came into play. Our combined human and animal instincts were the best gifts to protect us from danger. The fight-or-flight response was most effective based on vision, and intuition was a valuable tool when studying potential partners or mates.

In cyberspace, all this would change. In this impersonal technological playground you could fabricate everything—your age, your name, your looks, your occupation, your race, your gender, your sexual orientation, your personal history, and your personality itself. You could rearrange or reinvent yourself every time you logged on. If you were shy, you could be daring and flirtatious. If you were outrageously forward in person, you could come across as gentle and cautious. If you were fourteen and could bring off the act, you could appear to be much older and far more sophisticated than your years. If you were seventy-five, why not tell people you were thirty-three? Nothing was out of bounds. Anything went in this atmosphere, which someone once described as "Mardi Gras with typewriters." It was as if the technology itself had set loose something in the human mind or the unconscious, so that the old rules and forms of self-expression and self-control no longer applied. Here you could be whatever you or someone else wanted you to be. Here was a realm where you could finally let go. The technology seemed to encourage people to spell out—and sometimes to act on—their less civilized impulses.

If you were an ex-con in Kansas, you could present yourself as a caring farmer and successful entrepreneur willing to help those in need. If you were a woman who would never have ventured into erotic clubs or sex businesses in the physical world, you could now explore these places alone and unembarrassed, where no one even knew you were female. You were suddenly liberated from all the restrictions of the past and you were safe—or so it seemed—whenever you dipped your toe into this on-line pool or that one, gradually testing the waters without revealing much of yourself or taking the plunge.

In an office in Ohio, a female state employee grows bored in the afternoon lull of her workday and glances around to see if anyone is watching her. Her boss is out and no one else is looking her way. She turns on her computer screen and punches a few keys that are reserved for situations just like this. Within seconds, she's connected to a Web site offering hard-core pornography. She takes it in with furtive eyes, constantly peeking over her shoulder to make sure no one is approaching her desk; she's both fascinated and repelled by the images, unable to stare at them and unable to look away. If she's a little ashamed of herself for doing this on company time, she's also briefly entertained. A few minutes later, she returns to work, rejuvenated and ready to resume the tedious chores that make up her job. She's tried not to do this very often, but lately she's been checking in with the site every day.

In Louisiana, a man shares his marital woes and extra-marital fantasies with cyber-girlfriends in Sweden, Japan, Spain, and California. He long ago gave up on having intimacy with his wife, but this kind of romance invigorates him and allows him to be kinder to his spouse and children. Sometimes, he's convinced it makes him a better person. Initially, he likes to meet women in chat rooms, but then he breaks away from those settings and establishes one-on-one relationships with them. He asks them to send him pictures of themselves, which most of them are willing to do, and he keeps an extensive file of their photos and e-mails. His

wife never uses his computer. She doesn't have the password that would allow her to go on-line on this machine.
He's made it clear through remarks and attitude that he
doesn't want her in this office space, so she leaves him
alone and never asks him what he's doing during all those
hours he spends on-line in his basement. He doesn't reveal
what takes place in there and she doesn't really want to
know.

In New Hampshire, a stressed-out police officer stays
up all night with his "backup" women on the Net. He's
been fighting with his boss and with his wife and with
his mistress, whom he met on-line a few months earlier.
Now he's searching for a new connection out there—
someone fresh, someone who doesn't know his past and
won't judge him, someone who will find him interesting
and lively and funny, someone who will make him feel
connected to the world and good about himself. If he
hunts long enough in chat rooms and presents himself in
a favorable enough light, he knows he can find somebody like this because he's done it so many times before.

The man never tells anyone on-line that he's a cop, and
he doesn't talk about his looks or his age, either. He focuses
on his own mind and the thoughts and emotions of the
women he's speaking to. He knows how to be caring and
sympathetic, a good listener. He uses some of these same
techniques as a police officer when interrogating suspects
or witnesses to get them to tell him what he wants to
know. He's been doing all this for years on the job, and he
knows how to hook people by sharing his secrets with
them.

"The Net is like a confessional," he says. "You tell things
to people on-line that you wouldn't tell your closest friend.
You have someone to talk to who doesn't know you or your

family or your background. You feel incredibly free and alive and attached. Your Internet connections quickly become very intimate because you can unburden yourself of your deepest feelings without the idea that there will be any consequences. You can escape being an adult for a while, escape being a husband or a parent or even being a man. You can be anything out there—anything at all. And in some ways there usually aren't any consequences, but it still feels like cheating.

"The guilt is still there because you're talking to a stranger instead of talking to the people you live with. It erodes relationships at home because more than anything else you look forward to going on-line and spilling your guts to someone out there. It goes very deeply to that place that says somebody in the world can really understand and appreciate and love me for who I am. I think that's the deepest human fantasy of all—that someone can know us in the way we want to be known and see us the way we want to be seen. Someone can know our inner reality. Just that possibility is what keeps some people going. Without it, you feel very small and very alone.

"People on-line may want sex but they crave connectedness to others. The Net provides that in a global way. It's something totally new, and like all new things, it generates hope. Even if that hope ultimately proves to be false. It's like taking a little vacation from your own life— and everyone needs that once in a while."

XVI

A woman who enters a chat room and is willing to identify herself as a woman needs to be prepared for what happens next. Some people in the room will perceive her arrival as an invitation for sexual aggression. She might instantly be asked where she lives, her age, and the size of her breasts. Others will demand that she send them her picture. If she enters a chat room and says that she's young and blond, a feeding frenzy will ensue, with the woman immediately becoming the center of attention, regardless of who she really is or what she actually looks like. All this can be fun and flattering, but it can also, at least for many women, start to feel invasive, even like an assault. There isn't much chivalry in cyberspace. On-line you meet new people all the time, things get personal fast, and instant gratification is the common currency. It's easy to get addicted to the rush of having secret relationships with those who pay attention to you whenever you want this kind of attention. If you are primarily interacting only with yourself and your own emotions, for many people this at least seems as if you're connected to something outside you.

The Net has a remarkably seductive feel.

What often starts out as an on-line lark can lead to more serious consequences. Stories began surfacing everywhere about relationships and marriages dissolving because of cyber-romance. On the Net, personal interaction quickly moves from casual e-mails to intimate e-mails to sensual/sexual communications to the exchange of pictures to the decision to meet physically, to having an affair, to planning on bolting a marriage—and sometimes to divorce and breaking up households. As on-line love has become more popular, services have popped up offering to track your lover or spouse on the Net, without ever being detected, to see whom he or she is meeting in cyberspace. Private investigation has taken on a whole new meaning.

Many times an abandoned husband or wife never realizes that a spouse has been going on-line and carrying out hidden adultery via the Net for months or even years. Everything has unfolded just a few feet away from the wounded party and has taken place in total silence, within the electronic confines of a computer. Machines, as social critics had been saying for decades, are neutral. It's what you do with them that matters.

"Technology in any form," children's TV star Fred Rogers once said in *ON* magazine, "can be used for good or evil. It all depends on the hearts and minds of those who use it."

People's hearts and minds are now being tested in strikingly new ways. Instead of conducting just one illicit affair on-line, some users carry on four or five or six at once, with women or men in countries around the globe. When Internet lovers discover that their on-line partners are not involved exclusively with them, hell occasionally breaks loose. The old emotions of jealousy and rage are still the same; only the technology has changed.

Surfing the Net for love can easily become a minor

hobby that evolves into a major pastime that turns into an addiction that can be almost as demanding and consuming as a full-time job.

An altered reality had arrived at the close of the second millennium, and it would most frequently be compared to the Old West in nineteenth-century America, where many people were armed and dangerous and lawmen struggled to maintain order and protect the citizens of the new frontier. That era may have been wild and lawless, but it had not been driven by a rapidly growing, ever-expanding technology. Horses dominated the Western landscape, and both criminals and sheriffs used the same animals in their chosen lines of work. The outlaws and the peacekeepers were fairly evenly matched. When automobiles came along, criminals quickly adapted them to fit their needs, but once again law enforcement easily made the same adaptation. In the on-line world, the old patterns did not apply. Technology was changing so fast that the authorities simply could not keep up with it—at least not during the midnineties, when the Internet exploded onto the American scene. During those years, when dot-com businesses erupted everywhere and fortunes were made overnight, things really were wild in cyberspace.

Near the end of that decade, as law enforcement began to realize just how many different kinds of crime were being committed on-line, and how insidious some of those crimes were, they'd barely started to train or employ enough experts to fight back. They needed money for education, they needed funds for more and more sophisticated equipment because the technology turned over so fast, and they needed time to absorb what they were learning. Whenever they made progress, the technology surged forward again and was often being used for illegal activities. The great challenges that had always faced law enforcement, especially regarding the most serious crimes, had expanded once again.

Every year for the past decade the United States has averaged about eighteen thousand homicides. Some years we had considerably more and sometimes the number would decrease for a variety of explanations and theories. What has happened over the years is that the clearance and/or solution rate for homicides has decreased. In 1960, the clearance rate was approximately 90 percent. Today the average clearance rate is about 64–67 percent. In 1960, most of our cases were of the smoking-gun variety, which means the subject and victim knew one another. What gradually evolved were the "stranger" homicides or crimes without apparent motive. Due to a lack of resources, both technical and personnel, the bad guys were beginning to win.

Law enforcement responded by developing new forensic tests and other investigative tools. In the late 1970s, my colleagues and I began conducting our own research that would ultimately assist investigators and prosecutors in criminal profiling, assessments, proactive techniques, interview and interrogation techniques, and strategies for the prosecution. What compounded the investigative problem was the mobility of the criminal and the lack of technological tools to assist us in our investigations. It's hard to imagine that even today we do not have a common technological tool where law enforcement can share information with other agencies conducting similar investigations. We are a country with over seventeen thousand different and separate law enforcement agencies and departments. Many departments don't have the tools to link cases within their own community. How can they possibly link cases to crimes outside their jurisdiction? You have to rely on the hope that a law enforcement official takes a particular interest in a case, wait for the perpetrator to make a mistake, or get a lucky break.

In 1985, we had a formal ceremony at the FBI Academy for a new program called VICAP. This stood for the Violent Criminal Apprehension Program and was the brainchild of retired LAPD detective Pierce Brooks, who saw the need for it. Brooks would go to the library to review newspapers from around the United States to attempt to link and match unsolved cases. That was nearly two decades ago. VICAP still exists, but it will never be successful if it continues to be a voluntary program. For example, it does no good if the LAPD participates in the program if smaller departments in and around Los Angeles County do not participate.

With the advent of the computer, criminals have found an opportunity where they can for the most part remain anonymous and troll the Internet highways for potential victims. Law enforcement agencies are struggling to keep up with this new and potentially dangerous offender. Men like John Robinson know that it is difficult to catch them because no one central agency is coordinating the effort to fight these enemies, who can sit in the comfort of their homes seeking lonely and needy people who are only looking to improve themselves and make their lives better. People like Robinson believe they are superior in every way to the people they come in contact with on the Internet. These victims are merely objects to Robinson and predators like him. To kill someone whom they feel is inferior to them is like flicking a switch to turn off the lights. They feel nothing for the victims or their families.

★ ★ ★

Law enforcement was now playing catch-up against a foe that had infiltrated every corner of the Net. In decades past, the dark world of pornography and child pornography could be found either through underground mail or in the seedier parts of town at adult bookstores or other outlets. That era had now died. The Internet brought the most taboo sexual subjects right into the privacy of one's home or workplace computer. Everything from erotic photos of small youngsters to sadomasochistic Web sites to videos of rape and other forms of sexual violence were only a few keystrokes away. Sex had always sold and now it had found a huge new international marketplace. Money and desire were driving that market forward in every direction.

There were sexual newsgroups for just about every imaginable taste and some that went beyond most people's imagination. There were listings for those with a special interest in various ethnic groups, in cowgirls, in redheads, and in senior citizens. If one wanted to look at nude pictures of celebrities—including TV stars, movie actresses, and supermodels—services would provide these photos for a monthly fee. In some cases you might be looking at a star's head placed on top of someone else's body, but who really knew the difference? There were sites offering graphic pictures of violence being done to women and there were chat rooms where men performed virtual gang rapes on women—and virtual murders. There were pictures of dead people available for viewing.

As disturbing as these things were, they were not as disturbing as the on-line images one could find of small children. The Net offered still and moving pictures of girls five or six years old who were naked with their hands tied in front of or behind them. They were being sexually assaulted. There were pictures of girls with belts tied around their ankles and hanging upside down from the ceiling. Adults were doing unspeakable things to them, and there was money to be made in selling such images. By the midnineties, the Internet had an estimated five thousand worldwide child porn sites, and this number would grow exponentially during the next few years. Those who created and transmitted the images were extremely clever in their ability to hide where the pictures originated and how they were being sent to individuals around the world. In e-mailing a digital photo from, say, Detroit to Miami, it could be routed through Germany, England, and Turkey before reaching Florida. Those who knew their way around the Internet could make this kind of trafficking in child pornography almost impossible to track.

In the past, pedophilia had been viewed as perhaps the greatest taboo in modern society. People engaged in it usually had to pursue it alone and keep it extremely secret. The Net offered pedophiles at least some degree of privacy and had support groups for those interested in molesting children. These sites not only encouraged such predators but advised them on how to lure kids away from their parents and told them the best techniques to seduce children without getting caught. An entirely new criminal realm had exploded across the face of the globe, and it truly was, in every sense of the word, without boundaries.

Inevitably, scandals started to erupt. In 1996, in Belgium, several children connected to a pornographic ring were murdered. The next year another scandal was uncovered in Spain, and that same year 250 people were arrested in France for selling or possessing videotapes of small children being raped and tortured. In 1998, the Dutch police found a group of child pornographers in Zandvoort who were selling images of kids on the Internet to buyers in Europe, Great Britain, Russia, Israel, and the United States. These images shocked even the most hardened investigators of child porn.

"For professional reasons," an unnamed psychologist who worked as a police consultant on the Zandvoort case told the *New York Times,* "I have seen a lot of porn, but this left me speechless. It looks like the perpetrators are not dealing with human beings but with objects."

Predators become predators because they can turn people into objects—and they often save parts of their victims after the killing to remind themselves of what they've done. They keep vivid reminders of what they are.

As the twentieth century gave way to a new millennium, the people committing sex crimes on the Internet would cut across all racial, religious, economic, geographical, and professional lines. Doctors would be arrested for soliciting sex with youngsters, as would teachers, police detectives, priests, and a fifty-eight-year-old rabbi in Boca Raton, Jerrold Levy, who pled guilty in federal court to using the Internet to arrange a meeting with a fourteen-year-old boy in a parked car. Rabbi Levy's other counts of employing the Internet to e-mail child pornography videos were dropped. In 2001, the county of Gwinnett, Georgia, saw twelve criminal cases involving Internet child pornography or child sex.

For some people, the only thing stronger than the urge to express themselves sexually on the World Wide Web was the belief that they would not get caught. In the midnineties, this appeared to be true, because law enforcement was so far behind in detecting many of these developments and it would take years to catch up.

★   ★   ★

In the last half of the 1990s, with the Net entering tens of millions of American homes, criminals had begun using the new technology to commit fraud, theft, and many other violations of the law. At the same time both law enforcement and private agencies were beginning to study behavior—particularly sexual behavior—in cyberspace and were developing statistics about their findings. The results revealed that huge numbers of people used the Internet for some form of sexual exploration. Self-imposed restrictions were fading and people often did things on-line they might never have done anywhere else. The cyberworld had become the new sexual playground for countless Americans. Something had been released and was running through the Net—from the mainstream to the fringes.

XVII

Into this wide-open world of explicit Web sites, raunchy chat rooms, and cyber-sex came John Robinson, ready to apply the skills he'd been learning and honing throughout the past three decades. His ambitions, his libido, and his intelligence were stimulated by the new technology. He had to get educated about and involved in this new thing called the World Wide Web. He saw how it could be employed in his more legitimate businesses and used to expand his contacts with women everywhere. As always, he needed more money and was eager for more connections with the opposite sex. Now he could do some of the things he'd been doing elsewhere for many years without even having to leave home. If he was making plans to transfer his criminal skills to cyberspace, no one in his family suspected a thing.

Late in 1995, Robinson celebrated his fifty-second birthday with his wife and children at their home on Valeen Lane in Belton, Missouri, where his family had moved while he was in prison. One of the guests was the fiancé of his youngest daughter, Christine—a young man named Kyle Shipps, who worked as an officer with the Prairie Village Police Department. Of all his children, Christy, as she was called, seemed the closest to her father.

She was pretty, she was loyal, and she could be fiery. She admired and loved her dad, and in the future that love would be tested in ways most people never experience.

The party was festive and Robinson was in a good mood, as his fortunes seemed to be rising once again. He had money coming in from various sources, and he and Nancy had recently made a down payment on a $95,000, two-bedroom, ranch-style house and an adjoining lot in Big Pine Key, Florida. The Robinsons wanted to make this home a gift to their eldest son, John Jr., and his wife, Lisa, who'd just given them their first grandchild (there would eventually be half a dozen more). The new grandpa couldn't have been prouder.

John senior and junior went down to Florida to refurbish the property, which the younger couple eventually hoped to convert into a kindergarten. The senior Robinson intended for his son's family to live in the house, while he and Nancy would build a home on the lot. It was time, John had decided, for them to relocate in another state, far away from his troubles in Kansas City. It was time to start over where both his past and law enforcement were not hovering so close by (he still had to regularly visit his probation officer). He could always find new ways to do business, no matter where he lived, and the Internet would keep him in close touch with the world. Florida looked like the answer for his future, but then his plans went awry. The lot had a sinkhole and held old septic tanks that made building a home on the site off-limits. Robinson threatened to sue the Realtor who'd sold him the property, but when the Realtor made counterthreats, things fell apart and Robinson decided to stay in the Kansas City area. He was still edgy for change.

He and Nancy soon left Belton and moved into a

trailer-home park in Olathe, Kansas, called Santa Barbara Estates. The streets were named after California locales, and the Robinsons lived at 36 Monterey Lane, putting a double-wide home on one of the better lots. Nancy was hired as manager of the park's 484 mobile units, but her husband, as far as the neighbors could tell, did not have a job. They often saw him leaving his house, coming and going in his pickup. While he seemed unemployed, he also seemed very, very busy, constantly on the move, never having much time for conversation. His wife had become a well-known presence at Santa Barbara Estates, but nobody was certain what her husband did throughout the day. Occasionally, they saw him landscaping the backyard or putting in pink geraniums on the front patio or placing a statue of St. Francis in a flowerbed or installing a mock Liberty Bell on his property. A sign near the bell read "Grandpa's Place. We Spoil Grandchildren." During the summer, his lawn was immaculately kept, and when the holiday season came around, he called attention to his home by putting up the best Christmas decorations at Santa Barbara Estates.

Robinson would eventually try to boost his income by starting a new company called Specialty Publications, which featured a trade magazine, *Manufactured Modular Living,* about the mobile home industry. The periodical, which was free and survived on advertising, closely resembled another publication put out by John Woolfolk in the Kansas City suburb of Prairie Village. When Woolfolk became aware of this, he fired off a "cease and desist" letter to Robinson. Woolfolk was not the only one in the mobile home business who felt that his competitor was hurting the industry's reputation by telling homeowners to do things that were at best inappropriate, if not in direct violation of accepted standards. Robinson was unfazed and kept on publishing.

He brought the same friendly and charming personality to this field that he'd used earlier with Equi-II, Equi-Plus, and Hydro-Gro. He'd given up the suits and ties, replacing them with golf shirts and expensive loafers, and he talked about the mobile home industry with enough knowledge to disarm a number of people. If many of his professional contacts were taken with Robinson's new role and his casual wardrobe, some female residents at Santa Barbara Estates found him to be rude and flirtatious, often making sexually suggestive remarks. They thought he was just an irrepressible middle-aged man.

Nobody who lived next to Robinson—and quite possibly nobody who lived with him or spent time in his home—realized that each morning he waited until Nancy had gone to work at eight-thirty before turning on at least one computer (he had three desktops and two laptops). Then he went to his real job, which didn't have much to do with selling ad space for *Manufactured Modular Living*. He got on-line and surfed chat rooms and Web sites, establishing new relationships with women he'd never seen. He paid enormous attention to them, as he had to so many other women he was getting to know in the past, asking them all about themselves and then asking them to send him their picture. In time he would send out his own photo, by setting up a digital camera outside in the natural light and snapping pictures of himself dressed like a dude farmer. He wore a dark Western-style hat, cocked jauntily on his head, shiny black cowboy boots, crisply pressed blue jeans, a blue-jean shirt, and a bolo tie. He had an open, friendly smile and looked confident and approachable, exactly the way he wanted to look.

He assumed different identities in cyberspace, sometimes coming across as a highly successful entrepreneur and sometimes as a gentleman farmer. He called himself a variety of names, from Jim Turner to JT to a new name: Slavemaster, the same handle he'd once used when associated with the International Council of Masters. He used this last name when visiting sadomasochistic sites that had recently sprung up on the Web. He went onto them looking for women who said they enjoyed being submissive to a dominant male, and he often told them the same things that he'd once told Sheila Faith—all about his prosperous life in Kansas and his desire to help people.

He sprayed out into cyberspace the message that he was hoping to hook up with a member of the opposite sex because he wanted to be a lover and a friend and a supporter. He might become their provider or be able to find them a good job. He would help them come to Kansas and they could meet face-to-face for intimacy and perhaps something more. He established contacts with females all across the United States and beyond America's borders, offering them the chance to explore their on-line fantasies with a flesh-and-blood man. Some women did not respond to him, but others did, and they started thinking about taking up his offer. One day they would make plans to come see John Robinson or Jim Turner or JT for themselves.

Robinson was intrigued with all of the Internet, but he was especially interested in the sadomasochistic sites, with their emphasis on "masters" and "slaves." If the S&M world featured whips and chains, dungeons, dog collars, handcuffs, leather clothing, riding crops, and all manner of body restraints, it also had well-defined rules. Its rituals were about taking control and giving up control, and for many participants it was about learning to trust someone else in an alternative sexual encounter. Pain might occur, but the purpose was not to inflict permanent harm and certainly not to cause death. For many people, the world of S&M was a brief respite from the rest of life, from dreary routines or boring jobs.

The S&M subculture had its own lingo and "safe words." When those words were spoken, they acted as a signal that things had gone beyond what was agreed on and it was time to stop. Another type of S&M known as Gorean had no safe words and no rules; submission to the dominant was total. The Gorean concept had been laid out in twenty-five science fiction novels about the planet Gor, written by a philosophy professor named John Norman. On Gor, all the women were slaves to men and had to satisfy their every sexual desire. Since the books' first appearance in the 1960s, the Gorean novels had gained a cult following and were highly valued by book collectors. With the development of the Internet, Gorean adherents also had a strong presence on-line. Cyberspace was the perfect place to meet people with like desires.

Robinson was naturally drawn to the Gorean realm. He'd always relished being in control, especially in his relations with women. Now he'd found a locale where females willingly put themselves into submissive roles. Some would even go so far as to sign contracts for their "masters," in which they gave up not only control of their bodies but in some cases their financial assets. The three things that Robinson had pursued so relentlessly and aggressively over the years—money, sex outside of marriage, and power over others—were now literally falling into his lap or, more accurately, his laptop. He no longer had to create complicated baby-selling scams or business fronts that enticed young women who were looking for employment. He no longer had to pretend that he was an enlightened male who was interested in sexual equality, inside or out of the bedroom. Now he could be more of himself. The Internet provided him with a huge new arena in which to ply his trade.

Through ads in cyberspace and those in an alternative newspaper in Kansas City called *Pitch Weekly,* he looked for women who were interested in the games he wanted to play. He found one in the "Wildside" section of the paper, an attractive African-American woman in her late twenties named Alecia Cox. She had a velvety voice and what some people would describe as a sassy manner. Her personal ad in the paper read: "SBF [Straight Black Female] looking for mature male to take care of me—I'll take care of you." The aspiring radio personality was now working in Kansas City as a receptionist and had a young daughter who lived with her mother in Salina, Kansas. She wanted to get into the entertainment business; she had a professional head shot made up of herself with her résumé on the back. Her on-air name was Lisa Fox. She was ambitious but down on her luck. After Robinson answered her ad, they quickly reached an agreement: he would pay her as much as $2,000 a month, while she agreed to be his mistress. He wanted her available for sex whenever he desired it. When he arrived at her apartment, he demanded that she be waiting for him naked. He only visited during the day. He told Alecia that he was married but not having sex with his wife and he was about to get divorced. He also told her that he was a successful entrepreneur with a pool supply store and a hydroponic business. He bragged about knowing many important people, including President Clinton, whom he'd met during a flight on Air Force One. He also told Alecia that she was a "bright girl" who would make an excellent personal assistant. She was impressed enough by Robinson to join forces with him.

Their sexual encounters were generally conventional, but he did put clips on her nipples and a dog collar on her that restrained her hands. Underneath her feminine exterior was a tough, street-smart woman, cocky and self-assured, and for once, Robinson had met his match. Alecia wasn't afraid to ask for what she wanted and she asked Robinson for a lot. He didn't give her as much money as he'd originally promised and he occasionally reneged on his agreement to pay up, but the relationship lasted for a couple of years. On one occasion, when he demanded that she sign a slave contract, she complied, just to please him. For a while she worked at an athletic club where she had to disrobe in front of other people. Robinson wrote his initials on her hip with a pen, as if this were his private brand. The letters even resembled a brand, with the *J* and the *R* connected. He wanted other club members to see that she was someone's property.

He offered her gifts of clothing, which struck her as an unusual thing for a man to have. Many of the items weren't her style or size and looked worn. In the back of his pickup, she once saw an entire rack of women's clothes, and in the apartment he rented, he showed her other boxes of women's clothing. As Alecia sorted through the dresses, looking for something she might like, she wondered where all this apparel had come from, eventually choosing a white camisole, a black velvet shirt, and a green velvet dress. Robinson explained to her that the clothes had been left behind by ex-employees of his businesses. Alecia didn't ask too many questions and he didn't offer any more information. It didn't occur to her that the dresses had once belonged to women who'd gotten involved with Robinson, in much the same way that she was doing now.

Robinson gave Alecia a gold band and said he wanted to marry her. He also wanted her to tell him how much she loved him, especially when they were making love. He wanted to hear it from her over and over again during moments of passion. The words were as important as the sex. He may have been trying to hook her deeper emotionally, but she was satisfying some equally deep emotional longings within him. Robinson was profoundly entangled with women—a rage of need and desire and weakness and violence. He spent all his time with women, whether he was at home or somewhere else. Male friends did not figure into much of his existence, unless he was hustling them for gain. It was the company of women that he craved. And it was women whom he was always planning to get rid of.

In the fall of 1998, Alecia wanted Robinson to use his influence to help her get a job in entertainment. She gave him some of her publicity photos and he said he needed some documents holding her Social Security number. She gave up her apartment after he told her that he wanted to hire her to travel overseas on business with him. He wanted her to "schmooze" clients in London, Paris, and Australia. He put her up in a Best Western hotel before the trip commenced and said he'd take care of her passport application. The departure date kept shifting, and Alecia's family members grew skeptical about the job. Robinson asked her to write travel letters to her relatives on pastel stationery. When she asked why she needed to do this now, he explained that they would be so busy while abroad that she wouldn't have time for such details. He told her to date them in the future and gave her the actual dates, insistent that she do this.

The evening before they were supposed to leave for London, Robinson did something unusual, in spite of his decades of infidelity. He spent the entire night outside his home with one of his lovers. When he arrived at the hotel in his white Dodge Ram pickup, Alecia noticed that it had a trailer hitched to the back and a rack of clothing on the bed. The next morning Alecia woke up around five while Robinson was still asleep. She awakened him, which angered him. He was upset because she'd gotten up before him. She didn't understand why he was so annoyed. He jumped out of bed, showered, and quickly left after saying that he had errands to run. He told her to meet him at a restaurant at ten that morning to make final preparations for the trip. She went there and waited for him but he never arrived or called.

She phoned him again and again to ask what had happened, but he never responded. She was left without a job or a place to live and was forced to stay with relatives. A few months later, Alecia placed another ad in the same alternative paper and once more Robinson answered it. She was glad to hear from him, eager to resume their affair. Like many other women, she genuinely liked him, even when he wasn't giving her money. His attraction to women was so strong that some females found him irresistible. He explained to her that he'd bolted earlier because he was embarrassed by her behavior, accusing her of infidelity. He couldn't travel with someone he didn't trust. He couldn't tolerate someone he couldn't control. They restarted the relationship, and in the summer of 1999, Robinson convinced her to give him Power of Attorney over her affairs. By this time he was seeing a number of other women, so he and Cox gradually drifted apart.

Only much later did Alecia have a major revelation. She believed that the morning Robinson had angrily awakened next to her in the motel, he was making plans of a sort that did not involve world travel. She felt that he was going to kill her later that same day. That was why he'd wanted her to sign the papers and give him the Power of Attorney. The trailer on the back of his pickup, she realized, could have been used for transporting a body. She'd disrupted his plans by getting up before him, and he'd left the motel in a fury, something she hadn't understood for several more years. Then it made sense. Her accidental awakening that morning had saved her life.

XVIII

By the midnineties, Robinson stayed extremely busy romancing women of different ages, ethnic backgrounds, physical types, and educational and economic circumstances. If he'd seemed in a hurry before, now he was a whirlwind of activity, both on-line and off. He had cyber-affairs going on in, among other places, Texas, Kentucky, Tennessee, England, and Canada. He tried to persuade women in the United States and internationally to come to Kansas City and be a part of his life. Some turned down his requests but a few others would willingly and optimistically agree to uproot themselves and travel to meet this charming and persuasive country gentleman. He also asked a number of them to sign "slave contracts" similar to the standard one below:

SLAVE CONTRACT
This is a basic contract that may be used between a Master and a Slave.

Of my own free will, as of this day [date], I [name of slave] (hereinafter called "SLAVE"), hereby grant [Name of Master] (hereinafter called "MASTER"), full ownership and use of my body and mind from now until I am released.

I will place my sobriety/emotional sobriety first in all considerations in this relationship.

I will obey my MASTER at all times and will wholeheartedly seek your pleasure and well-being above all other considerations. I renounce all my rights to my own pleasure, comfort, or gratification except insofar as you desire or permit them.

I will strive diligently to re-mold my body, my habits, and my attitudes in accordance with your desires. I will seek always to please you better, and will gracefully accept criticism as a means for growth and not a threat of abandonment.

I renounce all rights to privacy or concealment from you. . . .

I understand and agree that any failure by me to comply fully with your desires shall be regarded as sufficient cause for possibly severe punishment.

I understand that for a training period indicated by you all punishment will be given at a 5 to 1 ratio to the offense.

Within the limits of my physical safety and my ability to earn a livelihood, I otherwise unconditionally accept as your prerogative anything that you may choose to do with me, whether as punishment, for your amusement, or for whatever purpose, no matter how painful or humiliating to myself.

The contract allowed the slave to use a "safe word" when things became too painful or harmful, either physically or emotionally. The slave agreed to finish any assignment within two full days and to answer all the master's communications within twenty-four hours. The contract continued:

I understand that if I use certain words which are deemed by you to be inappropriate for a SLAVE, the punishment will be automatic and then it is my duty to remind MASTER in the case that he fails to remember.

I understand that at all times I am to be honest with you and communicate my feelings (even if I perceive that you may not approve). I understand that no feeling I have can be wrong, and that they may indicate a situation which needs to be addressed. . . .

I understand that my MASTER has my ultimate physical, mental and spiritual well-being in mind and will strive to be worthy of his pride in all my endeavors. I will at all times maintain a safe, sane and consensual relationship.

To Robinson's delight and perhaps to his amazement, there seemed to be an almost unlimited pool of women willing to let a powerful figure take charge of their lives. For them, the "master/slave" relationship was based more on an emotional dependence than a physical one. None were looking for someone to damage them physically, but all were searching for an emotional escape through elaborate fantasies. They were easy targets for someone like the "successful entrepreneur" and "gentleman farmer" from Kansas.

Charles Manson, David Koresh, and Jim Jones all had personalities similar to Robinson's, but none of them had employed their skills in cyberspace. None had had the chance to control the world from a distance just by sitting at a keyboard and luring people in. All three were dynamic and articulate, but more than anything else, they knew how to read and exploit others. Each promised a better life to everyone who joined up with him. (As Manson once said in a prison interview, "Everyone is looking for something to believe in. You just have to find out what it is they're looking for.") Robinson quickly found out what these women were looking for, and over the years he was improving his skills as an astute "victim profiler," adept at speaking their language, whether he was addressing a mayor's assistant or a prostitute or a stranger on-line. His cherubic appearance, captured in digital photos of himself, made him seem nonthreatening, and he always turned this in his favor. Once he spotted weaknesses—and there are weaknesses inside every human system and every human being—he knew what to do next.

But what about the women who responded to him? What were they drawn to and why would they expose themselves to such a man?

Says a female who's dabbled in on-line romance herself, "In my own life, the more volatile a man was and the more he reflected anger or rage, the more I wanted to comfort and nurse him. Men have elevated aggression and sexuality. Women have elevated nursing and caretaking. The more of a caretaker you are, the more you will be drawn to a predator with aggravated sexual proclivities. Always with the idea of making him better, improving him. You always convey to him, in one way or another, 'If you can use my time, my skills, my brain, my body, go ahead. Everything I have is yours.' This is the mechanism of mating, of pair bonding, and you do it in order to make the best life possible together. That's hardwired into women. This holds true for Robinson's wife and for the other women, even those involved in the S-and-M world.

"The latter group wants to walk hand in hand with danger. That's the highest tightrope you can be on, the biggest thrill. It's like going to Las Vegas and putting all your money down on one roll of the dice. The risk is that you'll lose it, but it's no fun if you don't bet all of it. Being with a dangerous man is the highest thrill. And the more damaged and unstable you are, the more you will seek the highest thrill of self-endangerment. If a man can understand having all that sexual aggression and all the violent impulses that men sometimes express—but not using those things against women—then maybe he can understand how a woman could put herself in danger but not think that something will go wrong.

"There's a denial at work here, of course, and that's what enables you to take the risk. The denial comes from our relationship with the life force. That's a very large thing with women—that fundamental connection to giving and nurturing life itself. Some women over-rely on it when they are in very bad relationships. They say to themselves, 'Something bad won't happen to me. I will be saved.' They go into these things knowing they're putting themselves on the line, but they will somehow be protected and come out of it. The only thing that can really save any of them is their own decision to get out of these circumstances."

Says another woman who has engaged in cyber-sex, "For many women, fooling around on the Net is about power. You can create the fantasy and carry it out and stay in control of the situation. You can use your sexuality to have power over the man, but you can do it in the safety and privacy of your home. You don't actually have to be there with him. You don't have to have anyone lying on top of you, doing something you might not like. And if it gets to be too much, you can just log off and it's over. No questions asked."

Says another woman who's flirted in chat rooms, "Many, many women have been in relationships they knew were not quite right, because they wanted to be supported or helped out financially. Money caused them to go along with things they never would have otherwise."

Robinson was in some ways like a pimp with a stable of women both on-line and off. In the world of prostitution, a pimp has to assess each of his women's needs and vulnerabilities. Some have to be supplied with the drug of their choice. Others crave an emotional fix and to be told how much someone cares for them. Still others respond most deeply to fear. One way or another, the man must psychologically pinpoint the core desires and fulfill them to keep everything functional and running smoothly. The pimp's role requires innate intelligence, flexibility, resourcefulness, and a peculiar sensitivity to women. The police believed that Robinson had been involved with prostitution in the 1980s, and he now seemed to be transferring those skills to other realms. In the nineties, he was a father figure to some women, a lover to others, a husband to his wife, and even played the part of a fiancé. Virtually any need he saw in the women around him, he was both anxious and able to fill.

Robinson met a woman from Tennessee in a chat room and offered her a position working with computers at his new company, Specialty Publications. She was more interested in pursuing a personal relationship with the "Slave-master" than she was in taking the job. He had her sign a slave contract, and one of his demands was that she turn over to him about $17,000, including all the money that over the years she'd placed into an individual retirement account. She made a check out to Specialty Publications and he promised to reinvest her money, but she never saw the funds again. Later, when she questioned him about this and eventually tried to get her money back, Robinson ignored her inquiries and demands.

Like other women and men he'd conned, she was at first hesitant to come forward and go after her lost savings, because of the nature of their relationship. She didn't want to be embarrassed by the slave contract. But once her money had been withdrawn from the IRA, the Internal Revenue Service asked her to account for all of it (tax penalties for early IRA withdrawals can be quite stiff). She was stuck with trying to explain to federal agents what had become of her retirement account. She hired a lawyer to recover her losses but the money was gone.

While she was seeking legal recourse, Robinson was having on-line contact with a woman in Canada, who also signed a slave contract and agreed to follow his orders via the Net. One of his commands was to brand herself with his initials, which she said she would do but only if they met in person (they never did). On-line, he met a woman from Kentucky, a grandmother who owned a business. He'd started this affair by responding to her ad stating that she was looking for someone over forty-five and financially stable. Under the name Jim Turner, he e-mailed her back the standard photo of himself in cowboy attire smiling in a Kansas pasture, presenting himself as a wealthy, hardworking businessman and devoted father.

For about three months, the woman and Robinson e-mailed one another about their mutual interest in sado-masochistic role-playing. She claimed to be very independent in all parts of her life except the sexual arena. She and Robinson had found one another through a personal ad on a BDSM (Bondage-Discipline-Sado-Masochism) Web site and her screen name was Lauralei. She took up with Robinson not just because of their shared sexual tastes, but because he struck her as a sensitive man who was willing to talk, both on-line and by phone, about personal, emotional matters. He wasn't afraid of feelings or intimacy that went beyond just the physical. He cared and was willing to express it. After hearing about her brother's death from cancer, he consoled her at length, much as he'd done earlier with Sheila Faith when she'd spoken of her trials with Debbie's medical problems, telling Lauralei that she should lean on him because he was compassionate and strong.

He wanted her to come to Kansas and make their on-line relationship more than virtual. She found the offer alluring but needed to think about it.

During his conversations with Lauralei, Robinson mentioned another woman whom he'd met on-line, a young college student from Indiana. Robinson recounted to Lauralei how the student had left Purdue University and come to Kansas City to be with him. He described how her "gothic" appearance had startled and embarrassed him. She wore black lipstick and black clothes and had pierced various parts of her body. She was far more dramatic-looking, he confessed over the Net, than he'd imagined or hoped for. He was a businessman, after all, the head of a company, and he had to keep certain aspects of his life completely private. When they went out together in public, he tried to distance himself from her by claiming that she was a friend's daughter. Because of all these things, Robinson told Lauralei, he'd decided to send the young woman back to Indiana. Although he gave a vivid description of the college student, he never mentioned her name.

In time, Robinson failed to respond to Lauralei's e-mails and she asked him why. He said that he was away from his computer a lot because he was spending time at his recently purchased farm, about an hour's drive south of Olathe. He invited her out to see the farm, but she turned him down, in part because he never wanted to reveal much about himself or his background. Eventually, she lost interest in Robinson and stopped sending him electronic messages. She'd almost forgotten about this relationship until sometime later, when the police contacted her and wondered why her name appeared on his phone bill. She told them about their discussions regarding her brother and how thoughtful and sympathetic the man from Kansas had been after her sibling had died. Only gradually did she realize that Robinson had been sending the same cowboy photo of himself not just to her, but to women all across the country. When she tried to retrieve his old e-mail, it was too late.

XIX

The young woman who'd left Purdue University to come to Kansas City and be with Robinson was named Izabela Lewicka. She was born in Poland in 1979, and both of her parents had been scientists under the faltering Communist regime in that country. In 1993, when Izabela was fourteen, her family obtained permanent visas to the United States and moved to West Lafayette, Indiana, where Purdue was located. Her father, Andrzei, took a job in physics at the university, and her mother, Danuta, found work as a research assistant. Izabela was gifted at the arts—at painting, pottery, and fashion design—and pursued these things as a high school student in West Lafayette. Her rebellious instincts, her aesthetic passions, and the people she was drawn to all inclined her to take on an unconventional appearance. She was thin and petite with long brown hair, with a bohemian flair. She wore dark velvet dresses and mostly black clothes. She donned lots of silver jewelry and her nose was pierced.

At Purdue she met others with her interests at the on-campus Guru Java coffeehouse, a student-run hangout. She befriended Jennifer Hayes, who was a few years older than Izabela, and the two women shared their interests in theater, art, paganism, the gothic lifestyle, and the sexual world of bondage and discipline. Izabela told Jennifer that she had ventured to Chicago several times to explore some BDSM dungeons and playrooms. Izabela was fascinated with the darker side of life—with vampires and death imagery. The women liked to talk about the fine points of the BDSM culture and how bondage and discipline involved in-depth psychological games, while sado-masochism is about the giving and receiving of pain. Confidentiality was a big part of this world. Izabela and Jennifer were growing closer, but one did not share the details of "assignments" given by masters to their submissives.

Izabela was a gifted painter and seemed headed for an artistic career until something happened that altered her future. She may have been delving further and further into the world of BDSM but she was still living with her parents and her younger sister. At home she began surfing the Internet. Throughout the day or in the small hours of the night, when other students were sleeping or doing homework, she logged on and went into chat rooms, striking up conversations with strangers and meeting people from all over the world. She was already an imaginative person, and cyberspace allowed her to expand that part of herself.

"She was always thinking about something better," her mother said.

On-line, she could indulge her tendency for fantasy and be anyone she wanted to be.

It was intoxicating to sit alone in a room and make connections with people you'd never seen and could only envision. It was like living in a realm of make-believe, except that it was real. She was soon going deeper into some of the Net's less well known areas, visiting sexual sites and exploring different lifestyle options. Neither her parents nor her sister was aware of what she was doing; her mother and father only knew that her study habits were falling off and her grades were beginning to suffer, as she spent more and more time in cyberspace. The Net was like a huge game that got bigger and bigger the more one participated with it. Five contacts could easily expand into ten, and ten could grow exponentially.

Each time Izabela logged on, she might have new mail waiting or forwarded mail or she might make new connections on this endless web of people, all of whom were looking to be a part of something outside themselves. The Internet was unpredictable and exciting, the place to go to get a private rush. Every time she went on-line, she could visit new places and have more adventures with strangers. Some of those strangers might become cyber-friends. In 1997, during her many hours of surfing, she met a man in Kansas and decided that she had to meet him face-to-face. He'd told her that he was an international book agent who could employ her as a secretary. She told him about her artistic talent, and they both shared their sexual interests. He said he wanted her to illustrate some BDSM manuscripts he was working on. He presented himself to Izabela as an experienced dominant who was always looking for good students and was willing to teach her the subtleties of manipulating and controlling others. Izabela was hooked. Her ambitions of escaping Indiana, using her aesthetic skills, and becoming an apprentice to a BDSM master were about to be realized.

In June of that year, she stunned everybody who knew her by deciding to leave Indiana for the Sunflower State. When Jennifer heard about this, she cautioned her friend not to go, but Izabela was determined. She filled her old Pontiac Bonneville with her paintings, sketches, many books, family heirlooms, a Hungarian coffeemaker, and a Polish mortar and pestle, along with her clothes. One painting was a large orange impressionistic canvas. She also took several sets of sheets, one of which was dark green with maroon zigzag patterns given her by her mother. She'd told her parents that in Kansas she would be working at an internship with a man she'd met on-line, but she was vague. Her mother and father tried to dissuade her but couldn't. After arriving in Kansas City, she e-mailed her family that her new address was on Metcalf Avenue. She corresponded little with them because she felt they disapproved of what she was doing. Her father in particular had tried to convince his independent daughter to use caution, but Izabela was adamant about staying in Kansas and finding a new life.

For two months her parents waited patiently to hear from her again, and when they couldn't make contact, they drove west to look for her. They were surprised to discover that the Metcalf address was not an apartment but an Overland Park mailbox service. The company policy of the service was not to give out the home address of anyone who used their business. Discouraged and confused, the Lewickas spent only one day in Kansas City before going back to Indiana without finding their daughter or talking to law enforcement.

"We hoped she would be back for the beginning of the fall semester," her father once said.

Shortly after they returned home, they began receiving e-mails from Izabela. Her father, sensing something might be wrong, wrote e-mails to her in Polish to make certain that he was communicating with his daughter. He was only reassured after she responded to him in Polish with information that no one outside their family would know. Most of her messages were short and simplistic, saying things like "I'm fine, don't worry" or

"I want to live my life on my own." The words gave no specifics about her internship or her personal situation or the adventures she was having in Kansas City.

Andrzei Lewicka feared that if he acted on his suspicions or told the police about the e-mails Izabela had sent him, he would stop receiving them. Since this was the only link he had to his daughter, he decided not to speak to the authorities. Things remained muddy and in limbo, with uninformative e-mails continuing to reach the Lewickas, and with Izabela's parents continuing to keep whatever they'd learned about their daughter to themselves.

In 1997, not long after coming to Kansas City, the young woman had filed for a marriage license with a man calling himself John Anthony Robinson. Anthony was not Robinson's middle name, but the birth date on the application was the same as his. No record exists of their getting married. The following year Lewicka enrolled at Johnson County Community College using the last name Lewicka-Robinson. She took a beginning drafting class and wore a ruby ring on her wedding finger, which she showed off to her teacher. Izabela liked to brag that she was married to an older man. Robinson never publicly said that he was married to Izabela but introduced her to people as his adopted daughter or as his cousin from Czechoslovakia. Because of her outlandish gothic appearance—black lipstick, black clothes, and numerous body piercings—Robinson sometimes distanced himself from her when they were meeting with his business associates. Other times he openly groped her in public. When asked why she didn't live with her husband, Izabela said this wouldn't be "proper" and that people had treated the couple rudely so they thought it best to keep separate addresses. Since she was only nineteen and he was fifty-four, most observers would not understand or accept their age difference.

What neither Robinson nor Izabela told anyone was that she'd agreed to become his "slave." Their arrangement included a contract that apparently listed more than one hundred conditions that she had to meet, including the detailed sexual conduct expected of her. In return for her fulfilling these conditions, he would support her financially so that she could devote most of her time to her painting and her voracious reading of occult literature. Another part of the contract allowed Robinson to take nude photos of her, with a leather flogger lying across her stomach, her legs spread, while she reclined on a bed covered by the green-and-maroon-patterned sheets she'd taken from home.

In March 1998, Robinson rented an apartment in Olathe from a property manager named Jennifer Boniedot. He told her that he operated a business called Specialty Publications and that he would be using this space to train his employees before they went on to Nashville, Tennessee. He intended to bring in women from around America and they would be working in the apartment at night but would require quiet during the day. As far as Boniedot could tell, only one person ever moved into the apartment: Izabela Lewicka. Robinson told the property manager that the young woman was his adopted daughter and that he'd rescued her from abusive parents.

To fill up her days, because Robinson was so busy with other women, his businesses, and his family, Izabela began to meet other people. She frequented a used-book store in the Overland Park area that specialized in rare and out-of-print titles. The owner of the store, Robert Meyers, thought she stood out in this suburban community because of her Eastern European accent, her long black velvet dresses, and ornate jewelry. She also impressed him because she was so articulate, polite, and courteous. Izabela bought academic and art books, but was most interested in the world of the occult, purchasing tomes on the Salem witch trials, on poisonous plants and medicinal herbs, and on the history of witches and vampires. She bragged to Meyers that she was proud to have Eastern European blood because that was the land of Dracula. She told the proprietor that she was married to an "older man," and on one occasion she came into the bookstore with a male several decades her senior. If Meyers was struck by his appearance, which he once described as "corpulent," the bookstore owner was taken aback by Izabela's. She was wearing a spiked dog collar.

Izabela was becoming more daring in her looks and in her time away from Robinson. She met a young man named Eric Collins, who was part of a group that enjoyed vampire role-playing. The group was taken with Lewicka after she claimed to have roots in Dracula's homeland. They would get together outside a suburban shopping center and go into the nearby woods. Moving among the trees, they would act out a fantasy game involving driving a stake into someone's heart. The game had elaborate rules, rituals, statistics, but no violence. The stake was nothing more than a piece of paper with the word *stake* written on it. The game was great fun for the fanciful Lewicka, who could use her imagination and artistic bent in acting out these scenes. Her name inside the group was Special. Her parents could never have imagined her darting through the woods at night in this make-believe realm with her newfound friends. Lewicka also saw Collins at his workplace, Express Signs in Overland Park, where she went to order a banner for Specialty Publications. One day she came there with Robinson to pick up the finished banner. He met Collins and noticed a book on vampire role-playing by the cash register. Robinson was unaware that Izabela knew Collins and casually remarked, "My wife here plays that game too." Izabela said nothing, not revealing that Collins was one of the people she'd played with in the forest.

Robinson had moved Izabela into a fourplex at 901 Edgebrook in Olathe. He told the property manager, Julia Brown, that he needed an apartment to bring women from all over the country who would be training for his Specialty Publications business. He signed a year lease, but the only woman Brown ever saw occupying the apartment was the young girl with the exotic looks and European accent.

While Izabela was role-playing as a vampire with Collins and as a niece/daughter/wife/employee/slave with Robinson, her parents were growing more and more worried. She had stopped e-mailing them in Polish and declared that her future messages would be in English. She told them that she was getting married and would only be communicating to her relatives in the language of her American husband.

Her mother, Danuta, desperate for clues about her daughter, went into Izabela's room at home and looked closely at the few things she had left behind. Danuta came across a photo of an older man, dressed all in denim and boots, who was standing in an open field and smiling. She was surprised that Izabela would have a picture of this much older man and she wondered if the person in the photo was involved with her daughter now. She was puzzled and disheartened about why her daughter had moved away and couldn't understand her not acknowledging birthdays or holidays.

★ ★ ★

In the autumn of 1999, Izabela told her bookstore-owner friend, Robert Meyers, that she would soon be moving away from Kansas City and wouldn't be coming in anymore. He was disappointed because he was fond of Izabela and sorry to be losing such a steady customer. She told him that her husband would be buying books for her from now on.

Not long after this, Izabela's shocked parents received an e-mail telling them that she'd recently been married. When her parents sent her a message asking for their new son-in-law's name, she shot back that she wasn't going to tell them that.

"I am happy, I am wed. I want to be left alone," she wrote.

She also informed them she would never be returning to Indiana. Her husband was rich, worked for a big company, and traveled often. She would be accompanying him to China and Switzerland. These messages did not exactly sound like Izabela, but when her father e-mailed his daughter saying, "I'm not sure you're really Izabela," she responded by mentioning her younger sister's nickname. This convinced her father that he was really communicating with his daughter. Andrzei and Danuta then invited Izabela and her new husband to come home for Christmas. They received a reply saying, "Not possible, I'm busy." Another e-mail correspondence from their daughter around this time stated that she'd just been in Switzerland.

In anticipation of Izabela's twenty-first birthday on April 11, 2000, her parents mailed her a check. Three days later they got one of the last e-mails that had supposedly been written by their daughter: "We spent two weeks in the countryside of China. It is my birthday surprise." She went on to say that she was enjoying learning new painting and glazing techniques in the Far East. If the words were designed to show her parents that she was doing fine on the other side of the world, the e-mails did not allay their fears.

In Kansas City, Robinson was no longer seen around town with Izabela. He'd spent enough time with her in public that her absence was noticeable. He terminated the lease early at the 901 Edgebrook fourplex, saying that he'd moved out because of his concerns about the other tenants. When people asked him what had become of the colorful young woman with the dramatic appearance, he said that she'd been caught smoking marijuana with her boyfriend and deported back to Czechoslovakia.

Nancy Robinson noticed her absence too. Because Izabela had worked at Specialty Publications, Nancy had been quite aware of her and parts of her relationship with John. Nancy sensed that her husband was attracted to Izabela, and the older woman saw the younger one as a serious threat to her marriage. There had been many other infidelities in the past, but this one seemed more troublesome. John might actually leave this time. After all, the children were now grown and there was less to keep him at home or wed to her. Was he finally ready to break the bonds of his marriage and start over with someone else?

Like the rest of the world, and especially like many people in law enforcement, Nancy did not see her husband clearly, even though she'd lived with him for more than three decades. She did not yet understand what he was capable of doing, and she did not grasp the one thing he would not do: he was never going to divorce his wife. Their bond was beyond words and beyond understanding. It raised the uncomfortable possibility that love is more complex and stranger than anyone has yet defined.

The Killing Fields

XX

In summertime, the elm trees near La Cygne, Kansas, are infested with tiny bugs. They infiltrate the eastern part of the state and spin big white cocoons that hang on the branches like spools of cotton candy. They cling to the leaves and weigh them down, gradually eating away at their health and destroying the trees from within. The elms stand there, unable to shake off the disease, dead in the ground. The bugs, known as webworms, are not just lethal but ugly and off-putting in almost every way. In color, texture, and movement, they conjure up maggots and leave an indelible impression.

"They come here in hot weather and take the life right out of your trees," says a local farmer. "If you've ever opened up one of those cocoons and looked inside, you'd never forget it. It's gruesome. It makes you shiver. There are thousands of awful little things crawling around on top of each other. They stay with you afterwards and can bring on nightmares and thoughts of death. It makes you want to get a torch and put a flame to the whole bag."

The blighted trees detract from the subtle beauty of the landscape around La Cygne. Modest hills grow stands of maple and cottonwood, while the pastures are filled with brown-eyed Susans and red clover. Wild turkey and deer roam the underbrush, quail huddle in coveys in the hedgerows. The Marais des Cygnes River flows through eastern Kansas, bringing in fishermen and their steel canoes, which on warm days glide slowly up and down the wide banks of the silent steam. This countryside evokes another time and feels more than seventy miles away from Kansas City.

La Cygne has a thousand people and takes its name from the French word for swan. Legend has it that a beautiful Indian princess and a great chief fled her angry father and became lost in turbulent waters in this area, but were saved after turning into swans and surfacing in the river. The nineteenth-century French settlers in Kansas named the river Marais des Cygnes ("marsh of the swans"). Today images of swans are printed on the maroon-and-white banners that hang from the light poles on the two-lane blacktop leading into La Cygne, and Main Street features big planters shaped like swans. Nothing could look more innocent than this part of Kansas, but that innocence is something of an illusion. Back in the 1970s and 1980s, drug dealers specializing in marijuana were first drawn here because of its remoteness from the general population and from law enforcement. In time, their business grew and spread. By the midnineties, a handful of methamphetamine labs were operating in the state, but by the turn of the century more than seven hundred were up and running. That number would grow even more. Even out here on the Midwestern prairie, where coyotes howled at night at the clear black sky, things were never quite what they seemed.

In the late nineties, Robinson sold his property in Big Pine Key, Florida, and purchased sixteen and a half acres outside La Cygne. The land, which lay six miles northwest of the town and held some outbuildings and a pond, cost him $36,670. He eventually moved a trailer onto the property, installing a phone line inside it. The trailer sat back a couple hundred yards from the gravel road that ran in front of his acreage and was protected from view on one side by a row of trees. A pole barn stood on an edge of the land. People passing by on the road would barely notice the trailer or the outbuildings or the small body of water. The farm was an isolated escape from life in the city. Robinson enjoyed getting in his pickup and heading south toward the farm, sometimes stopping in La Cygne for gas or a meal at the town's café. He was friendly to the local people but kept to himself. In this rural setting he donned blue jeans and work shirts, unlike the preppy shirts and slacks he wore in Olathe. Among these folks, he portrayed himself as a weekend rancher, a man who left his urban identity behind in Kansas City by driving for sixty minutes. The problem was that he never really looked or sounded like a farmer.

Now in his midfifties, Robinson was balding, pudgy, and slightly below average height. His hair, what remained of it, was going either gray or white. He wore glasses that set off his baby face and clear blue eyes. He had no distinguishing features but looked bland, harmless. He looked soft in the body and cheeks, soft in the hands, like somebody who'd never done much physical labor. When he spoke, he did not stumble over words as did so many rural people or have to work to put together full sentences. He could talk fast about many different subjects, and his voice carried a trace of the Chicago area he'd come from. Upbeat and naturally exuberant, he had the demeanor of a natural-born salesman. But around La Cygne, he was usually subdued, never wanting to call attention to himself.

He didn't have much to do with his rural neighbors,

although he'd gotten into a fracas with one of them over a property line. Folks in the countryside rarely saw him out working on his land or fishing in the small pond near the trailer, and they never saw him taking pictures of himself. He liked to set up a camera outside in the open air, where he took photos of himself dressed as a dude farmer. Back in Olathe, while his wife worked all day as the manager of Santa Barbara Estates, he surfed the chat rooms and bulletin boards, constantly looking for someone new to send these pictures to.

His urban neighbors occasionally saw Robinson puttering in his yard or leaving in his pickup. They never imagined that he had five computers behind the walls of his home or that he was exploring Web sites they couldn't have conceived of. They viewed him as an energetic and pleasant businessman who was always busy, too busy to talk, always coming and going and sticking his hand out the window of his pickup to give them a wave. They perceived him as a community asset because he put up the best Christmas decorations, and that statue of St. Francis in his yard was reassuring. The Robinsons were churchgoing people, active at Santa Barbara Estates, and never caused anyone trouble—except for the occasional lewd comments that John directed at women in the mobile home park. But everyone had his little eccentricities, didn't he? In America's heartland, folks trusted one another more easily than in some other places and rarely bothered to look deeply into someone's background, as long as that individual made a nice appearance and seemed decent and sincere. Most people wanted to think the best of others.

Down at the farm, Robinson put up fences and cleared out underbrush and worked on the trailer's run-down deck.

At Santa Barbara Estates, he'd befriended a shy young maintenance man named Carlos Ibarra, who was originally from Mexico. Nancy had hired Carlos, and John had taught him much about repair work. Carlos was grateful for the job and the assistance. Sometimes the men fixed things together and the older one boasted to the younger one about keeping women in local hotels for sexual purposes. He showed Carlos a picture of a nude woman in a sexual pose, with her legs and hands tied to a table, telling Carlos that she was his girlfriend. When the two of them rode around Kansas City in Robinson's pickup, Robinson said that he'd like to have a pretty Mexican girl for a companion, implying that because of all the things he'd done for Carlos, the young man should now help him fulfill this desire. Carlos listened politely but didn't say a lot. He was in an awkward position. He liked Nancy Robinson because she'd given him a job, but now her husband was telling him about his affairs and showing him disturbing photos and seeking an uncomfortable favor. Carlos only wanted to keep working at Santa Barbara Estates and drawing a paycheck.

A Mexican girl wasn't the only thing Robinson asked him for. In time, when Carlos's mother, Lidia Ponce, came to visit him from Veracruz, Robinson told Carlos to ask her to take four or five light blue, light yellow, and light green envelopes and letters back home to Mexico. From there, she was to mail the letters to people in the States. Robinson gave Carlos $10 for stamps and explained that a friend of Robinson's owed money to a bank and was on the run from the authorities and wanted people to think he was in Mexico. Lidia did exactly what her son requested and mailed out the letters from the Fiesta Inn Hotel.

On three occasions, Robinson invited Carlos to go with him down to the farm. Once the young man fished in the pond, another time he helped Robinson move the trailer onto the land, and during the final visit he helped the boss's wife add a deck to the mobile home. Then Robinson asked him for another favor. He said that he wanted to make a fishing dock for the pond and needed several large barrels for the project. He asked Carlos specifically to find four eighty-five-gallon barrels built to hold fuel or other liquids, and to find lids for the barrels with holes in the top. The barrels would be used to keep the dock afloat. Carlos did not purchase the barrels himself but told Robinson about someone who could sell him just what he was looking for. The man, according to Carlos, was asking $15 per barrel.

XXI

In 1998, Robinson had reconnected with a Canadian woman he'd known since 1963, when he was nineteen and she was fifteen. Barbara Sandre was now in her fifties, with short blond hair, a heavy build, and a face that evoked Tammy Faye Bakker. In their youth, Robinson and Sandre had become friends and then written to each other for several years before losing touch. In 1969 or 1970, he reestablished contact by visiting her in Canada. She eventually moved to England, where she started a translation business, and they lost touch again. In 1993, Robinson rekindled the friendship by sending her parents a letter, which they forwarded to Barbara in Great Britain.

"He was in the States and I was in England," she once recalled, adding that she did not think it was odd to hear from him after a lapse of more than a decade.

The letter launched a new round of exchanges by mail and phone. She'd become separated from her third husband and he wanted her to visit him in Kansas City. He liked to regale her with stories about his life's adventures over the past several decades, telling her that he was connected to all kinds of secret organizations. He also told her that he had adopted grown children. He asked her if she would mind mailing some letters back to the States for his daughter Kim, after he'd sent them to her. He explained that Kim was collecting postmarks from Europe. Barbara mailed two letters for Robinson, both of which were sent to her already addressed. She did not look closely at the return addresses she mailed them from—one in France and one in Switzerland. Sandre willingly did other mailings for him, whenever he asked.

Barbara was a good listener and a good talker. She could speak almost as quickly as Robinson and had a sharp mind. She ran her own business, Berlin Associates, Ltd., which translated German into English and vice versa. Compared to some of the women he had become intimate with, she was practical, down-to-earth, and had her own financial resources. She had, in fact, given Robinson part of the money to buy the farm near La Cygne. She was not, however, perhaps so astute when assessing men or potential partners.

They began exchanging e-mails every day and she made a trip to Kansas to see him (her sexual encounters with Robinson did not involve S&M). Nancy Robinson figured out that her husband had taken up with a new woman and had apparently found something containing Sandre's address in Britain. Nancy was upset enough to compose a letter to Barbara and fired it off to England, telling her that she was Robinson's wife. Then Sandre fired off an e-mail to Robinson.

"I just got a letter from your wife," Barbara wrote him.

"What wife?" he replied.

Who is this woman, Nancy Robinson? Barbara demanded to know. He explained that she was not his wife but someone he had hired when his kids were small. This woman was now baby-sitting his daughter's children. Robinson implied that Nancy had been a problem in the past and said a court order was even in place so that she couldn't harass his family anymore. If this message seemed confusing and bizarre, it did not stop this businesswoman from making plans to uproot herself from England and move to Kansas City. She believed that Robinson was not married in spite of Nancy's letter, and she had another reason for going.

Robinson was, as she once described him to the police, "a caring individual." She felt certain that if she relocated to be near him, they would work well as a couple. In July 1999, she uprooted herself and came to Kansas City. Because of her alien status, she needed a cosigner to rent her first apartment and he performed this role. They opened a joint checking account and she worked at his publishing business, helping produce a mobile home magazine.

"He told me he had a government job," she once said. "He told me he worked for the CIA. He was an assistant director."

She soon moved again, this time to an unfurnished duplex in Overland Park. Robinson filled the new place with things he'd been keeping in storage: books, furniture, dishes, and other housewares. He told Sandre that some of the items had come from estate sales. He stocked the apartment with three hundred to four hundred occult-type volumes, the authors ranging from Anne Rice to Madame Blavatsky. Barbara found this choice of literature odd and was not interested in reading it, but she kept the books anyway. Robinson never told her where they had come from and she never probed. One household item he gave her was a Hungarian coffeemaker. Another was a Polish mortar and pestle, which she placed on the mantel of her duplex. Another was a large orange impressionistic painting, which she hung on her living room wall. She was especially pleased with the canvas because it had been signed by Robinson himself, and she believed that he was the artist. He also gave her some attractive green-and-maroon cotton sheets, which did not come with pillowcases.

To Barbara's disappointment, once she'd made a great effort to live near him, she didn't see nearly as much of Robinson as she'd hoped to. He only visited her during the day, and when he dropped by, they almost never left the apartment. They usually had sex and then he departed, but even that didn't happen often. She assumed that he was busy with his work and didn't push him to spend more time with her.

She filled her days by shopping for gifts for Robinson and making new acquaintances. When he asked for her help, she willingly gave it. Once she went with him to a run-down section of Kansas City, where he picked up a stun gun for a purpose that he didn't make clear to her. He'd ordered it over the phone but purchased it in her name, telling Barbara that "a colleague from another country needed it." Maybe this was part of his work for the CIA. She never saw the gun again.

On another occasion, in October 1999, she went with a friend to a Sam's Club. Coming down the aisle right in front of them were Robinson and Nancy, walking side by side, and he was pushing a cart. Barbara was startled to see him—and even more startled to see him with another woman.

"I'm going down a row thinking that looks like JR coming toward me," she has said. "I about ran over his toe."

The couple passed by Barbara so closely they almost ran over her foot.

"He looked right through me," she said, "like he'd never seen me before in my life."

Barbara assessed the other woman, taking in the color of her graying hair, her glasses, her age, her clothing, and her demeanor. She thought Nancy looked older than JR, as she always referred to him. Barbara immediately went home and angrily e-mailed Robinson, telling him that she'd just seen him at Sam's Club with another woman.

He denied even being in Kansas City and said that wasn't possible.

"I couldn't have been [at Sam's Club]," he wrote back. "I was in Russia."

This incident did not cause Sandre to stop seeing Robinson, but it did help motivate her to surveil him, just as Nancy had done in the past. Barbara had kept the letter that Nancy had mailed her in England, which had the return address of 36 Monterey Lane in Olathe. Barbara printed up a detailed map of Olathe off the Internet and enlisted a friend to drive with her to this address. She spotted JR's white Dodge pickup parked out front of the mobile home. She did not know where JR lived, but it looked to her as though he lived right here. When she confronted him this time with what she'd seen, he gave her a quick but complex answer, showing just how fast he could work. He told her that his daughter often used his truck and stored it for him at this residence when he was out of town. He said that relatives of his daughter's husband owned 36 Monterey Lane and that his daughter worked at a fire station nearby. Nothing in this explanation caused Barbara to end the relationship.

Robinson had been expanding his more legitimate Internet work by introducing himself to a local Web site designer named Steve Gwartney. He wanted Gwartney to help him develop an on-line version of Robinson's modular-homes magazine, and the designer produced a site that fit all his specifications. It linked browsers to both industry retailers and trade associations and had a feature called "J.R.'s Comments," which offered a picture of a smiling Robinson accompanying his advice. He wrote about the best modular home styles and tips for how they could hold their value. His presentation was convincing enough to make him appear like an expert in the field. Yet Steve Gwartney, who had a lot of Internet experience, felt that Robinson was an on-line novice who didn't know his way around cyberspace. Steve had no concept of the technical knowledge the man had gained in prison and no idea that he was currently running five computers out of his home and trolling various Web sites and chat rooms, under several names, including Slavemaster, Jim Turner, and JT.

Barbara Sandre didn't know Robinson was surfing these parts of the Net, either. She wasn't aware of his cyber-life or how many women he was interacting with daily in other parts of Kansas City. She'd wanted intimacy and love with Robinson but was settling for much less. What struck her most was how busy he always was, always running across town and taking care of a hundred details that he never talked much about. After a while, Barbara decided to move back to Canada, and she and Robinson had discussed that he might join her north of the border during the spring of 2000. They'd talked about living together in Canada because she had business contacts there and they'd be better off financially in that country. Most of her clients paid her in German or English currency, and the rates of exchange were not as good for her in the United States as they were in Canada. She and Robinson were thinking of pooling their resources, but she'd agreed, as she once put it, to be the main wage earner in their "family." She'd clearly taken the next step emotionally with him and had been led to believe that he had too.

He may have sensed that his time in the States was running out and that he was going to have to prepare for a future elsewhere. He needed an escape strategy because his life in Kansas City was getting more and more complicated, both on-line and off. And he was about to start making mistakes. The master juggler of identities, women, and relationships was finally overextending himself. There were too many needs to fill, too many people wanting his time and energy, too many stories to keep straight. His wife knew about Barbara Sandre too, and Nancy did not like what she'd learned about this latest affair. She and John were beginning to argue about Barbara and the arguments would only intensify. It was astounding that Robinson had been able to keep so many parts of his life separate and functioning for so long, but the web he'd woven around so many others was beginning to ensnare him.

Down on the farm, Robinson's neighbor to the west was Wayne Burchett. The men got to know each other and Robinson let Burchett run cattle on his property in exchange for Burchett's clearing out weeds on Robinson's sixteen and a half acres. Robinson's only stipulation was that the man not let his livestock in Robinson's barn. Robinson had plans for this barn that included more than agriculture. He once told Alecia Cox that he wanted to take her down to his "ranch," as he called it, for "lots of sex." He wanted to tie her up naked in the barn, have intercourse, and "come back and fuck" some more, as Alecia once put it. But she declined his offer. She never made it to the farm even though Robinson had once made plans to take her there. The morning that she'd awakened before him in the motel room—the same morning that she later believed he was going to kill her—he had told her that they needed to go to the farm to drop off her car before they left for Europe.

Robinson and Burchett agreed to their trade and rarely saw one another again. Things did not go so smoothly with Robinson's neighbor to the east.

Retia Grant and her husband lived on the other side of Robinson's property, and by the fall of 1999, these neighbors had yet to meet him. Entering middle age, Retia was a small woman with long, thinning brown hair. She was deeply religious and took the words of the Bible to heart. She was polite and unassuming and would go out of her way to avoid causing trouble with someone living next to her. One day after Bible study, she and a friend were out gathering bittersweet, a bunch of orange berries prominent in Kansas in autumn. After her friend left, Retia noticed that one of her sixteen cats, named Explorer, had wandered onto a far corner of Robinson's property, near his pole barn.

Retia and one of her eight dogs (named Montana) followed after. As they approached the barn, Retia heard a strange sound, a banging and clanging, as if metal were striking something hard. An orange car was backed up to the barn. Retia and the dog came closer and heard the sound again. Walking into the barn, she realized that she was not alone.

The barn had a skylight and the sun's afternoon rays were streaming down from it and illuminating a man holding a shovel. Robinson wore a dark shirt and dark jeans, with a ball cap on his head. He was standing in a knee-high trench. He'd been digging two large holes in the barn's dirt floor but was unable to go any deeper because the blade of his shovel had hit bedrock. As Retia and Montana came into the barn, suddenly the digging, the banging and clanging, ceased. It grew extremely quiet as Robinson looked at the woman and her dog.

As she tried to introduce herself, Robinson unleashed a string of profanities, telling her to get out of his barn and off his property—or he would "take care" of her animals. She tried to apologize but he was so enraged it did no good. He just kept yelling. The dog, sensing danger, moved in between Retia and the livid man. The shocked woman retrieved both of her pets and left as quickly as she could. After telling her husband what had happened, he was concerned enough to move their clothesline farther away from Robinson's property. The Grants went out of their way to avoid any more contact with their neighbor.

Months later, in March 2000, Retia saw Robinson once again carrying a shovel on his land.

XXII

On the Internet, Robinson met another Canadian woman, Lore Remington, from Halifax, Nova Scotia, who was in her early thirties and had a husband and children. Lore was pale and heavyset, with long, reddish brown hair and some defiance in her features. She had a tough, independent streak and was not entirely satisfied with the daily routines of housework. She had an active imagination and passion for other things and other people. In Halifax, Lore may have been isolated from much of the world, but the Internet changed that. It brought the world, or at least certain aspects of it, right into her home. Whenever she felt like it now, she could take a break from cleaning or cooking and log on to her computer, enter a chat room, and speak with others who were bored or lonely or searching for something to pick them up and get them through a long morning or afternoon. She quickly took to the Net and liked using its novel language: addie for "address," nick for "nickname," and LOL for "laugh out loud." She was a natural for cyber-interaction.

She liked to go into Gorean chat rooms for role-playing games with dominants and submissives. The games were stimulating and very adult. They were a kick, a way to escape the confines of her work and her home and her children for a while, and to meet others who shared her desires. On-line, she could use those parts of herself that were buried most of the time, but still very much alive. She could be whomever she wanted to be without having to leave the house. She could connect with the passions and secrets and fantasies of others just by logging on and joining in the action. When the game was over, she returned to her other persona of wife and mother.

In time she began speaking with others through the Internet realm known as ICG, a personalized service that told Lore whenever her friends were on-line. The service made a sound letting her know whenever a new message had come in. She would then usually pause in what she was doing and go to the keyboard and respond. The dialogue could continue for hours, back and forth across time and space, people staying in touch and sharing their thoughts and feelings through the electronic web. It was a way of not feeling alone, of always having something to look forward to. You never knew what the next message might hold or if you were about to meet someone new on the Net. You never knew what was going to happen next.

In 1996, she met a young woman who lived in Monroe, Michigan. Suzette Trouten and Lore talked for hours in cyberspace, finding out that they had a lot in common. Suzette was not married but was looking for romance and a relationship, and she was eager to make new connections. Like Lore, she had a fanciful bent, a large need for escape. The youngest of five children and the daughter of parents who'd married and divorced each other three times, Suzette had long battled weight problems and emotional troubles; she'd once attempted to end them by shooting herself in the stomach, but received only a flesh wound. If she'd struggled with many issues, she'd come through them very much alive. In her midtwenties, she was energetic, curious, open to experience. There was something vital about the young woman with dark curly hair, as if the life force and the death force had fought a terrible battle inside her and the life force had won.

She wanted to be a nurse, but needed more training and education. By the midnineties, she was employed as a home health care worker, helping the elderly and the infirm, and worked part-time in the Big Boy restaurant that her mother managed. Suzette's jobs were low-paying and repetitive and she had to repress much of who she was when on the clock, but once that part of her day ended, she went into cyberspace and met interesting people. She didn't have to get dressed up to interact with them. She didn't have to worry about her weight. She didn't have to do anything but log on and start typing. The aspects of her that were not finding expression anywhere else were welcome here. Millions of people just like her were out there, all over the world, people wanting something more and to feel connected to something larger, people who wanted to feel less isolated and more appreciated and understood and loved. It was sometimes difficult to talk to next-door neighbors because you didn't really want them to know who you were. But it was easier in cyberspace, where you were probably never going to come face-to-face with the other person anyway. Here you could let out the private side without so much fear. Here you could cut loose. Suzette struck up on-line friendships with numerous people and Lore Remington was one.

Tammy Taylor was another. She was from Ontario, Canada, and had met Suzette in a Gorean chat room. Tammy, Lore, and Suzette communicated on-line, sharing details about their daily lives and their interest in BDSM. Like so many others on the Net, they developed their own little community within the subculture of the chat room. Inside the group Suzette was known as Pandora. Her friendship with Lore grew to the point where they got together in Detroit for a week in 1998 and had an affair, although both of them were basically looking for relationships with men. In 1999, Suzette and Tammy met in person and also began a sexual relationship.

Lore had been searching the Net for a dominant partner and Suzette told her about someone she'd recently met on-line, a businessman out in Kansas who referred to himself as Master or JR. Suzette had first met Robinson in the spring of 1999 in the Silk & Steel Gorean chat room. When he told her that he was building a new Web site for the International Council of Masters, she was fascinated by the project and offered to assist him. They spoke via e-mail with some regularity and Suzette told him various things about herself, her employment, and her financial situation. He told her that he needed help with his elderly dad—a mysterious figure known as Papa John. JR said that he'd been looking for someone with health care experience to come to Kansas. He needed a nurse who was willing to travel, and a nurse was exactly what she'd long wanted to be. Would she be interested in taking a job in Kansas City, caring for Papa John? Suzette was intrigued with the offer and began thinking about making the move west. She was having trouble covering her rent and was falling behind in her payments. Maybe this was the break she needed.

She e-mailed Lore the cowboy photo of Robinson on his farm, and Lore herself eventually contacted Robinson through one of his cyber-addresses, which carried the handle "eruditemaster." This name, like so many other things in cyberspace, revealed the way Robinson wanted to be seen by others. It clearly showed his intellectual vanity (*erudite* means "deeply learned") and his belief that he was smarter than most people. In the late 1990s, everything was loose on the Net, so why shouldn't he let his egotism run rampant here? Why shouldn't he set himself up as a master of this new realm? There would always be people who swallowed whatever he said about himself—and people who believed he had the answers for them.

Perhaps because she was a wife and mother, Lore was quite cautious about actually hooking up with her cyber-connections in the flesh, but Suzette wasn't so hesitant. She'd meet people on-line and then go out with them, always willing to try something new.

When Suzette told her friend in Nova Scotia that she was in debt and looking into a lucrative job offer from a Kansas businessman, Lore was concerned. The position sounded too good to be real. When Suzette informed Tammy about the work, she got the same kind of response. Tammy was skeptical that something like this could be true. According to Suzette, the job paid $65,000 a year and included world travel to Hawaii and Hong Kong. Some potential conditions were attached to it; she was, after all, thinking about going to work for "eruditemaster," so she might also be expected to have sex with her new employer.

Lore advised her friend against mixing business with pleasure. That could get complicated fast, especially if master-and-slave rules were part of the relationship, but Suzette was not easily deterred. She was always hunting for the next thing that would take her mind off the miscarriages she'd suffered, or off her debts, always looking for something to satisfy her longings for a man who could love her for herself. The only creatures who seemed able to relieve her ongoing loneliness were her two Pekingese dogs, Hari and Peka. Suzette decided to follow her wanderlust and told Lore that she was going to Kansas to meet her prospective employer, but added her own note of caution. She wouldn't take the job unless she felt certain that he would be a good boss and the position offered her a future.

In the fall of 1999, after Robinson paid for her to fly to Kansas City, he had a limousine waiting to pick her up at the airport. Then he drove her by a mansion, which he claimed was his own. For several days, he treated Suzette royally, while constantly promoting the attractiveness of the job and her excellent qualifications. He'd even encouraged her to bring along her favorite companions, Peka and Hari, so the trip would be more enjoyable. It *was* enjoyable, but Suzette was not yet persuaded to give up her life in Michigan and take the job. She'd never lived anywhere but near her family. She was close to her mother, Carol, and had serious qualms about leaving her, but she wanted the opportunity to earn more money and eventually get a nursing degree. She liked helping other people, especially those who were ill or aging. Now she was being given that chance, while getting to travel and see the world. In November 1999, she made a second trip to Kansas to meet with Robinson. This was a good experience too. After going back to Michigan and weighing all the factors, she agreed to sign a year's contract with Robinson, not knowing that his father had been dead for about ten years. Suzette was ready for a change and the "eruditemaster" seemed like a generous and considerate man, even thinking about her attachment to her dogs. She would give Kansas a try.

In mid-February 2000, after a lot of hesitation and inner debate, she left Michigan, driving a truck that Robinson had rented for her. She took along some of her possessions, including her computer, and the two Pekingese, anxious to start a new life. For months, going west had sounded like a good idea, but she didn't actually know if she could say good-bye to her mother and the rest of her family. Through a series of e-mails she'd shared some of her worries with Lore about what she might find in Kansas City, but the positives would surely outweigh the negatives. Robinson had promised her an apartment in Overland Park and a leased car. He'd told her to get her passport ready because she could expect to be traveling to Europe soon. He'd let her bring along her dogs because they would make the transition easier for her. He understood her hesitation and appeared to be doing everything he could to alleviate it. He seemed to know that she was afraid of leaving home and needed to be eased out of Michigan.

When she arrived in Kansas City, on the afternoon of Valentine's Day, things were quite different from what she'd expected. The plans kept getting changed. She didn't start working right away with Papa John and she didn't move into the apartment and, after turning in the rental car, she didn't have a vehicle to get around town in. Robinson put her up in the Guest House Suites motel in Overland Park and told her to entertain herself for a few days before he could get the situation in order. Every now and then he would show up and want sexual favors or to take illicit pictures of her. Lore had already warned her about having sex with her boss, but it was too late to avoid that.

Suzette didn't do much of anything for a while, except to sit and wait for the action to begin, all the time sending out e-mail messages to her friends and family members. At least she had Peka and Hari to keep her company in these strange new circumstances. She was growing bored and passed the time by braiding the dogs' fur, but this distraction was only temporary. The motel did not allow guests to have pets in their rooms so she had to take the Pekingese to a kennel. Without the dogs, she felt even more isolated and homesick. She felt totally dependent on her new employer, but he wasn't paying that much attention to her and she didn't understand why the job hadn't started. She wondered if she'd made the wrong decision, but then in the last week of February, Robinson told her to prepare for her first business trip to California, before sailing on to Hawaii and Australia on his yacht.

One of her first chores was to sign thirty blank sheets of paper and address forty envelopes to her friends and relatives. Suzette had brought with her to Kansas not only the names and addresses of these people, but also some of their dates of birth so she could remember when to acknowledge them. Robinson carefully explained to her that she was about to be so busy traveling that she wouldn't have time to take care of these details. It was best to get them done now.

One day when they weren't working on the envelopes or the stationery, he came to the motel and set up a video camera. He focused the lens on the bed and prepared to turn it on. Both of them took off their clothes. The homemade movie began with Suzette lying naked on the mattress. A large painting hung above the bed and in the background a radio station played "Down Under" by the once popular Australian band Men at Work. Suzette wore a chain, held together by a silver butterfly pendant, that connected her two pierced nipples. She thrust a dildo into her pierced genitals, swaying and moaning into the camera. She pulled on the nipple chains and said, "This is what you wanted, master, to tell you I'm your slut. Your ass, your cunt, your lips, everything is yours."

"Who are you?" Robinson says, off camera.

"Your slut, your slave," she says.

"Whose pussy is this? Are you a whore, a slut? Do you like your cock, bitch?"

"Yes, master."

Robinson appeared on the screen, kneeling on the bed as Suzette gave him oral sex. He hit her several times on the back with a leather flogger. Then he spanked her and spanked her again. When they paused, it was to discuss how to use a piece of equipment known as a TENS (Transcutaneous Electrical Nerve Stimulation) unit, employed in football games or other athletic events to stimulate muscles after an injury. It's been compared in size and shape to a TV remote control and can be used during sex to stimulate the genitals with a small electrical charge. With the camera running, Suzette explains to him how it works and tells him that it feels like pinpricks.

"I want you to get your TENS unit set up," he says. "I want to see how it works."

After fiddling with it for a while, he tells her that you'd "have to be an electrical engineer to use this thing." Suzette giggles at him.

In some ways, she seemed more relaxed than he was, more casual about what they were doing, like a young person exploring the limits of her sexuality in an unabashed manner. She would come out of her slave character and talk to him like a friend and lover while he remained in the stern position of master. In her happy-go-lucky Suzette manner, she taught him about the TENS unit, but he remained gruff and harsh. Being in control was obviously not just important to him but an aphrodisiac. Her personality—her friendliness and openness, her playfulness and liveliness—came through until he began spanking her, and then she resumed her slave persona. To her it seemed like a game, but to him it was something more.

After putting aside the TENS device, he lay down on the bed on his back and she again gave him oral sex. When she mounted him, he talked to her almost nonstop, occasionally tugging on the nipple chain. He repeatedly used the most demeaning words a man can use with a woman, as if this would keep Suzette at an emotional distance.

"The most important thing you are in your life is my slave," he said, calling her a "whore," a "bitch," and a "slut." He moved around behind her and grabbed her hair and pulled back her head, entering her and continuing his tirade.

"Did you sign the contract?" he said.

She nodded.

"Would you give your life for your master?"

"Yes, master."

He spanked her again and kept talking to her in a flat and cold voice. When he finally ejaculated, he moved off camera. Suzette positioned herself in front of the lens and three golf balls dropped out of her, one by one.

As the encounter was ending, something else popped up on the videotape, something totally unexpected. Robinson had evidently not brought a new cassette to the motel, but had filmed the action over the children's movie *Willy Wonka and the Chocolate Factory*. The film clip was a perfect reflection of Robinson's daily life. When he wasn't carrying on S&M sessions in Kansas City motels, he was playing the role of doting grandfather.

XXIII

After Suzette had come to Kansas, she'd continued trading e-mails with Lore Remington. They talked about her new job and upcoming travel. At 2 A.M. on the morning of February 29, 2000, the two women exchanged e-mails. They didn't speak again on-line until eight o'clock that evening. Suzette said she was doing paperwork and they discussed her employment.

"Just don't fuck the boss," Lore wrote her at 8:42.

A minute later Suzette replied, "LOL. It would be screwing up a good thing if I did."

An hour later they communicated again, this time talking about one of Lore's former masters. Their dialogue continued off and on deep into the night. At 12:38 A.M. on March 1, Suzette wrote to her friend that she was not "doing" JR, but she followed this up with another LOL. While Lore was exchanging messages with Suzette she was also speaking with Badass One, another member of their on-line group. The banter went on until 3 A.M. Perhaps Lore and Suzette stayed on so long because this was the last chance they would have to speak over the Net for a while. Suzette and Robinson, according to his plans, were going to be leaving later that day for a trip to California and then a cruise to Hawaii on his yacht. Suzette had told her friends and family that she would be breaking down her computer for the trip.

In between her e-mails to Lore, Suzette called her mother in Michigan. It was 1 A.M. eastern standard time and Carol Trouten was getting ready to close the Big Boy restaurant she managed. She was totaling up the figures for the day when the phone rang. Suzette sounded lonesome, the same way she'd often sounded since leaving home for Kansas, but she was trying to remain optimistic. She told her mother the same thing she told Lore, that she was leaving for the West Coast tomorrow and a trip across the Pacific.

That morning, Robinson called Suzette at the Guest House Suites to say that it was finally time for them to leave, but he wanted to do one last thing before taking her out of Kansas. He thought she should see his property down by La Cygne. As Robinson came to get her, Suzette took apart her computer, which she felt would be placed in storage for the duration of her travels. Then she left.

At 11:43 that morning, a call was made from the number of the phone in Robinson's trailer at the farm. A little more than two hours later, he arrived at the kennel that held Suzette's Pekingese. He checked out the dogs, complaining about the size of the bill for their boarding: $477. An hour or so after that, he was captured on videotape paying the account for Suzette's room at the Guest House Suites. He also stopped by the unit he'd recently rented at Need Mor Storage in Olathe, where he dropped off some of the young woman's possessions. To enter the facility, he had to log in with an electronic card. At each location he visited on March 1—the farm, the kennel, the motel, and the storage unit—he left behind a trace, creating a timeline of his appearances.

After picking up the dogs, Robinson took Hari and Peka

back to Santa Barbara Estates and left them outside Nancy Robinson's manager's office in a traveling cage. Then he called animal control in Olathe to report the two dogs running loose at this address. That afternoon Rodney McClain, an animal control officer, came to the trailer park and saw the pair of handsome purebred dogs without collars freely roaming the property. He was struck by how well groomed and friendly the dogs were; they were clearly not strays. McClain picked up the Pekingese and transported them back to an animal shelter. According to Olathe law, if the dogs weren't adopted soon, they would have to be destroyed.

Hari and Peka were supposed to be put to sleep eight days later, on March 9, unless someone came forward to claim or adopt them. On March 6, Vicki and Dan Wagner, a local couple, took the female dog and named her Tara. That same day, Ginny Holbert, a volunteer at the Second Chance Pet Adoption, gave the male to Patty Lusher, a member of an animal care group.

On March 2, Robinson reassembled Suzette's computer and spent several hours going through her e-mail, searching for her passwords and other data. He wanted to know everything he could about how she communicated in cyberspace, whom she spoke to on-line, what their addresses were, and what sort of language Suzette had used when talking with her friends. Using this information, he would soon begin sending out e-mails to some of Suzette's acquaintances, the messages indicating that she and her dogs had finally left Kansas City behind and were off on a wonderful trip.

On March 6, Carol Trouten received what looked like a computer-generated letter on pastel-colored paper. It was signed by her daughter, but a number of things about it seemed wrong. Carol believed that it contained too much information, was written like a travelogue, and left out the kind of personal details that she would have expected from Suzette. More troubling, the letter had a Kansas City postmark. The letter had been written on February 28 and, according to what Suzette had told her mother, should have been mailed from the West Coast. The postmark implied that Suzette had sent it a few days later from Kansas City, which didn't make sense.

"She shouldn't have been in Kansas to mail that letter," her mother once said.

Carol soon received another computer-generated letter, this one postmarked from San Jose, California. It was typed and signed by Suzette and said, "Well, I'm off on the adventure of a lifetime."

"I knew this was not from my daughter," Carol said later. "There was no personality to it at all." These letters had no spelling errors and her daughter was notorious for getting words wrong.

In a strange way, Suzette's gregarious personality, captured on the videotape Robinson had made with her in the motel room, was leading her mother, who loved her the most, in the right direction. She knew what Suzette sounded like, she could intuit her absence behind the letters, and she sensed something had gone wrong. Robinson could do many things with many people, but he could not re-create the lively Suzette for those who knew her best. Little nuances in language were sending warnings to her mother; more were to come.

In 1996, a middle-aged woman named Jean Glines had worked with Nancy Robinson at a mobile home park. Back then she was married and got to know the Robinsons through her employment. A few years later, she divorced and moved to San Jose. In 2000, she called the Robinson home seeking a reference. She got John, who told her that he was divorced from Nancy and would give her a good recommendation for a new job. He immediately began flirting with her, calling her gorgeous and suggesting they become intimate.

"He wanted to have phone sex," Glines has said. "I told him that wasn't my bag."

Robinson began calling her often, asking her to move to Kansas City and be with him. Her own family was located in California and she had no intention of leaving them. Robinson was disappointed but stayed in contact. In March 2000, he asked her for a favor. He told her that he would send her some letters via FedEx and he wanted her to mail them out immediately from a post office in San Jose. The letters, he explained to her, were an effort on Robinson's part to protect a woman who was in a bad domestic situation. Glines agreed to help, and the letters were supposed to arrive at her home on March 24, but they didn't. When Robinson learned this, he "went totally ballistic," Glines recalls. When they finally did arrive she opened the package and saw three pastel envelopes, yellow, blue, and green. She would later remember that they were going to somewhere in the Midwest, perhaps Michigan, and the return address was either "ST" or "Suze." Her phone relationship with Robinson ended soon after she mailed them. One letter she sent was received by Carol Trouten, and Carol would get another letter that had been mailed by Lidia Ponce from Veracruz, Mexico.

By mid-March, Carol had not heard from her daughter by phone or e-mail for two weeks. On March 21, the anxious mother received an e-mail telling her that Suzette was about to take off sailing from California. This message, like the others, sounded all wrong—Suzette used different language and had a different tone. Carol was becoming frantic and decided that she had to contact the police—but whom should she phone? She asked another of her daughters, Dawn, to help her. Within a day, Carol had reached the Lenexa Police Department in Johnson County, Kansas (Lenexa is just north of Olathe).

A detective told Carol and her daughter to hold on to any e-mails they'd gotten from Suzette in recent weeks. When Carol was speaking to the police, the subject of the Pekingese surfaced and Suzette's mother told the detectives that her daughter took the dogs with her everywhere— even when she went shopping, carrying them in a large bag looped over her shoulder. Their small heads always stuck out and amused the other customers. If the dogs were not with her, that likely meant trouble for the young woman. Carol also said that Suzette had sometimes braided the female dog's fur with beads.

This last detail caught the attention of the police, and an officer began tracing any local dogs that had recently been adopted. This led him to Dan and Vicki Wagner. He called them and said he wanted to stop by their home and examine their new female Pekingese, which they called Tara. The Wagners were startled by the question, but invited him to come on out. The officer took hair samples from Tara and noticed that the fur around her ears was crimped and looked as if it had recently been braided. When he addressed the dog as "Peka," she immediately responded by cocking her head in his direction. The police were fairly certain they'd found one of Trouten's dogs, but where was Suzette?

Something besides the young woman was missing. She'd brought several pieces of furniture with her to Kansas City, but they'd disappeared as well. The police eventually traced her name to a storage locker business in Raymore, Missouri, just southeast of Kansas City and across the border from La Cygne, called Stor-Mor for Less. Because Robinson also rented from this outfit, they wondered if he might have some connection to Suzette Trouten. In March, they set up a surveillance camera at Stor-Mor in case he showed up and moved anything into or out of his locker. They also asked the Stor-Mor manager, Loretta Mattingly, to tell them about John Robinson. What sort of an individual was he? Had she noticed anything unusual about his behavior lately? How often did he come down to his storage units? Did he say much to her or to others? Had he aroused any suspicions in Loretta?

She did her best to convince them that they were pursuing the wrong man.

"When the police came out here in March 2000," she says, "I told them that they had to be after another John Robinson. It couldn't be mine. He was so personable and friendly. He was very energetic and knowledgeable. A happy person. He would always talk to me and he was always smiling."

Stor-Mor had four hundred ten-by-fifteen-foot units laid out on a flat lot behind the main office. While Mattingly enjoyed chatting with Robinson and had found nothing suspicious about him, she had noticed that in recent months he'd stopped coming to Stor-Mor even to pay his bill and had begun mailing in his checks.

"I just didn't think the police could be looking for the same man that I knew," she says, "but then they showed me a picture of him. It really was him."

The police didn't learn anything about Robinson during their surveillance of the business because he never showed up at Stor-Mor. They didn't learn anything of Suzette's whereabouts, either. Neither did her mother.

Carol Trouten was used to speaking to her daughter at least once a day, if not more often. The calls had stopped. Suzette's grandmother, Jenny Trouten, received a pastel-colored letter, posted from Mexico, signed, "Love, Suzette."

Before leaving for Kansas, Suzette had given her mother Robinson's home phone, cell phone, and pager numbers. This was out of character for what he'd done in the past, when he'd laid down strict rules for not giving out his personal information or even his real name. The appearance of these letters, combined with not hearing from her daughter, eventually caused Carol to pick up the phone and call Robinson. He was taken aback by this. It took him a while even to understand whom he was talking to, but he quickly recovered and told Carol that Suzette had not accepted his job offer but had taken off with a Jim Turner to sail around the world. Carol tried to be satisfied with this answer, but a short while later she paged him. Robinson tried to appease her by telling her that he'd received an e-mail from Suzette saying she was having a great time in her travels. Carol didn't believe him. Her instincts told her that Robinson knew much more than he was saying. She countered by saying that she was going to the police with her grave fears. He said there was no need for that. His own college-age daughter, he explained, had once gone to Europe and had acted much the same way toward her parents that Suzette was acting now. That's just the way kids were. As a mother, she had to understand that and accept it. But she didn't accept it.

For the first time Robinson knew that the veil of secrecy that had surrounded some of the women was falling away. When Carol Trouten said she was going to the police, the conviction in her voice told him that she would follow through. He was still inviting new women he'd met over the Internet to Kansas City, but he was also talking with Barbara Sandre about leaving the Midwest and relocating to Canada with her. The pace of all his activities was picking up even more.

XXIV

Carol was not the only one speaking to the police about Robinson. In late March, the Lenexa Police Department in suburban Kansas City had also learned about Lore Remington and Tammy Taylor and their connections to Suzette. The cops were quite surprised at what they were hearing. If most detectives did not know a great deal about the Internet or the world of BDSM, they were now going to learn about the subculture of dominants and submissives, of bondage and discipline, and of sado-masochistic role-playing on-line. They also learned that Suzette had had affairs with Tammy and Lore, and both women were now extremely concerned about her disappearance. Lore and Carol communicated about Suzette, and the women were developing their own strategies to break through Robinson's facade.

Lore knew Robinson in cyberspace as JRT or JT. After she began communicating with the police, she offered to use her on-line expertise to try to catch JRT in a lie or inconsistency. She would send him e-mail, get his e-mail in return, and forward it to the authorities. For the first time ever, a police department was using a civilian to investigate a homicide suspect in cyberspace. For decades, they'd used informants for other purposes, but they were now employing someone on-line to trip up Robinson.

As always, he was stimulated by the prospect of a new romance, thinking perhaps he could lure Lore to Kansas City. If she was interested in finding a great dominant in the cyber-world, he suggested, she should check out the address of eruditemaster, one of his on-line names. Lore followed through on this and the two began exchanging e-mails about establishing a master-slave relationship, but the trickery was about to take another turn. As they deepened their communications, Lore got a message from "Suzette," assuring her that eruditemaster was a tremendous dominant and she should get involved with him. Lore also received Robinson's favorite on-line picture of himself, the one of him standing out at his farm in his cowboy attire; he demanded naked pictures of Lore in return. The more Lore spoke to Robinson on the Net and the more that Robinson talked back—posing as both JT and Suzette—the more complicated the game became. Lore was certain that "Suzette" did not sound at all like herself, and she was increasingly worried that something terrible had happened to her friend. She was trying to "play" JT or JRT or eruditemaster to get a confession about a detail or a lie, but she was interacting with someone who'd eluded the authorities for decades when it came to connecting him with violent crime.

Lore expanded her strategy. She enlisted her other Internet friend Tammy Taylor to start e-mailing JT, to see if he would say anything to her that would confirm her own suspicions. Tammy posed on-line as a woman who was looking to become a submissive to a new master. She too was trying to play him for information and also wanted to pass the exchanges along to the Lenexa police.

Robinson was always open to more action and struck up a cyber-relationship with Tammy. If he was already extremely busy trying to keep all his identities straight and all his communications consistent, he suddenly got busier. He identified himself to Tammy not as JR or JT or JRT or eruditemaster but as someone totally new named Tom. He began instructing her in how to be a good slave and sent her e-mails from someone whom he claimed had been his submissive. The messages said glowing things about his prowess as a dominant and a human being. One such e-mail, from somebody referred to as "slavedancer," described Robinson as "a true MASTER and a wonderful man."

As the women tried to play their on-line target, he played them in return, step for step and move for move. Tom had become one more part of his multiple Internet personas. There was always someone else he was willing to be.

XXV

In March 2000, the police got a new tip about Robinson, from an employee at the Extended Stay America hotel in Johnson County, not far from the Guest House Suites. Robinson had brought another woman to Room 120 at this location, after he'd booked it for several days. He'd checked in and then she'd followed him to the room a short while later; they were holed up inside #120 long enough for the workers at Extended Stay America to wonder what was going on behind those closed doors. Their curiosity didn't amount to anything more than that until one morning when the woman came to the front desk and requested that the clerk do her a favor. She wanted him to make a copy of some sheets of paper, and he complied, but one page got stuck in the machine and he had to run it again. He took the mangled copy and threw it in the trash, then handed the woman the good pages, which she took back to her room. When she was gone, the clerk's probing mind got the best of him and he reached his hand down into the trash and pulled out the bad sheet. It was readable and looked like a contract of some sort—a document that said that a man was being given total control over a woman.

In Kansas, the authorities liked to know who was booked into long-term hotels, so each week these businesses provided the cops with a list of guests. When the detective came to pick up that week's list at Extended Stay America, the employee mentioned this incident and turned over the page to the officer. The slave contract was vivid enough to get the attention of the entire Lenexa PD, which was already investigating Robinson. Its detectives, led by Dave Brown and Jack Boyer, began looking into his background, wondering if he had a criminal record. They were amazed and extremely concerned at what they found, so concerned that the department, under the direction of Captain John Meier, put together a task force to look into his current business ventures and his private affairs. Before long, one of the detectives picked up the phone and called someone who'd been thinking about, if not exactly tracking, Robinson for the past fifteen years. It was a call Steve Haymes had never wanted to receive.

"We tried really hard in the 1980s to put him away for as long as we could, where he couldn't hurt people," says Haymes. "In reality, he did quite a few years. He was in prison pretty much from 1987 to 1993. I think the hope had been that maybe some of our fears weren't true and he was just more of a con man than anything else. And maybe the time in prison and the health issues had changed him, and maybe he was just burnt-out and tired and that was the end of it, but obviously, he'll play the game till the day he dies."

When his phone rang in early 2000, Haymes was about to be shocked by Robinson's behavior all over again.

"The task force contacted me," he recalls, "and said they needed to talk to me about somebody immediately."

Later that same day, the detectives drove out to see him. Haymes welcomed them into his modest office at the Missouri Board of Probation and Parole, located behind a gas station and mini-mart in Liberty. Behind his desk was a picture of his children, the same kids he'd felt compelled to protect from an angry, vengeful Robinson who'd been released from a Missouri prison back in 1993.

He brought out Robinson's files for the detectives on the task force and was surprised to hear what they were currently investigating.

"I'm not sure that in the eighties I believed that he would have done things with his own hand," says Haymes. "He had certain people that he associated with, and at that time he might have had someone do his dirty work. But clearly now, by 2000, the appearance was that he was doing things with his own hand."

Haymes was impressed with the task force—its growing size and seriousness—its determination to stop Robinson at last.

"They had a number of people working on it," Haymes says, "and were investing a ton of time. But it was still all low-key and being kept very quiet."

Part of the task force's job was to send Dave Brown up to Monroe, Michigan, to talk with Carol Trouten and with Suzette's friends and family members. They were desperate for information about the young woman. When Detective Brown told them that Suzette's dogs had been found living with new owners, their worry moved toward panic. Carol believed that her daughter would never have parted from the dogs under anything resembling normal or safe circumstances.

Detective Jack Boyer was in contact with Lore Remington via the Internet and had established a dialogue with her up in Nova Scotia. She was regularly communicating on-line with "JT" and then forwarding her e-mails to Boyer. He studied them for any indication of what had become of Suzette. Boyer also wanted Lore to give him information about and insight into the bondage or sadomasochistic lifestyle, especially as it got played out in cyberspace. As a cop for the past twenty-seven years, he was certainly aware of the S&M subculture, but couldn't claim much familiarity with it.

"We don't get," he says, "a lot of those kind of cases."

He asked Lore to give him a crash course in its rules and practices and wondered if she could recommend some things for him to read. She did this for him and he provided her with guidelines on how to deal with JT without letting him know he was under surveillance. As Lore spoke to Boyer about tricking Robinson, the suspect sent out e-mails under the guise of being Suzette. It was a time of cyber-manipulation and game-playing all the way around.

While Boyer and Brown conducted this aspect of the investigation, Detective Dawn Layman was following Robinson in her vehicle, trailing him around Kansas City and staying on him when he left town to drive south on Interstate 35 and then farther south on Highway 69, which led him down to La Cygne. On March 29, she tracked him through the small town and across the Marais des Cygnes River and on out to his farm, tailing all the way there unnoticed, before turning around and heading back to the Lenexa Police Department. She could see Robinson's property, but the trailer was set so far back from the road that she couldn't really get a good look. And neither the pond nor the pole barn was visible from the road. After discussing the situation with her superiors, Layman went back to the farm the next day to get closer and snap some pictures. She didn't have a search warrant and she would later claim that one wasn't necessary because there weren't any No Trespassing signs on his property and no fence. It was wide-open for anyone who wanted to park alongside the road and walk the several hundred yards back to the trailer and the pond.

She carefully looked around the property, taking note of the pond, two pickup trucks, and trying to peer inside the windows of the trailer, but they were covered with black plastic and newspapers. She took photos of the trailer and the trucks' license plates so she could later run the numbers and verify the owner. She also noticed a group of barrels, some blue and some yellow, standing by a small storage shed. After spending only about five minutes on Robinson's land, she looked around again and then left.

A couple of weeks later, on April 15, she returned to the farm with another officer, and both of them noticed that the property was now marked with No Trespassing signs and a makeshift gate. They speculated that perhaps Robinson's neighbors, who were fiercely protective of his privacy and their own, had seen her wandering on his land two weeks earlier and alerted him that someone had been snooping around his trailer and taking photographs.

Detective Layman couldn't help wondering if Robinson had figured out that he was under surveillance—being watched and followed and listened to when he spoke on the phone.

XXVI

The person in overall charge of the task force, which was expanding by the week and would reach almost forty members, was Johnson County district attorney Paul Morrison. For years his county had been one of the fastest-growing and wealthiest suburban areas in the nation. It had nearly doubled since the 1980s and was constantly adding new homes and businesses. Many people who had fled the complexities of city living had, like John Robinson back in the seventies when moving to Pleasant Valley Farms in Stanley, headed straight for Johnson County. The once rural landscape now felt like an extension of Kansas City, with its crowded developments, increasing traffic, and ever-present piles of upturned dirt, where more and more houses were under construction. To get away from the city and one's neighbors, one had—again like Robinson in the late 1990s when he'd purchased his farm at La Cygne—to keep going south.

The forty-five-year-old Morrison had been born in Dodge City, Kansas, the home of some legendary battles between Western outlaws and lawmen, but he'd grown up in the central Kansas town of Hays and in suburban Kansas City, Kansas. His father had been a railroad man on the old Santa Fe line. Burlington Northern–Santa Fe freight trains still blew right through the heart of Olathe all day and all night long; they rumbled directly across from the court-house where Morrison worked, and just a few yards behind the jail. Their whistles screeched to warn pedestrians and drivers to be alert and stay off the tracks, and amazingly enough, no one had been killed by a train here for decades. Morrison had grown up in working-class conditions, with early ambitions to be a police officer. He'd come of age in a tough Kansas City neighborhood and had closely watched behavior that had shaped his values, convictions, and career.

"There was a lot of bullying going on," he says. "People getting beat up at the bus stop every day. There were a couple of intimidators. One of them ended up in the penitentiary. I remember one day on the bus a friend of mine was sitting next to him, and for no reason he just turned around and knocked his front tooth out. Back then, that was just kind of shrugged off as bullying. In later years, I thought that seeing these things when I was young was one of the best things that ever happened to me.

"Johnson County is somewhat isolated. Kids grow up here thinking this is the way the world is, and it's not. So coming from a place like that gives you the ability to relate to many different kinds of people, which is a good thing."

Morrison was the first person in his family to have the opportunity to attend college, and he decided to pursue a degree in criminology. He still thought he wanted to be a policeman.

"While doing those studies," he says, "I realized that if I got to be a cop, I wasn't immediately going to be elevated to Sherlock Holmes status. I started to think about being a lawyer, with the idea of becoming a prosecutor."

His path to the bar was not straight. After one year of

One of the photographs that Robinson used to send to his women over the Internet. (Lenexa Police Dept.)

Catherine Clampitt
(Lenexa Police Dept.)

Robinson's mug shot.
(Lenexa Police Dept.)

Izabela Lewicka (Lenexa Police Dept.)

Lisa Stasi (Lenexa Police Dept.)

Suzette Trouten (Lenexa Police Dept.)

Debbie Faith (Lenexa Police Dept.)

Sheila Faith (Lenexa Police Dept.)

Paula Godfrey (Lenexa Police Dept.)

Beverly Bonner (Lenexa Police Dept.)

*Photos of some of Robinson's victims on the
Lenexa Police Department Task Force bulletin
board.* (Lenexa Police Dept.)

Detective Sergeants Rick Roth (left) and Joe Reed of the Overland Park Police Department Task Force. (Lenexa Police Dept.)

Edgebrooke, where Izabela Lewicka was murdered. Her apartment is at lower left, Apartment A. Blood found in the bedroom tested back to her through DNA. (Lenexa Police Dept.)

Suzette Trouten was put up by Robinson here at the Guesthouse Motel in Lenexa. (Lenexa Police Dept.)

When Lenexa detectives investigated this shed on Robinson's farm, they found the hidden yellow barrels by the toolshed on the left. This photo was very important in the trial because it confirmed that the bodies of Trouten and Lewicka were there at the time.
(Lenexa Police Dept.)

Sheriff's Deputy Harold Hughes of the Johnson County Sheriff's Department is the man who opened both yellow barrels.
(Lenexa Police Dept.)

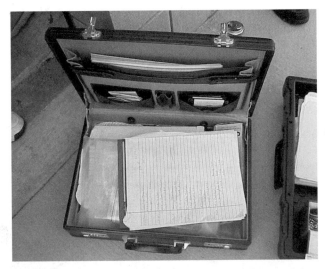

Police discovered this briefcase in Robinson's storage locker in Olathe. The legal pad contains e-mail addresses and biographical information on Suzette Trouten's relatives. (Lenexa Police Dept.)

Robinson's home office. (Lenexa Police Dept.)

college at Kansas State University in Manhattan, he dropped out to become a bricklayer's apprentice.

"I always tell people that if I'd been successful at laying brick," he says, "I'd be doing that instead of trying cases. But I got laid off and went back to school."

In 1977, he graduated from Washburn University in Topeka and then studied law there for the next three years. In 1980, he went to work as an assistant district attorney in Johnson County, where he quickly proved himself a good trial lawyer. With his balding head, full dark mustache, penetrating blue eyes, and folksy manner, he conveyed shrewdness, toughness, an aggressive competitiveness, and moral authority. Juries believed him and he was soon climbing the rungs of professionalism in the DA's office. He prosecuted the full range of felonies and became head of the narcotics unit. Then he began taking on the biggest murder cases in the office. He liked being in the courtroom and arguing in front of judges, developing an excellent reputation in law enforcement circles. He enjoyed talking to jurors and getting convictions against people who occasionally reminded him of the bullies back in his old neighborhood. He was hands-on at trials and wanted to keep things that way, but by the late eighties others inside the office were encouraging him to become the next Johnson County DA.

"I just wanted to try cases," he says, "but I kind of got talked into running for DA. I was actually very apolitical, but things turned out all right."

In 1989, he was elected district attorney and was now responsible for the cases generated by sixteen different police jurisdictions, yet he still found time to prosecute the major homicides himself. In 1990, he successfully prosecuted Richard Grissom Jr., a serial killer who'd murdered three young women. Their bodies were never found but Morrison was able to get a conviction and gained national publicity by using DNA evidence, considered novel at that time. Half a decade later, Morrison took on the even more notorious case against Dr. Debra Green, who tried to poison her husband and then deliberately burned down her mansion, killing two of her three young children (Officer Kyle Shipps of the Prairie Village Police Department, who was married to John Robinson's daughter Christine, played a small role in this case). Again, the DA won a conviction and solidified his reputation as an experienced prosecutor who was as good in the courtroom as he was in laying out legal strategy.

"In this business, you're only as good as your last case," says Morrison from his office in Olathe. Behind him a huge window reveals the new Johnson County administration building with its high clock tower and open courtyard, featuring a gazebo. In summertime, local people hold barbecues in the courtyard, which brings a small-town, homey feeling in the midst of these government buildings. Near the gazebo is a water fountain holding a sculpture of two young pioneer children who are looking optimistically out toward the future. The old Santa Fe Trail ran right by here, and the sculpture is meant to embody its spirit.

Something about Morrison conjures up an old-fashioned lawman. The Wyatt Earp coffee cup sitting on his desk reinforces this impression. The sound of a yammering police radio fills his spacious office, coming from his secretary's desk in the adjacent room. The radio is a symbol of just how closely Morrison monitors what's going on in his county.

"This is a great job," he says, leaning back in his chair and locking his fingers behind his head, "because the war on crime is a local war. The U.S. attorneys' job is important, but they don't affect things the way we do at this level. As I've gotten older, the good thing for me has been the opportunity to be a lot more involved with public policy issues."

In recent years, Morrison's office has created model programs that target high-risk offenders in the community, programs that focus on juvenile crimes, programs that focus on preventing domestic violence and on marshaling local citizens to get involved in crime prevention. Morrison has also been instrumental in innovative ideas for sentencing felons. And he has kept trying and winning cases, setting the example for the thirty other lawyers in his office. Their overall conviction rate well exceeds the national average.

Morrison has three children, and when not working, he and his wife, Joyce, are instructors at the Good Shepherd Catholic Church in Shawnee, Kansas. They teach young couples in the marriage preparation program about what to expect after their wedding.

"It's all about marriage," he says, "and it's not really very religious. It's about living together and getting along. People who have been married a long time tell you what to expect—and you're not going to get this from your parents."

By the late winter of 2000, all of his years of legal preparation and all of what he knew about being patient and thorough were going to be necessary tools for what he was facing in the early stages of the Robinson investigation. Nothing this entangled and multidimensional had ever before come across his desk.

"We had issues related to multiple states and jurisdiction," he says. "We had an investigation that had taken about fifteen years and some of it had occurred out of state. We had financial and computer issues. This case is almost as complex as it gets."

The DA, along with many other criminal justice personnel in both Kansas and Missouri, was painfully conscious that long ago John Robinson had managed to walk away from the disappearances of Lisa Stasi, Paula Godfrey, and Catherine Clampitt. Now it seemed that he may have returned to the game of hunting female prey and killing them by luring them to Kansas through the Internet. Morrison and those on the task force were extremely aware of the con man's ability to work the legal system to his advantage and to escape being connected to crimes of violence because of a lack of evidence. He'd slipped through their grasp time and time again, before going back to his old behavioral patterns. Instead of being changed or rehabilitated, he'd only grown into a more and more sophisticated adversary, which is typical of serial offenders.

For all these reasons, when Morrison launched the new investigation in March 2000, he was absolutely determined that if the man was arrested this time over the disappearance of Suzette Trouten, the charges had to stick. They could not proceed until they were ready and had solid evidence. As of April 2000, even though they were continually surveilling Robinson and had many suspicions, they had little real evidence to go on. They needed a break.

As in many other jurisdictions and many other cases, these dynamics created tension between the DA's office, the police investigating Robinson, and the families whose daughters were missing. Once Robinson had been singled out as the chief suspect in the Suzette Trouten case, there was pressure to move forward and see him arrested. Morrison would not be budged. The investigators still didn't have enough even to get search warrants for his home and farm. They needed witnesses and physical evidence before they could make their case.

If Robinson was arrested, Morrison himself would prosecute the defendant, along with Assistant DA Sara Welch. Morrison wasn't going to go to war until he was prepared and certain that he could win. This time there couldn't be any mistakes.

"I'm pretty invested in this case," Morrison once said, when talking about Robinson. "The amount of victimization that he has wrought on people is beyond comprehension. In so many ways, everyday people have been victimized by him, and from that standpoint, it's extraordinarily important that he be stopped."

XXVII

The task force was kept in constant motion that spring watching the frenetically busy John Robinson. They went to the Guest House Suites and spoke to employees. They had Carol Trouten page the suspect and get him to phone her back, so they could make a recording of the call in the hope that it would lead to the issuing of a search warrant (it didn't). They asked a judge to allow them to tap all his phones. They delved further into Robinson's criminal past and tried to unravel what his pattern of behavior had been and what it might be now. They considered going to Nova Scotia to talk with Lore and advise her on using the Internet to get Robinson to make incriminating statements. They researched more books and Web sites on the bondage lifestyle. They thought about sending a couple of detectives back to Quantico, Virginia, the home of my old FBI Behavioral Science Unit. Ultimately, the detectives did not travel to Quantico but spoke to some local FBI personnel.

"They were trying to help us figure out what kind of person we were dealing with," says Detective Boyer, "because John Robinson comes across as a typical family man with a wife and kids and grandkids. He's got a double-wide mobile home with a nice yard and toys and all that for his grandkids. The FBI was there to assist us and basically get a line on Mr. Robinson."

Profilers are generally brought into a case after all logical leads have been exhausted. However, I've worked numerous cases where I was brought in early in an investigation. In the early 1980s, I was brought into the child killings in Atlanta. While I provided on-site consultation, the killer continued to murder young children, "placing" them in areas where they could easily be found. In the kidnapping cases I've been brought into quickly, it was because time is everything. If you don't identify the kidnapper within forty-eight hours, the child will in most cases be killed.

What a profiler can provide depends on the type of case as well as the information you have to work with. For example, in a kidnapping, I could be working to develop a press release. I know from previous research that kidnappers, along with other violent criminals, follow the press. Therefore, the press release is critical. We do not want to scare or challenge the kidnapper. We want the kidnapper to know we have organized a task force and will ultimately find him. I want to emphasize finding the child and focus less on apprehending the offender.

In the Robinson case, profilers could have worked on interview interrogation strategies with investigators. This is an area in law enforcement where more training is necessary. An investigation may take two years of hard work, but when it comes to the interview/interrogation, maybe two minutes is spent on planning the strategy. The interview/interrogation is an acquired skill and a profiling team would be very beneficial in a case like this. In some respects the case was simple because forensics would link him to the victims. A profile is not necessary when the police have their man. In the Robinson case, it wasn't a question of who did it, but how and why he did these murders. Therefore, what a profiler could provide would be an assessment of Robinson, a complete look at his life and his behavior as a killer. The prosecutor could use this assessment during the trial so the jury would have a better understanding of the man being tried. Jurors would look at the accused and see a middle-aged, slightly overweight, grandfatherly man who did not look at all threatening. In contrast, they would also see photographs of the victims and the crimes that could sicken them to a point where some might have to look away. Profilers could help jurors understand how a grandfather could do something like this.

Early on in the Robinson investigation, research data collected over the years by my former unit could have been utilized in obtaining a search warrant—because crimes such as these are driven by fantasy, there is the need to perpetuate the fantasy. To do this, the killers become collectors. They have the need to keep mementos or souvenirs related to their crimes. In this regard, Robinson was no different from other serial murderers. He kept clothing and jewelry belonging to the victims. He made videos of his sexual encounters with at least one of them. A killer's souvenirs become key pieces of law enforcement's evidence. Research data collected by myself and others could have been used to strengthen the probable cause in a search warrant for Robinson's property.

In April, Lore Remington continued to play a submissive role on the Internet with JT, but she feared the worst. She understood the subculture of Gorean relationships, in which masters make submissives cut all ties with family and friends. By isolating the submissives, the masters hope to take complete control of their lives. One possibility was that Robinson had sold Suzette to someone in the

International Council of Masters. As bad as that might have been, at least it held out the hope that she was still alive. Remington kept receiving e-mails from Suzette, but they'd done nothing to ease her concerns.

While all these activities were swirling around Robinson, he continued his business and sexual pursuits on and off the Net, unaware that he was being closely monitored. He didn't know that the police were following him to Internet cafés, where he logged on and spoke to his contacts in cyberspace. These cafés were handy for people like him because it was far more difficult to track his on-line movements when he used a public facility than when he was on his personal computers. He didn't know that the Lenexa police were surveilling him at his mobile home from 7 A.M. to 11 P.M., seven days a week.

While one officer pretended to sunbathe in one of Robinson's neighbors' backyard, others posed as utility workers and climbed light poles to spy on his storage unit. He didn't know they were working with the local garbage collection agency to pick up his trash bags before dawn and replace them with someone else's bags that looked exactly like his. Then they took his bags to the police station and sorted through each piece, even those that had been shredded. They eventually found a mail receipt for the letters he'd sent overnight to Jean Glines in San Jose. He didn't realize that when he escorted women to motels around suburban Kansas City, officers tailed him and asked the employees to let them know if he booked anyone into one of their rooms for an extended stay. They were prepared with audio and visual equipment in case a new woman checked in.

Robinson didn't know that when he drove down to his farm near La Cygne, the police were right behind him in unmarked cars, staying with him until he pulled off the gravel road and turned into his long driveway. He didn't know they watched him ride all around Kansas City as he talked constantly on his cell phone. The police were amazed at how prolific Robinson was—going to the farm, driving down to his storage units in Raymore, Missouri, running several business operations, living and interacting with his wife in Olathe, interacting with many women in cyberspace, and continually starting up new relationships. Despite the aggressiveness of their surveillance, the authorities had thus far found nothing that would clearly implicate Robinson in a crime. Near the end of April, Robinson left Kansas City for a family reunion, and his sudden disappearance greatly concerned the task force. They wondered if he would come back. They needed a fresher contact to Robinson and one was about to arrive via the Internet.

Vickie Neufeld, an attractive, blond psychologist in her thirties from Galveston, Texas, had been exploring her interest in the S&M subculture for the past half decade. She had a master's degree in counseling and a Ph.D. in clinical psychology. By the spring of 2000, she'd been divorced for several years (she had two children) and was in an emotionally and financially fragile state when John Robinson answered her ad on a BDSM Web site. She'd been working with a geriatric population but lost her job on March 10, 2000, and was looking for financial support. Week by week, she was falling behind in her bills. Even though she was in the business of offering therapy to others, she'd lately been feeling bad about herself as a woman and as a professional.

She was taking antidepressant and antianxiety medications and had placed an ad on the Net to find a long-term, monogamous relationship. Neufeld had a spanking fetish and was seeking an arrangement in which a strong male would be her dominant and she would be his submissive. For many people, the desire to establish this kind of connection was not merely sexual or even necessarily monetary. It had more to do with emotional vulnerability than anything else. It was a chance to get away from your own life for a while and to let someone else make decisions for you. It was a break from adult responsibility. Neufeld had reached this place herself and hoped to find the answers to her dilemma in cyberspace.

She received a lot of responses to her ad, but the most promising one came from a man in Kansas City named J.R. He explained to her that he wasn't just any master, but belonged to an elite group of "dominants" and was highly respected in this subculture. Vickie was impressed with his qualifications and the two began exchanging e-mails and phone calls. She soon received his standard cowboy photo of himself on the farm. When Neufeld told Robinson that she was looking for work as well as a sexual relationship, he said that he was divorced and a prominent local businessman. He was financially secure, had many local contacts among doctors and psychologists, and could help her find what she was searching for. He asked her to send along her qualifications so he could get her job interviews in Kansas and Missouri. Perhaps he could help her get licensed as a therapist in Kansas. Encouraged, Neufeld accepted his offer and they decided to rendezvous in Kansas City. He wired her $100 to make the trip and she was eager to go. She had complex reasons for leaving Texas and starting up a new life a couple of states to the north.

"Sex was important," she would later acknowledge, but not her "underlying motivation." She was looking for help on just about every level.

On Easter Sunday, April 23, after driving seven hundred miles from Texas with her dog, Neufeld arrived in Overland Park and checked into Room 120 of Extended Stay America, where Robinson had arranged to meet her. He wasn't there and didn't make an appearance that evening, but some other people were on hand for her arrival.

Unbeknownst to either Robinson or Neufeld, the Lenexa Police Department had been tipped off that Robinson had booked his regular room at this hotel—#120—which indicated that a woman would soon be checking in here for at least several days. When Neufeld went to the room, detectives had already been on the premises for a day, taking two other rooms that adjoined #120 and setting up video and surveillance equipment. They watched her carry her luggage and a bag holding $700 worth of sex toys into the room. Like Neufeld, they were expecting Robinson to show up that first night but were disappointed. They maintained their vigil at Extended Stay around the clock and none of the officers were detected.

The following morning Robinson was going to show up after eight but didn't arrive until nine-thirty. He was carrying a large duffel bag and explained to her that he was always running late and had just arrived back in Kansas City from a business venture out of town. He would be off again soon for an important meeting in Israel. Neufeld was quickly impressed with his intelligence and charisma. He was well-groomed, well-spoken, and had a convincing way of presenting himself.

"I'd gotten dressed and wanted to look presentable,"

Neufeld says. "I'd made coffee and offered him some. I was dressed professionally. We both sat down. He asked if I'd gotten a slave contract and I said I'd downloaded it from the Internet."

Robinson wanted her to sign the contract but she said she had some reservations. On the other side of the wall, detectives listened to this discussion. She didn't care for some of the terms he was proposing—for example, that she would give her body to him in any way that he demanded. She had concerns about that. She wanted some addenda to the contract stating that if the relationship didn't develop well, Robinson wouldn't put her out in the street, that he would never hurt her dog, and that she could live with him until she could find work. After making these revisions, she signed the contract.

Vickie had taken some other precautions as well. Before leaving Texas, she'd told a friend that she was going to Kansas City to explore a new sexual relationship with a potential master. The friend, who was alarmed that an intelligent and accomplished woman like Neufeld would do this with a total stranger, insisted that Vickie have a system in place to ensure her safety. While she was in Kansas, Neufeld was to phone her friend every three hours to let this person know that she was all right, and if these calls stopped, the friend would notify the police and tell them to go to the hotel.

The conversation about the contract lasted twenty minutes. Then Robinson was ready for action. He told Vickie that if there was chemistry between them, they would pursue a relationship and she could stay in his five-bedroom home until a job came through (before coming to Kansas, she had sent Robinson her résumé and Social Security number). He took off his clothes and lay down on the bed, saying this was how they would find out if they connected sexually.

"He wanted me to lay down beside him," she says. "He unbuttoned my dress and took my clothes off. He said he wanted us to hug and be close to each other. He wanted me to rub his chest and I did that. He asked me to perform oral sex on him and I tried but he said I wasn't doing it right." He told her she was unsophisticated in her techniques.

Robinson brought out a camera and took pictures of Vickie while she performed fellatio.

"I didn't know he had a camera," she says, "and didn't want him to do this. He said, 'Let's try this a different way.' He got up and pulled me by my hair and he wanted me on my knees while he was on a chair. He moved my head back and forth until he ejaculated. He grabbed my hair and took pictures with his other hand."

By now, Vickie was "gagging and feeling kind of sick." Robinson asked her if his semen was sour and explained to her that if he ate celery, it would be sweeter.

Despite her fear and disgust, when Vickie later made contact with her "safe" connection back in Texas, she told her friend that she'd met Robinson and things were fine. She didn't call again, and she didn't stop the new affair because, as she once put it, "I wanted him to think that I was worthy of a job opportunity."

The police, meanwhile, continued listening quietly but intently to the whole scene in the next room.

Robinson abruptly got up, dressed, and prepared to leave, giving her $50 for food and other necessities. She was surprised at this paltry sum, as she'd assumed that he was a wealthy man; after they'd become intimate, she'd at least expected him to take her out to dinner. Before going, he opened his duffel bag and showed Neufeld what struck her as very serious sexual devices: chains, ropes, leather restraints, collars, and floggers. He left the bag in the hotel room. She wondered if all this was more than she could handle. She wondered if she should head back to Texas—now—but she'd signed a contract with Robinson and he'd taken it with him when he'd left the hotel.

After their initial meeting, the psychologist sensed potential trouble with this new man, but she didn't dwell on her feelings and intuitions. It was too late to change things now anyway, wasn't it? She'd agreed to most of his terms—and at the moment she was without the cash to return home. She didn't think her friends would wire her the money to get back to Texas, and she was reluctant to involve her family in her private life. She would stay a while longer and see what developed.

Robinson called the next morning to say that he was having problems with one of his overseas companies but would come by as soon as possible. When he arrived around 11 A.M., she was wearing jeans and a sweater. He asked if she'd looked at any of the sex toys he'd left in her room. She said she had and he asked if anything interested her.

"I told him he had heavy-duty stuff," she says.

He took off his clothes and asked her to take off hers and put on some spike heels.

"He was laughing as he said this," she recalls. "I was feeling uncomfortable."

She didn't remove her clothes or put on the heels.

"He sat there for a while and got very angry and told me to take my clothes off. He pulled off my sweater. I was afraid. He wanted me to get on the bed on my knees and

I did. He put a leather collar around my neck and I said it was a bit tight. He told me to put my hands behind my back and I did. He put cuffs on me. I was afraid."

The cuffs were attached to the collar.

In most of Vickie's other BDSM encounters she had had negotiations and talked about what was going to happen. Robinson dictated and forced the next moves. With a collar around her neck and her hands clamped behind her, he again sat on a chair and took pictures of her.

"I told him to stop," she says. "He laughed and my fear became anger. I said if you don't stop, I'll leave and go back to Galveston. He stopped taking pictures. He came over and undid everything and put his clothes on. He said if you want to go back, that's fine, but if you want a job offer, you'll have to do what I tell you to do."

Once more Robinson informed her that she was unsophisticated and didn't know anything about the S&M lifestyle or what it meant to be a slave. She shouldn't be bothered by his taking pictures of her. Perhaps she should reconsider their contract, because she wasn't fulfilling her agreed-upon role. Perhaps she wasn't ready to make a commitment. If she didn't change her behavior, he would renege on the job interviews he'd set up for her next week. They argued for a while before he left the hotel.

Later that day, Neufeld called him and apologized for how she'd acted. She'd had time to cool off and think about things, and she'd decided that she wanted to continue the relationship. He accepted her apology and explained that the photos he'd taken of her were solely for his personal use and she didn't need to be concerned about them going out to others on the Net. She just needed to relax and enjoy what he had to offer. He suggested they meet tomorrow at the hotel and then instructed her to be wearing a velvet ribbon around her neck to symbolize their relationship. Vickie followed his lead, driving to a local mall and purchasing the ribbon. When he arrived at her room the following day, she was wearing it and hoped he would like how it looked.

"I wanted him to perceive me," she says, "as he wanted to perceive me."

Once Robinson was in the room, he laid her down on the bed. Then he began doing what he always did—slipping into his master persona and talking the talk.

"He said, 'How does my slave want it?' I said nothing. He took his hand and slapped me as hard as I've ever felt. Then he slapped me on the other side of the face. You only do in the S-and-M world what you've agreed upon."

In Vickie's mind, she certainly had not agreed to be slapped this way. Robinson again wanted oral sex and she hesitated but then went ahead. After Robinson was satisfied, he said he had to prepare for a meeting in the Middle East. Things seemed better between them now so they discussed her going back to Texas to make arrangements for her belongings to be packed up and shipped to Kansas. She could take care of this while he was abroad. The plan appeared to be a good one, but then something happened that angered Vickie again. Just before Robinson left, he grabbed her bag of sex toys and took them with him.

"You don't need these," he told her, adding something that underscored his fear that she might go down to Texas and never return to Kansas City. "This is one way to get you back."

The toys had been given to Vickie as gifts and held considerable sentimental value. She wanted them back but didn't want to start trouble now.

The detectives next door waited patiently and listened to Robinson and Vickie, wondering what would develop next with the couple in Room 120. They heard slapping and barking and wondered if this was just part of the S&M sex play (the barking turned out to be Neufeld's dog).

When Robinson drove away from the motel with the toys, he didn't realize that he'd just made another mistake. One had occurred when Suzette Trouten had given her mother his phone numbers. Another had taken place when the employee at Extended Stay America had discovered the slave contract in the trash basket and passed it along to the police. Another had unfolded when he'd taken the dogs back to Santa Barbara Estates and they'd been handed over to the authorities and given new homes. This told everyone who knew anything about Suzette that she wasn't merely a missing person, but was most likely dead.

But why had she needed to disappear? She didn't have any monetary resources to steal. She couldn't be cashed out, not unless he'd sold her to one of his underground connections. With all her doubts about what she was doing in Kansas, couldn't he have simply packed up her things and sent her back to Michigan? Or did she know too much about Robinson's past and his secret life? Had he told her or shown her things that were too dangerous to be revealed? Or had he simply reached a point where he believed that he was invincible and could get away with anything with women? So far, he had every reason to think that he could. But the sheer number of women he was juggling and the energy it took to manage the ever-growing complexity of lives and lies finally began to unravel his plans.

Along with everything else, some of the women he was encountering were, like Vickie Neufeld and Alecia Cox, stronger-willed and more resistant. He needed more compliance, needed women who wouldn't talk back. You couldn't have dissension and keep playing his game.

Hitting Vickie Neufeld in the face or hog-tying her in the hotel room may have been experiences that she wasn't quite ready for, but they hadn't pushed her to call on her safety net or contact the police, but stealing her $700 worth of toys was another matter. They were expensive and losing them in this manner deeply offended her, and if he didn't bring them back, she was going to take action.

XXVIII

Before she left for Galveston, Robinson gave Vickie a little cash for the trip. While she was making plans to move north permanently and find a job in Kansas City, she e-mailed him about putting together references and referrals whom he could contact in setting up interviews for her. He provided her with several addresses of prospective employers but not their phone numbers. Vickie soon received a response from a female who was apparently a nurse; she told Neufeld that Robinson had helped many professional women and that Vickie was lucky to be associated with him.

"Fifty slaves," she said, "would love to be in your shoes."

A week passed and Neufeld was still in Texas, not feeling very lucky at the moment. She was waiting to hear from Robinson that a van was about to arrive at her front door and move her furniture to Kansas. Robinson was supposed to have provided this service, but he hadn't followed through and seven days had evaporated. She concluded that he wasn't going to help her and she wasn't going back to Kansas to find a job. The relationship wasn't going anywhere. Vickie called him and left a message on his business phone, saying, "I feel that you used me. Please send my stuff back."

He replied with a message of his own, stating that he'd been in Israel, that he was really a colonel in the air force, and that Vickie "needed to think on her own and trust him." When they got together again, he was going to punish her because she'd doubted him. Confused, she e-mailed the nurse, seeking some clarity.

"Slaves," the nurse sent back, "don't argue with masters."

Robinson began avoiding Vickie's calls but left her messages that the move was still on. Desperate, Neufeld finally got hold of him, but his timetable for her coming to Kansas remained slippery. Looking for sympathy or maybe just to stall her, he told Vickie that he'd recently been in Tulsa and that his week-old grandchild had had open-heart surgery. She doubted this; she'd checked out his earlier story about flying from Kansas City to Israel and discovered there were no direct flights between the two places.

She was ready to break off all contact with him but wanted her sex toys back. If he didn't return them, she was going to the police. As soon as she'd made the threat, she started receiving hang-up calls that intimidated and spooked her because they came during the hours when Robinson usually tried to phone her. Each time this happened now, she was prepared for it and blew a whistle into the receiver as hard as she could. Eventually, the hang-ups stopped.

Then Robinson called and told her that if she continued to harass him about the toys, his attorney would let the professional association of licensed psychologists in Texas know that she'd come to Kansas City for an S&M relationship with him. He would expose the nude pictures of her that he'd taken in the hotel room, and these photos

would destroy both her personal and professional reputations. (He'd once made a similar threat to Alecia Cox,
telling her that if she wouldn't commit to marrying him, he
would show her mother the nude photos of her that he'd
taken; he was, of course, already married and had shown no
intention of leaving his wife, but it was a way to keep Alecia off-balance and uncertain, more vulnerable to his
demands.) Robinson's threats to Vickie were enough to
make Neufeld stop trying to get the toys back—at least for
a while.

After thinking about it, she wasn't willing to back off
and decided to call the police, unaware that they already
knew that she'd been in Kansas City with a suspect who
was under heavy surveillance. He was being surveilled
because of the actions of a group of women, of mothers
and daughters and friends and lovers, from almost all
points on the compass. From the north, Lore Remington
and Tammy Taylor were attempting to get Robinson to say
something incriminating over the phone or the Internet.
From the east, Carol Trouten was also trying to get information out of Robinson. And from Texas, Vickie Neufeld
was thinking about filing criminal charges against a man
she believed had stolen from her. In some cases, the
women did not know of one another or what each was
doing, but all of them would use their resources to help
law enforcement close in.

While Robinson was seeing Neufeld, he was building yet
another on-line relationship with Jeanna Milliron, a
divorced accountant from Texas in her thirties. She was
currently unemployed and, like Neufeld, had placed a
personal ad on a Web site seeking a relationship in which
she would be a submissive. During the past ten years

Milliron, a full-figured woman with a soft voice and brown hair framing her baby face, had explored the S&M lifestyle, but she was not interested in experiencing significant degrees of pain. She soon received a response to her ad from "James Turner." They exchanged basic information and he told her that he ran a couple of businesses—involving publications and growing hydroponic vegetables—and they discussed her going to work for him as well as having a sexual relationship. Because she felt they had similar tastes, she became more comfortable communicating with the man. They began talking on the phone and decided to get acquainted in person to see if the attraction was real.

In early May 2000, Robinson made arrangements for her to come to Extended Stay America and check into Room 120. Once more, the police were told and made preparations to surveil the couple. Milliron arrived in Kansas City by bus and Robinson was there to meet her. She immediately recognized him from the cowboy photo he'd sent her over the Net. He bought her some groceries and took her to the hotel, explaining that he was divorced with grown children. They talked about her being a book-keeper for his businesses and taking care of his house. She wouldn't get a salary but he would handle her expenses and pay her bills. When he said good-bye to her after this first meeting at the hotel, he left behind his bag of floggers and cuffs.

The next day they had a sexual encounter at the Extended Stay America, but only after he'd beaten and punished her because she hadn't assumed "the position" when he'd shown up—she was supposed to have been naked and kneeling in the corner. He was infuriated because when he'd gotten to the room, she'd disobeyed him by having locked the door. In his mind that violated their agreement, so he hit her on the back and breasts. He hit harder than she was anticipating. When the sex was over, he quickly left.

Milliron spent that weekend alone at the motel without hearing from Robinson, which seemed to be part of his pattern with a variety of women whom he'd brought to Kansas City. He would pay extremely close attention to them for a short while, then abandon them in a strange place for several days. By the time he came back, they were eager to see him. When he showed up on Monday, he asked Milliron for her Social Security number for insurance purposes, but this request alarmed her. Jeanna's instincts told her to give him a false set of numbers, so she did. He then handed her $100 and told her to return to Texas, close out her bank accounts, and be prepared to move back to Kansas City around Mother's Day. Milliron did as she was told but kept in touch with the man through e-mail. He informed her that he was busy selling one of his companies and affectionately signed his messages, "Hugs, kisses and lashes."

After storing most of her belongings in Texas, she drove back to Kansas in mid-May. Robinson met her at the Guest House Suites in Overland Park and they continued their sexual relationship (the police were not conducting surveillance at this location as they had been at Extended Stay America). Whenever he arrived at her room, he expected her to be kneeling in the corner naked and wearing makeup, with her hair pulled back behind her head. Even when she complied with his demands, he hit her hard across the breasts and then took pictures of the marks he'd left on her chest. She didn't want photos snapped of the bruises but he took them anyway. After the sex and violence were over, he would disappear again.

When she complained that she was getting bored being left by herself, he told her to go to the local mall to pass the time. She didn't want to do this, and during their next encounter he exploded because she wasn't following his advice. He told her to go back to Texas and that he'd stashed another $100 in the cabinet of the hotel room that she could travel on. By now Milliron had begun to realize that neither the job nor the relationship was going to develop, and this left her feeling angry and humiliated. He'd simply used her. Her hopes for establishing a bond were gone. Jeanna had to do something to strike back at him, even if it was dangerous.

After their last encounter, Jeanna, shaking and in tears, went to the motel lobby and approached a clerk. He showed her a copy of the driver's license of the man who'd paid for her room, and his real name was not Jim Turner but John Robinson. Milliron went to a phone and tried to call the police, but she was too upset to dial. The clerk took the receiver and helped the nearly hysterical woman make contact with the authorities. A few minutes later, Detective David Brown pulled up in front of the Guest House Suites. He spoke to Jeanna and heard the now familiar details that had come from other women who'd been involved with Robinson. As he listened, Detective Brown was encouraged. He knew that he was closer than ever before to having what the police needed—a live witness who could describe how Robinson operated and tortured his lovers, perhaps before killing them. Unsure if Robinson would return to the Guest House Suites, Brown thought it best to relocate Milliron to a safe house, where she stayed for several days.

On the morning of May 20, Brown spoke to Jeanna at

length, and other members of the task force interviewed her as well. They were gathering more information and passing it along to the district attorney's office, hoping that Paul Morrison was ready to give the signal to arrest Robinson. The DA could not afford to be rushed but the task force was ready to act.

"We always get antsy," says Jack Boyer, "and we always get a little bit anxious to get things rolling, but there's a procedure. I don't care how long you've been doing police work, you learn a great deal about impatience and you learn to adapt, but you still get anxious. You want to see things roll along, especially if you've been working hard. Paul Morrison is a damn good district attorney and he's very sharp and he makes sure all the *t*'s are crossed and all the *i*'s are dotted. I have no complaints about his work at all. Paul was right there with us all the way. We didn't do much without him knowing about it and making sure everything was okeydokey."

The task force, which had grown beyond thirty members, kept pushing forward. Boyer went down to Arkansas, where Vickie Neufeld was staying, to speak with the woman, while Lore Remington kept communicating with Robinson and reporting back to the Kansas City police. The detectives continued their surveillance of Robinson and were beginning to suspect he knew he was being watched. In recent weeks, he'd put security cameras around his home at Santa Barbara Estates and had installed an alarm system on his Dodge pickup. He had also given Barbara Sandre the go-ahead to pack up the apartment she'd being occupying in Kansas City and start the move to Canada. She was under the impression that he was finally ready to commit to her and would join her up north at the end of June.

Unbeknownst to Lore Remington, who had maintained an on-line dialogue with JR or JRT, she was about to be recorded having a phone conversation with Robinson. They had tapped his ground line, and on May 25 he called Lore in Nova Scotia and identified himself as James. His tone was bright, friendly, and breezy. He talked fast and dirty. He told Lore that he'd been trying to reach her all day and then went into some instructions that a master would give his slave. He talked about her putting electrodes on her rectum and vagina and said, "It can be a lot of fun." He told her that she'd been "a bad girl" and that a master doesn't want a slave "fucking anyone else." Lore went along for a while with the sex talk, and even though she didn't know the call was being recorded, she then turned it toward Suzette. Robinson never missed a beat. In the same glib manner, he told her that he hadn't "heard squat from anyone as far as Suzette is concerned." He said he had a private investigator looking for her. From the PI he'd learned that Suzette and her lover had taken a boat and had gone sailing around Mexico. The investigator was trying to trace Suzette through credit cards and gas receipts, and Robinson claimed that Suzette had stolen $10,000 from him. Robinson told Lore what a liar Suzette was and how she'd led some people to believe that she had cancer.

"I didn't know her," Lore responded, "she played me."

Then Robinson launched into how promiscuous Suzette was with various men who were paying her bills.

"The private investigator told me," Robinson said, "that she gave blow jobs to cover the rent, that was the interest her landlord charged."

As Lore listened to this disparagement of her missing friend, she had to control herself to keep the act up.

Robinson continued, "I'm getting a profile of a fucking psychotic bitch who was fucking people for money and being a prostitute."

Then Robinson explained how a friend of his in Kansas City had received a call from Suzette's mother— "The weirdest call he ever got." In recounting this, Robinson sounded put upon that any of the missing woman's relatives would be disturbed enough to make phone calls about her.

"I wish Suzette would do the right thing," he said to Lore, "and tell people what's going on." Their conversation ended with Robinson telling Lore what she needed to do for her slave training during the weekend, which included putting golf balls inside herself.

Glib or not, Robinson's hostility at the persistence of people asking him about Suzette could not be suppressed. For years he had managed to keep his real identity concealed. The unspoken code of silence surrounding the master/slave contracts and his insistence that Beverly Bonner, for example, tell no one his real name had kept him operating in secret. But Suzette had violated the code. Despite her raunchy proclivities, she had taken the practical step of giving her mother Robinson's phone numbers before she left for Kansas. The pattern had at last been broken.

XXIX

M emorial Day, May 29, 2000, was a hot day in Kansas City. When he left the house, Robinson was tailed by the task force as he drove around Olathe and went to a grocery store to buy hamburgers and hot dogs. He was in charge of overseeing the annual Memorial Day barbecue at Santa Barbara Estates, and if he felt that he was being surveilled or might soon be facing arrest, he tried not to show any of his concerns to his friends or neighbors. They would see only the upbeat Robinson, who was always fast with a quip and a smile. Wearing a golf shirt and swim trunks, he stood by the side of the community pool and cooked the dogs and burgers for all who attended. None of those at the party could have imagined that detectives were sitting on the outskirts of the mobile home park following all his moves with long-range cameras, shooting pictures of Robinson telling jokes and enjoying the moment.

The next morning, the task force reported to Paul Morrison, and the detectives wondered if he was now ready to make the arrest. He wasn't. The DA understood the full complexities of the situation and knew that if Robinson was ever charged with any of the murders of various women who'd been disappearing around him for fifteen years, this might well become a capital punishment case. In earlier decades, Kansas had had the death penalty but had gotten rid of it and then readopted it in 1994. Since then four men had been convicted of capital crimes, but all had had their death sentences set aside because of legal technicalities. No one had been killed by Kansas since the last hanging in 1965. That year had seen a series of executions, including the deaths of the *In Cold Blood* killers, Perry Smith and Dick Hickock. Morrison knew better than anyone else that getting a conviction in a death penalty case was only half the battle.

"Sixty-six percent of death penalty cases," he was quick to point out, "are overturned on appeal. People don't realize that. They just pay attention to the first conviction."

He was absolutely determined to pay attention to every detail and was still not satisfied that he had all he needed to arrest Robinson and search his properties, his vehicles, and his storage units. In spite of the enormous suspicions that Robinson had generated for so many years, there was no physical evidence that he had committed a single violent crime. It was entirely possible that if search warrants were executed on his properties, nothing would be found. Once again, the authorities would have to release him to continue his on-line and off-line games. Morrison could not take this chance.

Over recent weeks, Suzette Trouten's family members had received more computer-generated letters that had been mailed from Mexico and held Suzette's signature. The letters claimed that she and her companion, Jim Turner, were having a grand time sailing the sea. Morrison was aware of these letters and also aware that the task force was itching for him to act. Robinson had been very active lately and there were concerns that he might leave town. If he departed the state or the country, everything would become much more complicated. The pressure was mounting on Morrison but he still wasn't ready. It took one final set of developments to push aside his doubts that something had to be done.

The district attorney had learned from investigators that Robinson had recently hooked up with a woman from Tennessee on the Internet. She was divorced yet still living with her ex-husband and had an eight-year-old daughter. Robinson had convinced her to come to Kansas with her child and to bring the title to her car. By late spring, she'd packed her belongings and was ready to make the trip with the girl. In addition to this, the detectives knew that Robinson had met a seventeen-year-old mother who had just given birth. Her circumstances were so desperate that she and the infant had been living in her vehicle. If she would become his mistress, Robinson had promised the teenager, she could move down to his farm near La Cygne. The situation was strikingly similar to that of Lisa Stasi with her newborn daughter fifteen years earlier, right before the young mother had disappeared forever.

It was one thing, the authorities believed, to watch and listen as Robinson lured adult women to Kansas City motels and had violent, consensual sex with them. The police didn't feel they could do much to protect these women—at least until a crime had been committed. Babies and children, however, were another matter. Youngsters had no choice in coming to Kansas or in taking up residence at Robinson's farm. They were at the mercy of the adult world, and investigators tracking the suspect had every reason to believe that when it served his purposes, Robinson would have no compunction in disposing of them. The DA had seen enough. It was time to move.

On June 1, as Morrison's office began preparing the arrest warrant, Robinson was busy at Santa Barbara Estates. Something annoying was going on in his neighborhood and he wanted the police to help him out. A teenager and some of his rowdy friends had been playing rap music loudly, and Robinson simply could not endure the sound. After Robinson had asked a seventeen-year-old to turn it down, the two of them had exchanged words and gotten into a scuffle. Robinson called the cops, who showed up and took a statement from him about the rudeness and violence of these young people. The officers handling the call had no idea that they were speaking with someone who'd been under constant police surveillance for weeks. They took his complaint and arrested the young man, placing him in the Johnson County Juvenile Detention Center.

Robinson went to bed.

XXX

The mobile home park where Robinson lived held mostly pastel-colored trailers set quite close together. Lots were cramped and lawns were sparse. Although many families had lived here for years, the place retained a feeling of transience and everything about it seemed a long way from Santa Barbara, California, or the notion of an estate. The Robinson residence at 36 Monterey Lane had a screened-in porch, which gave it more style than most of the others, yet it still appeared unsubstantial. A late-afternoon tornado of the kind this part of the country was known for could easily rip through the park, uproot the homes, kill the inhabitants, and instantly turn everything into rubble.

At just after 10 A.M. on Friday, June 2, plainclothes detectives pulled up in front of Robinson's address and quieted the engines of their nine unmarked police cars. Law enforcement surrounded the property, which held pink geraniums in front, a prominent statue of the Virgin Mary in a flowerbed, and a shed for gardening out back. As Robinson's next-door neighbor Henry Timmons, a seventy-nine-year-old man who'd come outside to take a walk, looked on in disbelief, several detectives knocked on Robinson's door and were let inside. Timmons could never have guessed what was going on inside the Robinson household.

Detective Jack Boyer was one of those who entered the home that morning, and he'd been waiting a long time to do what he did next. By now Boyer had his own investment in the case. He'd spoken with people whose relatives were missing or dead, and he felt some of what they were feeling. He'd spent almost three months tracking Robinson and had been amazed at where the trail had led and how many lives were disrupted by the man. Boyer had had to control his desire to make this arrest but now the moment had come. For a while, the men spoke politely with one another, Robinson uneasy about what these men were doing in his home. His day had already gotten off to a rocky start. That morning, he and Nancy had argued over Barbara Sandre. Nancy knew that her husband was still involved with the woman she had once sent a letter to. But she didn't know that her husband and Sandre had talked about leaving the country or that Sandre had already gone ahead and started looking for a furnished apartment for the two of them in Toronto.

"I left early that morning for work," Nancy has said. "I was very angry with John over Barbara Sandre. She'd been in and out of our marriage for thirty-five years. I tried to tell Barbara that we were married. I sent her a letter and explained our life in chronological order and explained about our children. We were getting ready to have it out."

Robinson was preparing for another day of managing all the other women in his life when someone knocked on his front door. The police were standing in front of him and he let them inside his home. They had a search warrant for his properties.

"We told him why we were there," Boyer says. "We told him we wanted to talk to him about a couple of complaints that we'd received about him. He sat down and talked to us about that and he got a little nervous."

The longer Boyer spoke, the more Robinson's agitation increased, in his facial expressions and body language. The detective noticed the man's growing discomfort and was pleased to see it. For once Robinson was not so glib or talkative. He was used to being in control of things, particularly at home, but his discomfort was about to get much worse. The detective started to explain why they were paying this unexpected visit and how a couple of women had come forward recently and accused him of sexual assault. His threatening tactics against Neufeld had backfired. She'd gone to the police, despite his having nude pictures of her. And his rough treatment and dismissal of Milliron had caused her to contact the authorities as well. They were not so intimidated by the man that they'd refused to seek some help and some justice. Someone had finally decided to fight back.

"When I mentioned some of the charges," Boyer says, "I think he was a little shocked."

Then Boyer shared a few more details from the months-long investigation into Robinson. He looked much more surprised a few minutes later when the detective brought up Stasi and Trouten. He went pale and got quiet. The glibness he almost always used with strangers had entirely disappeared.

"Now he was really shocked," Boyer says. The shock deepened when they arrested him, cuffed him, and led him outside.

Robinson's neighbor Henry Timmons watched what was unfolding and wondered what the man next door had done to generate so much attention from law enforcement. To Timmons, Robinson had always seemed friendly but preoccupied, in a hurry to get someplace right now. But this morning, as he was being escorted outside by the cops to one of their cars, he'd lost the quickness in his step and the confidence in his eyes. He wasn't smiling at anyone. He was frowning straight ahead and looked stunned, perhaps even ashamed, as he quietly ducked into the car and was driven away to the Johnson County Adult Detention Center. It was set right across from the courthouse holding Paul Morrison's office. In early June, the courtyard separating the courthouse from the administration building was filled with people sitting in the sun and talking or eating their lunch or having a cigarette. The fountain holding the sculptures of two pioneer children was shooting a stream of water into the air. The quaint, innocent scene at first appeared to be an unlikely setting for the lurid stories that were about to emerge from Olathe.

Later that day, Robinson was questioned in a conference room with Trouten's photo on one wall and a map with directions to Robinson's farm on another. He was booked on sexual assault charges against Jeanna Milliron and for stealing $700 worth of sex toys from Vickie Neufeld. He was placed in solitary confinement and his bond was set at $250,000.

As the police continued their work at Santa Barbara Estates, other Robinson neighbors came outside to stare at the activity and to gossip among themselves. A few of the women had heard Robinson make suggestive or salacious remarks to them, but none had regarded him with genuinely serious suspicion. What could he possibly be involved in that was dangerous enough to provoke this kind of response?

Detectives Dawn Layman, Dan Owsley, and Mike

Lowther went through everything inside Robinson's home and cataloged or carried out one item after another, including his five computers and the floppy disks he'd used with them. The office was cluttered and held two computers, a printer, and other business machines. So many framed documents were on the wall it resembled a doctor's office. They spent about five hours taking photographs of the property, rummaging through the mobile home's belongings, searching his office and white pickup truck, dusting objects for fingerprints, and collecting evidence. They found a blank sheet of stationery that Lisa Stasi had signed way back in January 1985. Robinson had kept it for more than fifteen years. There was an envelope addressed to a Marty Elledge, later discovered to be one of Lisa's relatives. The police also retrieved receipts from the Rodeway Inn— pieces of paper showing that Robinson himself had checked Stasi out of that hotel on the day she'd vanished during a snowstorm.

The office also contained Social Security forms for Debbie and Sheila Faith, and e-mail addresses for some of the women Robinson had been speaking with on-line. The Lenexa police found a credit card bearing the name James Turner. There were two sets of computer-generated business cards for Hydro-Gro, Inc., one set with "James Turner, Vice-President—Finance," the other with "John E. Robinson, International Operations." They located an application for articles of corporation for this company from Beverly Bonner. There was also a fax of a credit application to Gateway 2000, signed by B. J. Bonner and dated May 11, 1998. They uncovered documents from the Drug Enforcement Administration, the U.S. Department of Justice, and the State Department. There was a checkbook issued under the names of John Robinson and Barbara Sandre. Two books were also retrieved about how to find foolproof ways of changing your identity in modern America.

The police took away coolers, large popcorn tins, and a toolbox from his gardening shed. They hauled off his truck. They carried out a fax machine and cardboard boxes, all of which were turned over to other authorities at the police department. One man prepared to do an "autopsy" on Robinson's hard drives and disks. A computer forensic specialist in Kansas City named Mike Jacobson was assigned to decipher and list everything contained on Robinson's computers that might be relevant to his crimes. Jacobson was confronted with a mountain of work—the computers held ninety-one thousand potentially relevant files—and all of Jacobson's labor was surrounded by questions. What data or names or pictures inside the machines might give clues to the suspect's behavior or cyber-connections? Which e-mails might open a doorway into his experiences with women outside his marriage? With whom had he been communicating on-line and for how long? Had Robinson used aliases and what chat rooms had he visited? Were there any links between his computers and any of the women who'd disappeared?

The challenges of doing this kind of autopsy were enormous, if not unparalleled. Like everyone else legally connected to the Robinson case following his arrest, Detective Jacobson was quickly placed under a gag order. He could not talk about his involvement in the investigation, but others with similar expertise could.

Special Agent Dave Schroeder worked with the high-tech investigative unit of the Kansas Bureau of Investigation. He had a bachelor's degree in criminal justice and had been with the KBI for nearly a quarter of a century. Schroeder, who turned forty-two in 2000, was stocky, brown-haired, and wore a mustache. In years past, he'd been in the narcotics unit, but in the midnineties the KBI expanded its field of expertise to include computer forensics. By 1997, it had created the high-tech investigative unit, with four agents and a supervisor, to combat this new criminal realm. Computers were a hobby of each person in the unit, and to add to their knowledge they attended every training seminar they could. Schroeder is a member of the International Association of Computer Technologists, which offers certification and a networking system for people investigating high-tech crime. Because the Net crosses all jurisdictional boundaries, in his current job he'd worked on national and international cases. The evolution of his career mirrored the evolution of American society and crime at the start of the twenty-first century.

"We're involved with almost any type of crime you can think of," he says, "but mostly we're involved with child pornography. We also deal with homicides, fraud, securities fraud, consumer fraud, and narcotics cases. Computers store information about who owes money and store recipes for making the drugs. These things used to be put on paper but now they're stored electronically."

Schroeder's workload had expanded greatly in recent years because computers had become cheaper and people were buying more equipment and becoming more computer savvy. But they still didn't know that much about how to destroy e-mails or potential evidence. Most people believed they were getting rid of information on their hard drive when they simply deleted it from their system. They weren't—at least not until the space it occupied had been overwritten. And this was true for the space in as many as five distinct locations for one e-mail: on the sender's hard drive or backup disks; on the sender's Internet server; on the other servers of the Internet service provider and the major telecom provider; on the e-mail recipient's server; and on the recipient's hard drive or backup disks or any other system that the recipient may have forwarded the e-mail to. Once in cyberspace, an e-mail has a long-standing life that can be traced.

E-mails aren't deleted, according to Schroeder, unless people take "fairly extraordinary" measures to remove them for good. Without those measures, technologically sophisticated detectives can retrieve them.

"We go in with forensic tools," he says, "and change the way of thinking in the computer from 'It's not there' to 'Yes, it's still in there and we want to recover it.' There is software written strictly for data recovery, and people can go in for a substantial fee and recover what's apparently been lost."

The computer can also find what's seemingly been deleted by searching through what is known as "ambient data." Computers operate by filling up voids based on size parameters. To fill a given void, which has been created by a given command, the computer will grab data from a memory bank and use it to fill up the cavity. The information it grabs may apparently have been deleted in the past, but not completely deleted, so it can still be randomly accessed during this process. Computers, like any machine, run on technical commands, and one command is that until it fulfills its space requirements, it can't move on to the next function. The ambient data that can be retrieved by forensic specialists often contains information important to criminal investigations.

"To the average user," says Schroeder, "none of this process is visible or known. But that randomly selected memory could hold a blackmail attempt or an extortion plot or a murder scenario or child pornography or a critical conversation between two adults."

When doing an "autopsy" on a computer, after someone has been arrested and that individual's property has been seized, the authorities have to follow meticulously the Constitution's Fourth Amendment rules regarding reasonable "search and seizure" or the evidence will never stand up in court. This creates enormously time-consuming tasks and complexities. Most law enforcement people are used to getting a search warrant and going out and looking for a particular item. What happens if you obtain a warrant for someone's hard drive but then you find things on the disk that you were not specifically hunting for? What if you are investigating one kind of crime but find evidence of several others?

"Let's say that I'm looking for things on narcotics on a hard drive but I find some things connected to child porn," Schroeder says. "I have to stop what I'm doing because this isn't covered by the search warrant. Then I have to go get another warrant. These are all new areas for law enforcement, and new case law is being made daily because of these Fourth Amendment issues. In addition to that, you've often got local, state, federal, and international laws involved because of how the Net works. People might be sending e-mail about criminal activities all over the world.

"We are starting to catch up with this criminal frontier. We've been behind the curve because of funding and not knowing what the future will hold technically. Once you see a problem, it takes the government time to respond, so you end up in a reactive stance, and the learning curve is enormous. The Internet keeps growing and new viruses are being written each day. No one person can keep up with it. You need one individual for each aspect of this kind of investigation, and you need a hundred people but only have four. So you feel understaffed and everyone who does this work feels that way."

Schroeder was not involved in the John Robinson case but was familiar with the work done by Mike Jacobson, who would receive an award from the Kansas Association of Chiefs of Police for playing a critical role in this investigation. One of the most intriguing questions surrounding Robinson's upcoming trial was how his computers would be used to prosecute him and what they might reveal about his connections in cyberspace. How these questions were answered in the Olathe courtroom would set precedents for future legal proceedings.

The object of conducting a computer autopsy, Schroeder says, is not necessarily to discover every single item on a hard drive—one drive can now hold millions of pages of documents—but to preserve the data precisely as it is. It can take weeks, even months, to locate a single name on a hard drive, something that nontechnical people in law enforcement often don't understand. They often think that you can seize the computer today and have the evidence ready by tomorrow, but everything is more complicated than that.

The moment you turn a computer on, you change the configuration of everything that's in it, which is to say that you can alter the evidence of a crime. The windows and the files "start cookin'," as Schroeder says, and when that happens, you've likely ruined some of the raw data that you most wanted to preserve. Instead of getting the computer and immediately turning it on, which seems to be the natural thing to do, specialists like himself have learned to copy everything off the hard drive first, making exact duplicates of the evidence and then working off the copy and keeping the original data intact.

"Ninety percent of the time," Schroeder says, "what the criminals think they have erased is still there. It just takes another technique—a trade secret—to get it back. But the search to do that may take two months."

Prosecutors are not the only ones now eager to retrieve data on the Net. Defense lawyers have also started rummaging through old e-mail to see if they can find messages from police or witnesses that might contradict what someone has said under oath during a legal proceeding. Detectives have to be extremely careful what they commit to this electronic web, because much of it can be found and potentially used against them. What might before have been said in a phone conversation that they were certain was not being overheard is no longer secure in cyberspace. Every word must be weighed before being sent out.

As the Robinson case so well demonstrates, the Internet has become an opportune hunting ground for violent criminals. Investigating these cases is difficult because of jurisdictional problems as well as the lack of training in Internet crimes. While the emphasis in most departments is on child pornography, this case was not about child pornography. Victims came voluntarily to Robinson. In a sense, Robinson was a profiler, a "victim profiler." His manipulative mind discovered while in prison that the Internet could be another tool for him to use. He also discovered that there are a lot of unhappy people in this world who have needs to fulfill. He saw that he could use these needs to his benefit, both sexually as well as financially. The Internet was a safe harbor for him. When he felt he had the right victim, and the risks of getting caught were low, he would come out from behind his computer and attack.

How many more Robinsons are there in this new technological world? How many other people are there who have been harmed in some way and we don't know anything about them? I've been asked many times how many serial killers there are in the United States. It is difficult to know exactly the actual number of serial killers. Every year approximately ten to twelve serial killers are identified. These are primarily men who kill two or three victims or more over time. There is a cooling off period between the homicides that can last days or many months. Serial killers are different from mass murderers because the mass murderer kills four or more people, and sometimes himself, during one event. With the clearance rate for homicides being approximately 64–67 percent, and with eighteen thousand to twenty thousand victims per year, and with over seventeen thousand law enforcement agencies not connected technologically to share crime and criminal information, we've created a great opportunity for anyone who wants to hurt or murder someone. At the very least we have thirty to fifty serial killers in the United States at any given time. We have hundreds of unidentified dead in morgues. The Internet can be a great tool, but unfortunately it has become a foe to the law enforcement community.

The anonymity of the Net has clearly bred many more crimes. By the 1980s, the U.S. Customs Service had pretty much eliminated child pornography through the

United States Postal Service because it had simply become too risky for the perpetrators to send illegal material through the mail. The pornographers needed physical contacts outside of themselves to distribute their goods. In the 1990s, with the arrival of digital cameras, computer transfers, and the availability of widespread Internet connections, child predators could now do everything alone and reach a marketplace that covered the entire globe.

You could now do all this without seeing or having to trust anybody. Most Internet service providers don't check to see who you are when you ask to use their service. You could be anyone, even the president of the United States, and they wouldn't necessarily know this. The Net has created the sense for users that no one knows who they really are, so they can take on a different persona in cyberspace. That feeling of anonymity encourages the feeling that they won't get caught doing something illegal. They do it once and get away with it, and then they do it again and again.

Laws surrounding explicit sexual material vary from country to country and from state to state—certain kinds of pornography are legal in some nations—and this makes prosecuting these cases even more challenging. If you're living in Kansas, for example, and in possession of child pornography received from overseas, you are committing a crime, even though the material may have been legal where it was created. In the late 1990s, law enforcement and other local groups lobbied the Kansas legislature until they changed the law so that possessing sexual images of individuals under the age of eighteen was illegal. A more uncharted realm is computer-generated images that may depict an actual person—or not.

"We've seen pictures," says Schroeder, "where someone

has cut and pasted body parts together—using arms, legs, breasts, and genitals. Is this a picture of a real child or not? This is a gray area for us."

Some people use credit cards or checks to buy child pornography. Others employ a much older form of commerce, created centuries earlier in the open marketplace: bartering.

"Let's say that you have a criminal with a five-to-two ratio," Schroeder says. "This means that for every five pictures you download from my system, you have to upload two back to me. These ratios are even automated in computers now, so they are programmed to do it exactly this way. Let's say your interest is very detailed and graphic. I send you some pictures and you say, 'I like this one but I already have that one.' So you save what you have and trade the duplicates, and this is how bartering is done. It's just like trading baseball cards."

A fine line exists between policing the Net and invading privacy or restricting freedom of expression. Most everyone wants the Net to retain its great feeling of experimentation and to remain an alternative to mainstream media, but few people want it to encourage or protect serious criminal activity. The most important thing you can do is to be in control of yourself and aware of the pitfalls when you log on to the World Wide Web. Nobody can any longer afford to be naive when it comes to cyberspace. Too many people have gone out into the fantasyland of the Internet looking for sex or romance without an awareness of what they were encountering. Not all of them survived.

XXXI

On June 2, 2000, after scouring the Robinson address for evidence, two of the Lenexa detectives executed another search warrant at Need Mor Storage in Olathe. Dan Owsley and Dawn Layman used bolt cutters to open the padlock on the space rented by the suspect. The locker held a trove of information and written materials connecting Robinson to some of the dead women: Suzette Trouten's passport application, birth certificate, and Social Security card, plus forty-two preaddressed envelopes to members of her family and thirty-one sheets of pastel-colored paper signed at the bottom, "Love ya, Suzette." The detectives also found a stun gun, a slave contract signed by Trouten, birthday cards, e-mails addressed to J. Robinson, and computer disks. There were several pictures of Suzette and the video he'd made of them in February 2000. They found her journal with a yin-yang symbol on the cover plus a brass unicorn, a jewelry box, and a Mickey Mouse watch.

The locker also contained a Kansas driver's license for Izabela Lewicka, her Purdue University ID card, and a typed-up slave contract entitled "Basic Slave Rules," outlining 115 directives for her to obey. Owsley and Layman saw Lewicka's name on documents for a 1987 Pontiac Bonneville and Alecia Cox's name on other pastel letters and envelopes. They uncovered the cowboy picture that Robinson had routinely sent out into cyberspace, along with images of women in bondage and a photo of Izabela Lewicka lying nude on a bed with green-and-maroon-patterned linens. These were the same linens she'd brought from Indiana to Kansas.

A black leather case was opened, and inside were several leather floggers, a dark blindfold, clothespins, and three white golf balls inside a small plastic baggie. There were also wooden paddles, an electrical unit, a metal speculum, and lubricants. Vickie Neufeld's sex toys were also stashed in the locker. In addition to all of the other Robinson personas, he was also a pack rat, having saved things that many people would have long ago thrown away, especially if they were evidence of a crime. Fifteen years of evidence was stacked up in both his home office and the storage locker.

While all this was taking place, Nancy Robinson, sitting in her office, noticed some police activity down the block and assumed that a park occupant had gotten into trouble. It was probably an arrest for a petty offense; these days, that sort of thing happened more often than she wished it would. She was surprised when two detectives, flashing guns and badges, came to her manager's office and told her that they needed to speak with her—in private. She was much more than surprised when they told her that her husband had just been arrested for sexual battery. She wanted to talk in the parking lot but they insisted on going to the station. During her interview, they asked her about her own sex life. The subject of BDSM Web sites would also come up in her talks with the authorities. In 1998, she would one day reveal, she'd first learned that her husband was surfing these sites. She could tell where he'd been and what he'd seen. When she asked her husband about this, he told her nonchalantly that he'd been exploring the Internet and that was the end of their conversation.

Nancy was quickly released and would not be regarded as an accessory in any of the charges that would be filed against her husband. She tried to go back to work, but in the days ahead she would find that more and more difficult. Reporters kept calling, wanting information about her family or her husband or herself, and this was starting to interfere with her job. Then the media began bothering her employer, the owner of Santa Barbara Estates, and that was more than her bosses were willing to accommodate. She was soon unemployed.

Nancy disappeared from the mobile home park's managerial office and did not come back. If she or her children felt they'd received bad publicity in years past because of the actions of their husband and father, they were not prepared for what was coming. It would dwarf anything they'd experienced as a result of their connections to John Robinson.

The police had released Nancy without further questioning, but in the upcoming days and weeks her behavior would arouse a lot of speculation at Santa Barbara Estates and beyond. Residents throughout the park wondered aloud if she was involved in any aspect of the things her spouse was being accused of. And if she wasn't, how could she have lived with someone for as long as she'd lived with Robinson and not have known or at least sensed what he was doing with all these other women for a decade and a half? How could you be that close to someone and not realize who he really was? Who could possibly be this blind?

Communities, especially small communities, hate being

fooled—particularly by those they've come to like and trust. Once fooled, their old feelings of affection and trust often curdle into a disappointment and anger that spill out onto anyone who might have destroyed their innocence or helped protect a perpetrator. They don't like being shocked, and the shock waves were just beginning at Santa Barbara Estates. The following day the entire city and region would get a nasty jolt. The waves would spread all across the nation and the Internet.

For decades Robinson had been an extremely busy man. The authorities were about to see just how busy he'd been.

XXXII

Saturday, June 3, was unusually hot for eastern Kansas. By 9 A.M. the sun was scorching and the air would turn more oppressive with each passing hour, pushing the thermometer past ninety. A few hours earlier, a band of police cars had left Olathe and driven south on Interstate 35, then turned onto Highway 69 and kept going south, passing through the town of La Cygne and moving on to the farm owned by Robinson. Present were the Lenexa and Overland Park Police Departments, the Kansas Bureau of Investigation, criminologists, and the Linn County Sheriff's Department. The group had brought along trained German shepherds, known as cadaver dogs. They'd brought shovels and gloves and all manner of forensic equipment, ready to set up a makeshift crime lab right on the premises, if necessary. They'd brought divers to look in Robinson's snake-infested pond. The cops shot at the snakes throughout the day.

While the Linn County sheriff's deputies were securing the perimeter of the property, others walked the entire sixteen and a half acres. It looked like an ordinary farm, with garden hoses, a wheelbarrow, and ladders stacked up against the side of the trailer. Johnson County officers videotaped and photographed the two trucks, the trailer, the shed, and the pond. They flew overhead and took aerial photos of the land, the layout of the buildings, and freshly moved dirt. Others examined the holes Robinson had dug in the pole barn and noted a two-wheeled dolly inside the structure. (Another dolly would be recovered from Robinson's Dodge pickup in Olathe.) Investigators would eventually bring in a backhoe to tear up the barn floor, and sections of the walls would be dismantled. Others would lay out, in an open area, long pieces of plastic sheeting found inside the shed and examine them closely for organic material, such as blood or human tissue. As one group looked at the barn, the dive team peered through the muddy waters of the pond searching for anything unusual. (Later, when the pond was drained, they found an abandoned truck sunk by one of the previous owners of the property to prevent his ex-wife from getting it in a divorce settlement.)

Sergeant Rick Roth of the Lenexa Police Department used a pry bar to force open the locked door on the east side of the trailer. The interior of the trailer contained a couple of lawn chairs and numerous boxes filled with cleaning supplies. The carpet had been removed and the floors were bare except for a few patches that had been covered with white paint. The criminologists started scraping underneath the paint to look for blood.

The sun rose higher and hotter until it was overhead at noon. Some of the officers were growing discouraged. All were hot and getting hungry. Their enormous amount of work had turned up little. Maybe there wasn't any real evidence at the farm.

Just before 1 P.M., Johnson County sheriff deputy Harold Hughes was working in the trailer when someone told him that one of the cadaver dogs had picked up a scent. Hughes went outside, where he and Sergeant Roth moved toward the gathering commotion by the shed. As they came nearer, they saw that the storage shed was surrounded by tall grass. In these weeds were lawn-mowing equipment, an outboard motor, some blue plastic barrels, and behind all this, two eighty-five-gallon, bright yellow metal barrels. As Roth studied the barrels, a German shepherd came up and sat down in front of them. The dog sniffed the air and then sniffed it again aggressively, a sign that it had picked up a strong scent. Roth was joined by Overland Park police sergeant Joe Reed, who studied the dog and looked over at Hughes.

Roth approached the yellow barrels, eased the first one away from the cluttered area, and rolled it on its edge. He laid it on its side and moved it to a clearing. As he set the barrel upright, he noticed a reddish liquid oozing from the lid and down the side. A German shepherd ran up and put his paws on top of the barrel. Roth went for the second barrel but didn't lay it down as he brought it toward the clearing. Hughes joined Roth by the barrels and noticed a distinctive scent that he'd become familiar with during his twenty-eight years in law enforcement.

"It smelled like dead or decomposing something," Hughes has said.

Police photographers snapped pictures of the dead flies, leaves, and mold covering the lids of the barrels.

Hughes, the leader of the crime scene investigation team, took out a pair of pliers and applied pressure to the metal band around the lid. He applied some more, gradually prying open the barrel. As he removed the lid, a vile smell hit him in the face, causing him to lurch backward. He regrouped and came nearer, looking down into the barrel. Roth did not detect the smell until now and would later describe it as "horrendous." Hughes peered inside at what seemed to be decomposing flesh—a body with its head pointed down, sitting in about a foot of rancid fluid. It was bloated and purplish. The video photographer immediately climbed up a ladder and shot down into the open barrel, as flies buzzed around the rim. Then Hughes resealed the barrel and turned to the second one. Hughes and Roth put on latex gloves.

Following the same procedure, Hughes opened this barrel and was again hit with the smell of death. He glanced in and saw another mass of decomposing flesh. Inside, a pillow lay on top of the remains, which appeared to have been there longer than the first body. The video photographer, who was also a criminologist, shot more footage of the contents of this barrel. Then it was resealed and both barrels were processed for fingerprints.

Captain John Meier of the Lenexa Police Department was at the farm throughout the search. He'd watched Hughes opening the first barrel and was nearby when the detective popped off the lid.

"I've been a police officer for twenty-six years," Captain Meier said later, "and I'd never seen anything like this. There wasn't much body left inside."

As Meier watched Hughes work, he speculated that Suzette Trouten might be one of the people in the barrels. At least that would tell the investigators that they'd been on the right track when conducting their surveillance on Robinson. But who was the other person?

The barrels were heavy—so heavy that the officers needed a winch to hoist them onto the back of a truck for the two-hour drive to the state capital in Topeka for autopsies the next day. The weight of the barrels, when they held a human body, would begin to raise questions that were never fully answered. Would it take more than one person to lift and transport the barrels, even if he had a dolly?

The discovery of the bodies set off a new round of procedures back in the trailer. Criminologists, who'd been collecting trace materials from the floor with clear plastic tape, now ran luminol tests for blood and other searches for biological matter. It had been a long and gruesome ordeal at the farm; toward evening the trailer was relocked and yellow evidence tape was placed around the buildings and the entrance to the property. The crew drove to La Cygne and back to Kansas City, preparing for more work tomorrow.

XXXIII

Once the bodies arrived in Topeka, a crane unloaded the barrels onto a wooden pallet at the morgue in the county's law enforcement center. Care was taken not to stir up the contents. Dr. Donald Pojman, a pathologist and the deputy coroner of Shawnee County, Kansas, conducted the autopsies. The first barrel had been marked Unknown 1, and after it was reopened, Dr. Pojman saw that it contained a nude human form in the fetal position. He drained out the fluid, slid the body onto a plastic bag on the floor, and saw a female whose long dark hair was pulled back in a ponytail and whose genitals had been pierced with rings. The body was adorned with nipple rings connected by a metal chain held together with a silver butterfly pendant. A piece of cloth, like a blindfold, partially covered her face. The cloth was held in place by a rope. The left side of her head had sustained a severe injury. After the scalp had been cut open and peeled back, Dr. Pojman determined that the wound had fractured the skull and was consistent with a hammer blow. The "circular punch-out" was 1¼ inches in diameter and had left bone debris in her brain. Dr. Pojman also noticed the lack of defensive wounds, suggesting that the victim had never fought back against her attacker. The doctor estimated that she'd been dead anywhere from a couple of months to a year. He cut off her hands so that others could process them for fingerprints. One of her rib bones was removed for DNA testing. Within the next few days, a forensic odontologist, relying on dental records from Michigan, identified Unknown 1 as Suzette Trouten.

When Dr. Pojman opened the barrel marked Unknown 2, he found a female with long matted hair, clad only in a sheer black shirt. Her head hung down in her body fluids and she was partially covered by a green-and-maroon-patterned pillowcase. Floating in the fluid were several fingernails and three pieces of silver duct tape. The doctor also peeled back her scalp where there were two overlapping holes in the skull above the left ear. The impact of the blunt trauma had left a hole measuring 2½ by 1¾ inches. These were also consistent with a hammer blow. She had a hairline fracture of the jaw and no defensive wounds. A rib was again removed for DNA testing. Dr. Pojman observed a more advanced state of decomposition in the second victim and estimated that she'd been dead from six months to two years. Her prints were so diffuse that they could not be processed and her hands were not removed. Unknown 2, later identified by dental records, proved to be Izabela Lewicka.

Detective Harold Hughes was present during the autopsies. From Suzette Trouten's body, he was given the genital rings, the nipple rings with chain, the blindfold, and a dark-colored hair tie. From Lewicka, he was given the pillowcase, the shirt, and the three pieces of duct tape. Some of the cloth items were taken to a biohazard lab where they were frozen and preserved as evidence. Hughes also took the hands and rib bones and distributed them to other criminologists.

Rick Sabel, an eleven-year veteran of the Kansas Bureau

of Investigation, took photos of the autopsies as they were being conducted. Like Captain Meier, he'd never seen or smelled anything like this before. He'd worked on many drug investigations and violent crimes, but he was now encountering what seemed to him almost a new level of evil. As he was snapping pictures of the bodies, a syringe holding the fluids from one of the victims accidentally slipped from the coroner's hand and pricked Sabel's flesh. It didn't draw blood but raised the fear that he might have contracted AIDS or hepatitis or some other potentially fatal disease. He underwent six months of rigorous medical testing before he was pronounced healthy.

As the investigation continued that Saturday, a policeman phoned Steve Haymes to alert him of the discovery of the bodies. Like others who'd been pursuing Robinson for months or years, the Missouri probation officer was both appalled and relieved at what he was hearing. His intuitions about the suspect's deep criminal past and his homicidal tendencies looked as if they were finally, a decade and a half after Haymes had first begun investigating, tragically proving to be correct. Haymes wondered how many more bodies were out there.

If the police had been busy during the first two days of arresting Robinson and examining some of his properties, they now got busier.

With the autopsy results in hand, forensic teams had a better idea of what to look for. They returned to Robinson's farm on Sunday and spent almost a week taking blood and other biological material samples. The trailer, barn, and shed were scoured for murder weapons. They recovered nine hammers, two picks, and a chisel. Inside a small plastic trash can in the trailer, they discovered a roll of duct tape with bloodstains on the side. A piece of paper towel in the kitchen sink held bloodstains as well. Some of the evidence would be collected and sent to a crime lab in Kansas City, Missouri, for more thorough testing. They also found blood on the baseboard in the bedroom, containing hair and human tissue. Bits of the hair, when examined closely by the forensic team, had forcibly been pulled out. Several small bloodstains were examined and one was found to be an "impact stain" as opposed to a contact stain. (In an impact stain, the blood's trajectory creates a splatter, as a hammer blow would make.) The blood on both the paper towel and the wallboard along with the hair and human tissue would turn out to be Trouten's.

XXXIV

With two barrels recovered from Robinson's farm, Johnson County DA Paul Morrison now prepared the largest and most detailed search warrant his office had ever created. It listed Robinson's alleged involvement in numerous homicides, his widespread Internet connections, and his penchant for the S&M lifestyle. Before its execution, the warrant was presented to the Cass County, Missouri, district attorney's office, headed by Chris Koster. This step was necessary because Robinson also maintained a rented locker at the Stor-Mor for Less in Raymore, Missouri, and law enforcement wanted to search this location as soon as possible. If any further evidence was found at Stor-Mor, that would only add to the already massive complexity of the case, bringing in not only a new jurisdiction but a second state as well. If Paul Morrison had a lot of experience handling large and complicated criminal matters that were headline news, DA Koster had little. Morrison was older and ran a much larger operation out of Johnson County—his office employed ninety-five people and processed about nine thousand cases a year. He was a veteran at dealing with the modern media. Koster was handsome, fresh-faced, and—some people said—quite ambitious, always looking for the next career booster.

On Monday morning, June 5, a cool day in Missouri,

another caravan of legal authorities, led by DA Koster, made its way across the countryside, past the white picket fences and horse farms, on its way to Raymore. Cass County deputy attorney Mark Tracy executed this warrant on locker E-2, which had the letters SM written on its padlock. As police and investigators stood around waiting for the locker to be opened, uncertain what to expect, a van filled with warm pizza and hot coffee showed up. The food and drink would be necessary to keep the workers energized throughout this long day.

That chilly Monday morning, Loretta Mattingly, who ran the Stor-Mor office, was prepared for the arrival of law enforcement. She understood that they were coming to look inside the unit she'd rented to John Robinson.

"That weekend," she said, "I'd seen the news that they'd found the bodies in the barrels on the farm, so I knew they were heading this way."

Loretta had blond hair, bound together in a tight permanent. She kept a big plastic frog near the front door of her business, which croaked loudly every time somebody came in or went out the front door (on June 5, there was a lot of coming and going, and a lot of croaking, in her office). She was one of the few civilians present when law enforcement opened locker E-2 at Stor-Mor for Less.

"The police sealed off the place," she recalled months after Robinson's arrest, "and went out to his locker and cut the bolts and opened it up. No one had ever done that before. They quickly realized there were barrels in there. Three of 'em. With a dead woman in each one.

"They called the crime lab in Kansas City and told them to get out here. Then they went in and out of the locker the rest of that day and night. The prosecutors from here in Missouri, from Cass County, showed up and then the media. They came at three-thirty that afternoon. I was there when they first opened up the locker. One barrel was leaking because of chemicals in the body. The body had leaked out acids and the acid ate right through the barrel and it smelled bad and it still does out there. We bio-cleaned it but the acid from the body ate into the concrete floor of the locker and we had to replace the floor. I don't know if we'll ever be able to rent that space again. The police stayed all that night and did a test in the dark to look for blood . . . then came back with a second warrant. They thought there might be a hatchet or a hammer in there because the coroner said that a blunt blow had killed the women.

"Everybody was here that day. Three county sheriffs and Mr. Wonderful—that's DA Koster from Cass County. He's from Harrisonville. That's down the road and the county seat. He was grandstanding for the media. He said I needed to testify soon because I was getting old and needed to testify before I forget things. I'll be sixty this year and that's not old. You don't forget these things.

"I never noticed what John Robinson brought in here. I never saw him transporting any barrels. He had a white short-bed pickup and I watched him come and go, but I never saw anything unusual. I wonder about his wife, Nancy Jo. She had her own rental unit out here and I met her at least once. She made no impression on me, not like he did. She left the area right after the bodies were found. I think she went down to Tulsa because she still has her unit and she's sent in a check from there. I wonder if she's really innocent about all this.

"I think those barrels here were brought in a long time ago—back in '93 or '94. Those women might even have been killed here. They were dressed up and had blindfolds on. I told the police that I think they were killed five or six years ago. All I know is, they'd been dead a long time. They were antiques almost. I had two customers leave here because the smell was so bad. But we didn't notice it before they found them. It took them about an hour just to cut the bolts and open the unit. I watched this for a while, but then I came back in after I found out there were bodies in those barrels."

Mattingly would one day testify that she did remember seeing Robinson cleaning out his unit sometime before his arrest, saying that a raccoon had gotten in there and created a mess.

Kevin Winer, a senior criminologist with the Kansas City Crime Lab, helped execute the search warrant at Stor-Mor. Among the items in Robinson's storage unit were luggage, wood chips, a pink kiddie pool, paint supplies, and three barrels. The barrels were hidden by the clutter in the locker, much as they had been at the farm. Newspapers dating from 1992 were found near them. Two of the barrels were wrapped in thick, opaque plastic and further wrapped in duct tape and placed in the corner. All were sealed and had items stacked on top of them. One barrel was off by itself and had "rendered pork fat" written across its face. Opening Barrel #1, Winer observed a shoe, a brown sheet, and a pair of glasses. He lifted up the shoe and saw that a leg was attached to it. The barrel was quickly resealed. Two of the barrels were leaking badly, and Kitty Litter from a torn-open bag had once been spread around their bases in a vain attempt to mask the smell. Fearing that the barrels would leak further when lifted, an officer was dispatched to go purchase three children's wading pools at a local department store. The barrels were then placed in the pools for transport to the Jackson County medical examiner.

Thomas W. Young, M.D., was the chief medical examiner for Kansas City and had overseen more than thirty-eight hundred autopsies. In Barrel #1, he found clumps of dark hair, a folded yellow bedsheet, a crumpled brown sheet, earmuffs, and a fully dressed corpse. The female body was dressed in size 14 stirrup pants, a tweed jacket, panty hose, underwear, a blouse with a multicolored scarf, and gloves that covered her hands. The woman had on one ornate earring and a Bulova watch with the time stopped at 1:22. Blunt-force injuries were on the left side of the head and on the forehead, but there were no defensive wounds. Dental records would eventually determine that Barrel #1 held the remains of the former Missouri correctional-facility librarian Beverly Bonner.

In Barrel #2, Dr. Young found another deceased female, this one with long dark hair and dressed in jeans, socks, white shoes, and a T-shirt that read "California, A State of Mind." Her upper denture had been broken in half and fractures were on the back of her head and face. The injuries were consistent with hammer blows, and this body had a broken right forearm, a defensive wound. The triangular-shaped hole in her head was the size of an orange. When dental records failed to provide good enough information on the bodies found in Barrels #2 and #3, Michael Finegan, a forensic anthropologist at Kansas State University, was brought into the case. He'd once helped identify the remains of outlaw Jesse James and now looked at the evidence pulled from the storage unit. He determined that Barrel #2 held the body of Sheila Faith. Barrel #3 contained another, younger female, this one upside down, with long brown hair and wearing green knit pants, a green pullover shirt, and one sock. The final victim was a teenager with a degenerative condition and a misshapen pelvis: Debbie Faith, Sheila's daughter. Like the other two females, Debbie had suffered multiple severe blows, about the size of a golf ball, to the side of her head, and her body showed no defensive wounds. Dr. Young thought that the three women, due to their advanced stage of decomposition, had not been dead for months, but years.

"I'm not accustomed," he said, "to looking at bodies in barrels."

With the discovery of the two bodies in Kansas and then three more in Missouri, Robinson's bond was immediately raised to $5 million, the highest ever set in Johnson County. The investigation into the man's on-line and off-line activities now mushroomed, with the task force growing to nearly forty members from both Kansas and Missouri. Some detectives traveled to Florida to look at his former property at Big Pine Key, others kept searching for more evidence at the farm and at Santa Barbara Estates, while still others made contact with many different people who'd once interacted with the suspect. A number of them had connections to the on-line world of sadomasochism.

"Some people came forward to talk to us," says Detective Boyer, "and I'm sure some haven't."

As part of the education of Boyer and the Lenexa Police Department, the detectives became familiar with what had been described as the bible of the S&M culture: *Screw the Roses, Send Me the Thorns*.

"Some people are very embarrassed by the lifestyle," Boyer says. "There are a lot of people in it, whether you realize it or not. They're in it, but they don't flaunt it. They kind of keep to themselves and they don't want to be drug out by the media."

But the media was suddenly intrigued with this subject and was all over the Robinson case. The *New York Times,* the *Washington Post,* and *USA Today* published stories that the nation's—if not the world's—first Internet serial killer suspect had just been arrested in Kansas. The tiny village of La Cygne was quickly overrun with journalists from national newspapers and magazines looking for details and insights into the man who'd often passed through their community on the way to his farm. The problem was that virtually no one in La Cygne had been aware of John Robinson. Most people couldn't have picked his photo out of a lineup or ever recalled meeting him. He'd kept to himself, quietly grabbing a meal or a tank of gasoline in the town before going about his business on the farm. The locals had had no idea who he was, and this was the last kind of publicity that La Cygne, with its colorful banners of swans hanging from light poles and its big white swan planters standing on street corners, wanted for itself.

As reporters scoured the Kansas countryside, police began searching for women who'd spoken with Robinson in cyberspace or traded pictures with him, but getting them to come forward was proving difficult. Any woman was naturally reluctant to admit that she'd once been interested in pursuing sexual or financial connections with someone who was about to be charged with killing at least five other women. Some officers tried to match photographs found on Robinson's computer with real women, and others attempted to match names they'd downloaded from his hard drive with the names of other potential victims. Robinson had used at least three cyber-aliases—Slavemaster, James Turner, and JT—if not many more. He'd sought out new women on numerous Web sites and chat rooms. All of this amounted to a massively entangled criminal investigation that would take a long time to unravel and catalog.

While some detectives hunted on the Net, others contacted Alecia Cox, who drove them to a fourplex at 901 Edgebrook in Olathe. She told them that back in 1999 when she was still involved with Robinson, the two had gone to an apartment here, which Robinson claimed to own. Alecia had seen that the apartment was unfurnished except for a few boxes, a computer, and several articles of women's clothing. Robinson had told Alecia that the girl who used to live here had moved away with her boyfriend. Robinson and Alecia had had sex at the apartment and she'd picked out a few pieces of the used clothing. Alecia next drove the police to another apartment in Overland Park where Robinson had put her up for two or three days. This furnished apartment was where Barbara Sandre had once lived, and Robinson had told Alecia that it belonged to a friend of his who was out of the country. While snooping around in Sandre's closets, Cox had noticed clothes that were conservative, dressier, and made for someone quite a bit larger than herself. If Cox had given the investigators some good leads into Robinson's involvement with several women, she herself was shocked to learn from them that her ex-lover was a serial-murder suspect.

And she'd been living with, if not wearing, a dead woman's garments. The evidence recovered from Alecia—a white camisole, a black velvet shirt, and a green velvet dress—would later be identified by Danuta Lewicka as having belonged to her daughter, Izabela.

Julia Brown, who'd once rented the Edgebrook apartment to John Robinson, told the officers that when the man had moved out in 1999 and the apartment had been inspected, the only thing left behind was an empty fish tank. The living room and bathrooms were filthy, with cobwebs everywhere and even the beginnings of a termite tunnel. The bedrooms, however, were meticulously clean and looked as though they'd been freshly painted.

"It looked like someone sucked all the dirt out of the area," Brown told them.

Before forensic analysts could do testing on this apartment, the family living at the Edgebrook fourplex had to be temporarily relocated. Then investigators found blood splatters on one bedroom wall, and this blood, along with that from the duct tape taken from Robinson's farm, proved to be Lewicka's.

Another part of the task force contacted Barbara Sandre, now living in Toronto, who gave them permission to search the duplex in Overland Park. Like Alecia, Barbara was stunned to learn that she was part of a homicide investigation. Some of her possessions were still packed up at the duplex, waiting to be moved to Canada. Items seized from this location included an antique coffee grinder, a brass mortar and pestle, and several pieces of artwork, some signed "John 2000," others "John '92." There were over a hundred books, most with occult themes. All had belonged to Lewicka. At the duplex, Sandre had neatly packed her linens inside a large plastic garbage can, which held some green-and-maroon-patterned sheets. When Detective Dawn Layman, who helped execute the search warrant at this address, spotted these sheets, she immediately recognized that the pattern matched that of the pillowcase from the barrel holding Lewicka.

On July 10, Detective Hughes executed a search warrant

on Robinson while he was incarcerated in the Johnson County jail. The warrant allowed him to take samples of Robinson's blood, saliva, and head and pubic hair. Robinson cooperated fully, pulling out at least one hundred of his own hairs.

By August, the police had accumulated reports on Robinson that ran to eleven thousand pages and would one day double that figure.

"This case," Paul Morrison had announced to the media in one of his first public appearances after Robinson's arrest, "has to do with the suspect having numerous contacts throughout the United States who share similar interests, over, among other things, the Internet."

He added that there was a significant financial aspect to the investigation.

What Morrison didn't say and what he couldn't have known at the time was that Robinson's wild ride on the Internet had almost exactly paralleled the dot-com boom that flourished throughout the late 1990s. Some investors made millions of dollars almost overnight and many people grew rich through the inflated stock prices. But then the bubble burst. One reason, analysts later speculated, was that everything had happened too fast and people had simply gotten greedy to make more and more. They'd overreached, and what had gone up began to come down. Now fortunes were lost as quickly as they had been made. Robinson had gotten greedy too. Before the arrival of the Internet, he'd managed to hold all of his scams and identities together. He'd been somewhat limited in the number of women he had access to at one time. Cyberspace had changed all that.

He'd used the Net to auction himself off to an unlimited number of female contacts. Then he'd picked and chosen among the most vulnerable or desperate, but his reach had also finally exceeded his grasp. By the spring of 2000, just as the dot-com businesses were starting to level off or tumble, Robinson could no longer micromanage everything and everyone he needed to. His hunger for more and more women finally consumed him. And then his bubble burst.

Before long, investigators had linked to Robinson a sixth missing person, Lisa Stasi, and then a seventh, Catherine Clampitt, and then an eighth, Paula Godfrey. No one knew what the final number might be. Apparently, no one knew much about Robinson, either, including his wife and children. Following his arrest, they released a statement saying that they did not recognize the person whom media reports were making out to be a monster, the epitome of evil in cyberspace. That was not, as far as they could tell, a description of their husband or father, not the man who'd married or raised them. He couldn't have been torturing and killing young women who were about the age of his own daughters, not while he was doing everything else with them, could he?

That kind of beast was not anyone his family had ever seen—and they'd been living with or interacting with him throughout the past several decades. If the reports were true and Robinson had really done these horrific things to the victims, then he must have been someone very different from the person they perceived. His life must have had parts that were never allowed to touch one another and that were always kept separate inside.

The police in suburban Kansas City had uncovered the trail of a serial killer, which in modern America was not that uncommon. As mentioned previously, the FBI has estimated that at any given moment there are between thirty and fifty serial killers in the United States, of whom ten to twelve are identified. Many of the unsolved cases are called "stranger homicides," meaning that there is no relationship between the killer and the victim. These victims are quite easy for the violent offender to locate; every major city that has prostitution, runaways, drug addicts, and street people/homeless will have unsolved homicides. For years in Vancouver, for example, there were missing women who had worked as prostitutes. Until 2001, law enforcement believed that they must have moved on to another city, then four of these women were found murdered and authorities began looking for around fifty more who they felt might be victims of a serial killer.

Many people believe that all serial killers fit the same mold and follow similar patterns of behavior, but at the FBI, we discovered that this image is false. When I was transferred to the FBI Academy in 1977, I began doing research in the area of criminal psychology and the criminal mind. The majority of the research was from a rehabilitative perspective, correctional perspective, or probation/parole perspective. No research was available from a law enforcement or investigative perspective. Criminals were identified and labeled with psychiatric/psychological terms such as *psychopath, paranoid, schizophrenia,* etc. To complicate matters, when I interviewed people like Charles Manson, they were sometimes categorized as psychopathic and at other times as schizophrenic. These terms meant little to the law enforcement community and me. I teamed up with colleague Roy Hazelwood and together we came up with three categories for violent crime: disorganized, organized, and mixed. A disorganized killer is very much what the name implies. His crimes are random and a lot of forensic evidence is left behind because of the killer's state of mind. Mental illness, drugs, and/or alcohol may affect the offender, and this will in turn affect the appearance of the crime scene. An organized killer, on the other hand, carries out well-planned and premeditated homicides, and little or no evidence is left behind linking the suspect to his crime. The mixed category often occurs when more than one offender is present at the scene or when a crime starts out well planned but then something or someone interferes with the perpetrator and things become too unpredictable or messy to control. By describing criminals and crime scenes in simple, understandable terms it became easier to profile crimes of violence. Although we had these categories, we found criminals may at times show elements from more than one category.

For example, the Nicole Brown Simpson case showed elements of both an organized and disorganized offender. The killer brought a weapon to the scene and wore gloves and a knit cap, all of which fit the organized category. However, the method and manner of Ron Goldman's death was different from Brown's. Some believe there may have been two killers and that would explain why Nicole and Ron were killed differently. It is my opinion this double homicide was the work of a single killer. Ron Goldman put up a stronger fight, and the killer did not expect this to happen. Goldman was slashed, cut, and stabbed before collapsing and bleeding to death. Nicole Brown, on the other hand, was struck in the head and was unconscious when the killer cut at her throat with such fury that she was nearly decapitated.

John Robinson appeared to be the organized type and in some ways conjured up John Gacy, who murdered thirty-three boys and young men in Des Plaines, Illinois. By day Gacy was a building contractor, was engaged in local politics, and had even had his photo taken with President Jimmy Carter's wife, Rosalynn. Gacy dressed as a clown for charity benefits and was married, but by night he was a serial killer. He was very organized during many of the murders, but he finally grew careless and was eventually arrested. Serial killer Robert Hansen (fifteen victims) was from Anchorage, Alaska. The owner of a bakery, he was married and had two children, but when his wife and children went away on trips, he turned into a different human being. He took prostitutes in his private plane into the Alaskan wilderness, and after landing at a remote area, he stripped the women naked and had them attempt to flee by giving them a head start in the woods. Then he doggedly tracked them down, like a wild animal, killing them with a high-powered rifle.

Robinson was different from these men in one primary area: his long criminal history as a scam artist. Serial killers often have pasts that involve other violent crimes, but Robinson had seemingly evolved toward violence over decades. He'd graduated from one type of criminal to the next. He was always a work in progress.

The Kansas City area had seen serial killers before, but what it was encountering in June 2000 was different from anything in the past. No one had ever heard of somebody transferring his seductive and homicidal skills directly onto the Internet. No one had seen this coming. It appeared that the world's first known on-line serial killer had just been uncovered in a mobile home park in a Midwest suburb. By the first week of June 2000, people were starting to ask a lot of questions about John Edward Robinson. What had he really done for a living? Where had his money come from? How long had he been able to get away with committing crimes? How had he fooled prison psychologists so completely? Did his wife know more than she was saying? How could he have evolved from a petty con man into the person the public was reading about in the paper—what had driven him toward such brutal acts? Why hadn't anyone understood what lay behind his facade? And what was going on in cyberspace that the average on-line user knew nothing about?

Information about Robinson began pouring in from every side. As the facts piled up—outlining his long criminal record and a string of victims going back more than thirty years—the story stretched credulity almost until the breaking point. The facts also conveyed two fundamental warnings: monsters aren't necessarily born but are made over time, and you never knew who you might encounter in cyberspace.

While the media looked for new angles and the police continued their investigations, the twin prosecution teams from Kansas and Missouri tried to find a way to work together to bring Robinson to trial. Almost from the start there was conflict. The case involved a myriad of crimes, five bodies found in two states, several different jurisdictions, three missing persons, a baby that had never been located, and a pair of DAs with distinctly different styles. If Paul Morrison resembled an old-fashioned lawman, Chris Koster evoked a handsome kid just out of college who was looking for a role on a TV show about law and order. Their backgrounds and experience added to the natural rivalry that had long existed between Kansas and Missouri—a rivalry that was about to resurface following Robinson's arrest. Morrison had grown up in Kansas City,

Kansas, while Koster, who was nearly a decade his junior, had been born on the other side of Missouri, in St. Louis. After graduating from the University of Missouri with a law degree in 1991, he'd gone to work in the Missouri attorney general's office and then taken a job at a Kansas City law firm. Three years later, his public ambitions emerged when he won the district attorney's job in Cass County, roughly half an hour's drive south and east of Kansas City. In 1998, he won the office again.

While Morrison represented one of the fastest-growing suburban areas in his state, Koster's jurisdiction had a rural feel and constituency. Morrison was used to managing and trying high-profile murder cases himself; Koster's county hadn't even had a homicide for the past couple of years. Morrison worked in a large office in a square, bland, modern-looking government building in Olathe. Koster worked in a small space across the street from the elegant nineteenth-century Cass County Courthouse, located in the town square in Harrisonville, which conjured up nothing so much as the antebellum South. With its stately courtrooms, immaculate wooden staircases, beautiful wainscoting, and crowning bell tower, the courthouse brought to mind another era and another period in the history of criminal justice, when men were summarily hanged for stealing horses. If Johnson County seemed Northern and urban, Cass County retained vestiges of the Old South. In the spring of 2000, such comparisons wouldn't have meant much if things had gone smoothly after Robinson was taken into custody—but they hadn't. Shades of the old interstate feud, fueled by the Civil War, were being rekindled.

Morrison's task force had wanted to do everything exactly by the book so that Robinson would not only eventually be convicted but later lose when he tried to appeal his conviction; he'd wriggled free of the legal system far too many times in the past. This was one reason the DA had waited so long to arrest him. What Morrison didn't want was anyone tampering with his view of how to handle the case. In one form or another, the greater Kansas City area had been victimized by this man for about thirty-five years, and unless due process was diligently carried out now, he might find a way to beat these charges. That simply could not be allowed to happen.

The first sign of trouble between the two jurisdictions came on July 6, about a month after the arrest. Chris Koster announced to a local newspaper, the *Democratic Missourian,* that his county was "ready to go" in the prosecution of Robinson. By this time, a preliminary hearing for the defendant in Kansas had already been postponed, until October, and postponed in Missouri as well. Koster went on to say that to speed things up, he was formulating a plan to transport Robinson back and forth across state lines so he could attend hearings in both states. The young DA, now taking on the biggest case of his career, seemed to be getting impatient with the process. If Kansas got to try Robinson first, and Missouri didn't get to bring him to Cass County and try him for several more years, witnesses might forget what had happened and their testimony would end up being stale or something worse.

This was all it took to push Morrison's legal and emotional buttons. These public statements were the kind of thing that could torpedo the best-laid courtroom strategies, even before they were initiated. If Robinson could somehow manage to turn this conflict to his advantage and go free again. . . . Nobody inside the Olathe courthouse wanted to contemplate that possibility. When informed of Koster's quote, Morrison fired off his response in the pages of the *Kansas City Star:*

"My understanding is there are serious legal problems with bringing a prisoner back and forth across state lines. We just can't control the variables, and it would be an understatement to say we would be playing with fire if we attempted any of that."

What Morrison didn't come right out and say was that his county had been working nonstop on the Robinson case for the past four months and had done all the legwork leading to the suspect's incarceration. It had employed numerous police and other investigators, had traveled around the nation hunting down leads and spent a lot of money doing this, had gone into the nether reaches of the Internet to find out what Robinson had been doing online, had uncovered the two bodies on the farm, and had obtained the search warrants that had led to the discovery of three more victims in Raymore. The Cass County DA and his people had shown up—after all the frustration and sweat and expense—and then reveled in the glory of the arrest and the attention of the media. There wouldn't be any case in Harrisonville, the Johnson County DA's office knew, if Morrison's crew and the Kansas cops hadn't done their job well. Because they had been diligent and successful, Robinson was locked up in one of their jails, and that was where they wanted him to stay. Until he'd been tried and convicted in Olathe, the state of Missouri and Cass County and Chris Koster could just wait.

It wasn't long before the *Kansas City Star* jumped into this controversy and came down on Morrison's side, while giving the younger DA a public spanking.

"Koster's scheme," the paper wrote, "to haul Robinson back and forth across the state line so Koster can score some prosecutorial points before Morrison should be halted in its tracks."

In the end, Johnson County prevailed and Robinson stayed put in the Adult Detention Center. He would not be traveling anywhere for a long time, except to cross the street for his court appearances. His preliminary hearing was set for the fall of 2000, but it would be postponed for months. The Cass County DA could not have imagined how long he would have to wait.

XXXVI

The next delicate issue confronting Morrison concerned Tiffany Stasi. The Johnson County DA was now faced with informing several people that the baby Don and Helen Robinson had "adopted" from his brother for $5,500 back in 1985 had not come by normal channels or from a mother who'd committed suicide. The state of Kansas was not simply charging Robinson with the capital murders of Suzette Trouten and Izabela Lewicka. In late July, the DA's office also accused him of first-degree murder in the death of Lisa Stasi and of aggravated interference with the parental custody of her infant daughter, Tiffany. In addition to these four counts, there were four more in the original indictment, ranging from sexual assault on Vickie Neufeld and Jeanna Milliron to the theft of the former's sex toys.

That summer Morrison had approached Carl Stasi, Tiffany's biological father, with the news of what had happened (Carl then submitted to a DNA test to prove that he was in fact her dad). To the relief of everyone, Carl hoped to be able to see his daughter but would not try to win custody of her. Morrison's office also informed Don and Helen Robinson where Tiffany, whom they'd renamed Heather, had come from. This led to the very touchy subject of whether Heather, now fifteen and living in the Midwest, should have her name and picture revealed by the media. Both Morrison and the Robinson couple tried to protect her, but the secret was quickly out and the *Kansas City Star* ran her high school photograph on the front page.

At a press conference, Don and Helen went public for the first time with their feelings about what his brother had done back in 1985. They did not deliver the comments themselves but had FBI special agent Dick Tarpley read them to the media:

"We too have been betrayed. . . . We have and will continue to cooperate with the authorities investigating the allegations surrounding John Robinson. We love our daughter very much. Since her adoption, which was never kept from her, we have always assumed that as she became an adult, she would be curious about her birth family. Because we were unaware whom her birth family was, it was our intention to assist her in any way possible in her efforts in identifying and locating them.

"The circumstances surrounding the investigation of John Robinson are as distressing to our immediate family as they are to the other families victimized. Our daughter is aware of the investigation and we are doing our best to help her through this difficult time."

The *other* Robinson family, comprising Nancy and her four children, put out its own statement after their husband and father's arrest. They didn't appear to have had any more grasp of his nature than did the strangers he'd been interacting with in cyberspace. Their remarks read:

"We, as a family, have followed the events of the last week in horror and dismay along with each of you. As each day has passed, the surreal events have built into a narrative that is almost beyond comprehension. While we do not discount the information that has and continues to come to light, we do not know the person whom we have read and heard about on TV. . . . [John Robinson is a] loving and caring husband and father. . . . We wait with each of you for the cloud of allegations and innuendo to clear, revealing, at last, the facts."

Robinson's daughter Christy, who was a medical emergency worker and married to a police officer, was the most aggressive in her defense of her father. The young woman was about the same age as some of the females whom Robinson had allegedly killed. She attempted to ward off strangers who tried to visit her father in jail and apparently sent out e-mails that extended her dad the presumption of innocence in the face of countless media reports that portrayed him as the Internet Slavemaster who may have killed up to eight people. (Privately, officials in Johnson County wondered if he hadn't gotten rid of some people whom they'd never heard of.)

Christy had an endless and unenviable task in front of her. Almost as soon as the news broke of Robinson's arrest, the local and national press offered up stories detailing Robinson's long criminal record and his more recent adventures into the world of on-line sex. As these reports filtered out into the metropolitan area, people rushed forward to talk about being wronged by Robinson down through the years, usually in financial ways. Some of them called the police, but others were too embarrassed to do so.

In recent years several famous murder investigations, including the O. J. Simpson case and the JonBenet Ramsey case, had generated oceans of conversation and speculation on the Net. Everyone with a computer and a modem could now play amateur detective in solving these killings, while instantly sending his or her opinions around the world. The Robinson case, the first major one with a tangible Internet connection, immediately set off a heated debate in cyberspace. The *Kansas City Star*, which took the lead in covering the arrest, set up a chat room where people could offer their views about Robinson and the murders. The dialogue centered not so much on his guilt or innocence as on alternative sexual lifestyles, which had received a lot of attention in the days following the discovery of the bodies. Some people who were a part of the S&M subculture insisted that Robinson's behavior in no way reflected the ideas or actions of members of that group. Those in the S&M community in and around Kansas City were appalled to learn of Robinson's activities. They adamantly denied that he represented anything about them and stated that they would have reported him to the authorities at once—if they'd only known what he was doing.

The key thing in S&M relationships, the posters said, was not danger but trust; you were able to enter into these situations and explore them because of the confidence and the belief you placed in another that you would not be hurt. It took more faith and more trust to do this, they suggested, than to engage in conventional relationships. In the wake of the discovery of the bodies at Robinson's farm and in his storage locker, the Internet was proving to be an educational forum, and people logging on to the *Kansas City Star* chat room gave hints for avoiding trouble in cyberspace. The main one, underlined again and again, was to meet your potential partner in a safe and public setting *before* getting involved sexually—because you never knew who this person might be.

Some of those who entered the *Star*'s chat room felt that anyone who was fooling around with sexual alternatives or with men like John Robinson was naive and inviting danger. Others said that they'd lost a relationship or marriage because their lover or spouse had hooked up with someone on-line. Others argued that these postings were nonsense because they'd developed good relationships from Internet contacts. And others accused some chat room participants of being Robinson family members in disguise, who'd logged on to explain or defend the accused man. Still others said that they'd known Robinson personally and he'd either seemed harmless or he'd swindled someone inside their own family.

The most intriguing posting came from a close relative of Suzette Trouten's, who dismissed the notion that all of the victims in this case were either looking for trouble or were self-blinded or ignorant individuals. This poster contended that Suzette was not a trouble-seeker but an intelligent young woman who was not easily taken in. According to this person, Trouten had met Robinson at least twice before getting close to him, and the man had worked the situation diligently before Suzette had agreed to take up with him. Robinson was not an obvious deviant to be avoided, but a clever man with a remarkable ability to appear normal.

Following the opening of the barrels and the identification of the victims, almost all of the dead women were described by those who'd known them as smart and resourceful people. What they had in common was that they were looking for something—or someone—to remove them from their circumstances, and especially from the economic circumstances they found themselves in. They were searching for somebody who could rescue them and offer a fast escape into a different life. In the days and weeks after the bodies were found, the papers were filled with articles from psychologists and other experts about the dangers of hunting for romance on-line. Women from coast to coast were advised in the strongest possible terms to be careful when surfing the Net for love or other forms of support. It had taken a grotesque tragedy to bring these warnings to the surface. Cyberspace had a dark side that could no longer be denied.

While all of these activities were unfolding outside Olathe's Adult Detention Center, Robinson sat in his cell and began devising his legal strategy for beating seemingly insurmountable odds. He was being charged with three murders in Kansas (of Lisa Stasi, Izabela Lewicka, and Suzette Trouten), plus three more in Missouri (of Sheila Faith, Debbie Faith, and Beverly Bonner). Chris Koster was also charging him with fifty-six counts of fraud and forgery linked to his financial scams in Missouri. As Robinson pondered the charges, the Burlington Northern & Santa Fe trains ran right behind the jail, blowing through town all day and all night long. The screech of the whistles startled some people and for others evoked freedom and movement. There was nothing like the sound of a train, especially at night, to make one feel lonesome or want to be someplace else. The constant whistles must have been maddening for Robinson, who had pursued his passions and his freedom so relentlessly. His uncounted hours of driving all over Kansas City, of cruising back and forth to his farm, of spending full days locked in conversation with women in cyberspace, of planning the next seduction, had suddenly ended. All he could do now was think and wait and try to come up with a way to win his trial. If he lost, he was looking at being the first person executed in Kansas since 1965.

Immediately after his arrest, he declared himself indigent and unable to afford legal counsel. All he had for income, he told the court, was a small government check and his wife's salary. The court accepted this claim and appointed him a three-man team, headed by Ron Evans, from the Topeka-based Kansas Death Penalty Defense Unit. The lawyers in this office, as in other similar offices across America, did this kind of work exclusively and were often regarded as the best possible defenders of those being tried on capital murder charges. They were usually not only excellent at parsing the legal fine points of capital cases but had strong personal feelings against the government putting people to death. Robinson, by saying that he could not pay for an attorney to defend himself against the state of Kansas, was given three of them who were thoroughly committed to keeping him alive.

The arrival of the death penalty team indicated not only that Robinson would be well-defended during his trial—for free—but that he was focused not so much on winning his case as on what would happen if he was convicted. Often defendants bring in death penalty defense experts only after they've been found guilty; Robinson was effectively bringing them in right after his arrest. Because the case was so complicated, and because it had led to the creation of more than twenty thousand pages of documents and had potentially eight hundred witnesses, his attorneys soon asked for more time to prepare for the preliminary hearing. They also filed forty motions challenging the evidence against their client and questioning the validity of the Kansas death penalty law. The motions were heard in the chambers of Judge John Anderson III, the son of a former Kansas governor. He ran a no-nonsense courtroom that was committed to moving through the process as quickly and efficiently as possible, but even he would come to understand that nothing in this case would happen fast. And at times, it seemed that it wouldn't happen at all.

First, Robinson's lawyers sought a delay for the October preliminary hearing. It was pushed back to November 2000. Then they sought another delay and it was pushed back further, to February 2001. Despite these developments, Robinson did make an occasional trip from the detention center to Judge Anderson's court. For these appearances, he donned a sharp blue suit and tie, looking like the legitimate businessman he'd so many times claimed himself to be. He sat quietly and calmly, gazing at the judge or the prosecutors or taking notes with a pensive expression. He grew paler and thinner, his hair going grayer and then whiter. His eyes seemed to retreat farther into their sockets. He revealed none of his gift for banter that had charmed so many people over the years.

He allowed no one in court to see his flash point of rage, which lay just below the surface of his bland expression or his smile. In an instant he could transform himself from a pleasant-looking businessman into a red-faced, foot-stomping boy throwing a tantrum. His fury emerged when he was surprised by someone (as Retia Grant had surprised him that day when he was digging a big hole in his barn) or when he came up against something he couldn't control. Now, sitting in jail, he would try to devise a strategy to control and orchestrate the legal circumstances surrounding him. Now he would do whatever he could to delay the process. His penchant for busyness had a new focus.

Fighting Back

XXXVII

John Robinson's was the most spectacular crime yet connected to the Internet, but it was only one of thousands that were being uncovered at the turn of the new millennium. In recent years, the biggest explosion of on-line lawlessness had occurred in the realm of child pornography. In 1999, the FBI had opened up fifteen hundred new cases of child porn in America alone, and many experts contended that it was the fastest-growing criminal frontier in cyberspace. In 1998, five thousand child porn Web sites had been identified by police working in high-tech crime units. By 2000, the number had grown to twenty-three thousand and the next year it climbed to one hundred thousand. Mainstream magazines like *Newsweek* were now running cover stories on the dangers of letting youngsters explore certain corners of the Net, and Web sites were providing tips and clues for how parents could protect their children from on-line predators.

By the end of the nineties nearly every week saw arrests of suspects (almost always men) who'd gone on the Net looking for a pedophilic connection but who'd instead made contact with an FBI agent or a police officer posing as a minor. When the adult tried to hook up with the "child," in a physical location, he got busted. The authorities had become adept at setting traps for these men. Even citizens were playing a role in these stings. In 1997, Randy Sluder, a Disney employee, snared a predator in Florida named Billy Charles Burgess after Sluder had told Burgess via the Internet that he was a blond-haired, blue-eyed, thirteen-year-old girl named Maggie284.

In 1998, the U.S. Customs Service broke up the largest Internet child porn ring yet uncovered. Called Wonderland, it had buyers and sellers in at least twelve countries and thirty-two American cities. Numerous professional people were involved in the ring, and some of them could not cope with the consequences of their actions and the public humiliation that came with charges of being a pedophile. Within a few days of their arrests, four men associated with Wonderland—a veterinarian and a former military officer among them—committed suicide. The need for fantasy and exploitation had always existed—just as it had for John Robinson—but the Internet afforded countless more opportunities for people to explore these desires. Unlike Robinson, some of those arrested for on-line crimes were shamed into self-destruction.

In September 1999, an even bigger bust occurred when a team of computer specialists and U.S. postal inspectors entered the home of Thomas and Janice Reedy of Fort Worth, Texas. Investigators soon determined that the Reedys' Internet business, Landslide Productions, provided access to three hundred child porn sites around the globe, reaching thousands of people across the United States and nearly 320,000 clients worldwide. Thirty federally financed task forces were involved in the dragnet against the Landslide owners. The Reedys, parents of a nine-year-old daughter, were earning $1.4 million a month from Landslide, and at the time of their arrest, the family was living in a large suburban home and driving a Mercedes-Benz. The uncovering of this business caused postal inspectors to create Operation Avalanche, a much larger investigation into on-line child pornography, and a year later the operation led to one hundred more arrests.

Thomas Reedy was the main focus of the allegations and was given the opportunity to work with the FBI to catch other child pornographers, in exchange for a twenty-year sentence. He declined the offer and chose to go to trial, perhaps thinking that successfully prosecuting on-line child porn charges was a new and difficult case to make. He was wrong. Reedy was convicted on eighty-nine counts and his wife on eighty-seven, although she was viewed as an accomplice and received only a fourteen-year sentence. He got 1,335 years in prison—the first life sentence ever given in a federal child porn case where the defendant was not accused of actual molestation of a youngster. With Reedy's arrest and subsequent conviction, the government had made a huge statement to potential on-line predators: you didn't have to harm children physically to be put away forever. You only have to take illicit pictures of kids or buy and sell their photos on the Internet.

In March 2002, the FBI announced the breakup of yet another vast Internet child porn ring, arresting eighty-six people in twenty-five states. Those busted in the government's Operation Candyman—Candyman was the on-line name of this group of offenders—included two Catholic priests, six other clergy members, a child photographer, a school bus driver, a preschool teacher's aide, and at least one police officer. In August 2002, the government broke up still another American and international on-line gang called the Club, which had allegedly sent out about a million child porn images, many of them depicting group members molesting their own children. By now it had become clear that those engaged in such crimes were no more obvious or exotic-looking than John Robinson. And it was frighteningly apparent that these types of criminals were proliferating at an alarming rate. But it was just as clear that the government was catching up with the cyber-criminals.

"A new marketplace for child pornography has opened up in the dark corners of cyberspace," Attorney General John Ashcroft said at the time of the Candyman arrests. "There will be no free rides on the Internet for those who traffic in child pornography."

Sex wasn't the only growing criminal realm on the Net. There were many elaborate check-kiting scams as well. In a popular one throughout the Midwest, con artists were going to the yellow pages and scanning logos from well-known corporations. Then they added that logo to a phony check they'd created by using Internet software. Then they wrote a payroll check to themselves and cashed it at a local convenience store. A small group of people would quickly do this in one major city, cashing a lot of checks at many different locations, before leaving town for the next score. In one day, they could easily cash $10,000 worth of checks. The method worked well because most convenience-store employees would not think of refusing to cash a check with a logo from a Fortune 500 company, especially not when a respectable-looking person was asking them to do this. Corporations weren't the only entities having their identities stolen. The country's largest personal-identify-theft ring, which was using databases to carry out their scam, got busted in New York in November 2002.

In the spring of 2000, the U.S. attorney's office in New York City filed charges against 120 persons, including several prominent members of organized-crime families, who were charged with allegedly swindling stock-market investors out of more than $50 million. Among those named were

Anthony Stropoli and Frank Persico, reputed associates of the Colombo crime family, and Robert Lino, an alleged capo in the Bonanno family. According to the authorities, the suspects used phony press releases to falsely hype certain stocks over the Internet to boost the price of securities that they already owned. As soon as the stock prices had been inflated, those generating the false information sold their securities and left other investors with shares that were basically worthless.

In September 2001, the use of the Internet to create much larger crimes became shockingly apparent after international terrorists flew planes into the twin towers of New York City's World Trade Center and drove another commercial aircraft into the Pentagon in Washington, D.C., killing thousands of people. Investigators eventually discovered that the terrorists had left "footprints" in cyberspace, communicating with one another through the Internet and writing cryptic messages behind on-line pictures. The attackers had employed the ancient Greek practice known as steganography—a method of placing secrets on the back of images. Following the deadliest attack ever on the United States, FBI agents set about obtaining records from Yahoo! and America Online, as well as confiscating computers that the terrorists had allegedly used in Florida and Virginia. As one part of its response to the September 11 attacks, the Bush administration created a new high-level, high-tech office designed solely to fight cyber-terror.

The age of on-line innocence was over. In less than a decade since it had achieved mass popularity, the Internet had revealed an astonishing range of abilities. It could be used as a global tool for the highest purposes of communication and education—or as a force for mass destruction. It was as good or as evil as the human beings who were punching its keys.

XXXVIII

As crime had spread across the Net, law enforcement had begun to gain ground on those using the Web for illegal ends. In 1996, the Computer Crime and Intellectual Property Section of the U.S. Department of Justice created the Infotech Training Working Group to investigate on-line violations of the law. This office evolved into the National Cybercrime Training Partnership (NCTP), and the NCTP worked with various levels of law enforcement to develop long-range strategies, raise public awareness, and build momentum to combat the problem on many different fronts. The National White Collar Crime Center (NW3C), based in Richmond, Virginia, offered operational support to the NCTP and functioned as an information clearinghouse for cyber-crime (on-line white-collar crime involves identity theft, theft of assets, or fraud). All these agencies worked together to generate more funding to help law enforcement keep up with the ever-changing computer world. Those in charge of policing the Net looked upon their mission as a battle that they could not afford to lose.

"The technology revolution is here and it is not only assisting law enforcement, it is working for the criminals," said Richard L. Johnston, the director of NW3C. "There is very little time to accomplish a lot with limited resources. We are at a crossroad. The sense of urgency to focus on program coordination, deploying a plan quickly, and underwriting every initiative with a solid base of training is real because the window of opportunity for law enforcement to keep pace with cyber-crime is not only short—it's closing."

One problem for the authorities was the difficulty police departments had in competing with private companies for computer expertise. Trained technical personnel could usually earn far more money in the private sector than working for public agencies. Near the end of his second term as president, Bill Clinton took measures to alleviate the situation by announcing plans for congressional funding for scholarships to those who studied computer security and then agreed to join the Federal Cyber Service after graduation. The program was modeled on the military one that had been successfully used by the Reserve Officers' Training Corps on college campuses.

In 1999, the FBI and hundreds of police departments around the country began using software called the Violent Criminal Apprehension Program, or VICAP, so they could share information to track kidnappers, rapists, and murderers. The software allows the agencies to send requests for information electronically and to cross-reference their investigative work, and it has led to a database holding eighty thousand cases. The program has connected vital clues found in different locations and helped solved many cases. Two examples are the Rafael Resendez-Ramirez, the Texas Railroad Killer, case, and the Samantha Runnion murder case in California. VICAP now churns out about eighty leads a month.

Also in 1999, the Training and Research Institute of

NW3C conducted an in-depth survey on white-collar violations of the law. The institute found that in part because of the recent emergence of the Internet, one in three American households were now the victims of white-collar crime. Traditional street crimes were falling in many places around the nation, but high-tech crimes were on the rise. The institute also found that only 7 percent of these on-line victims contacted a law enforcement agency. To boost this figure, in May 2000, the FBI, the Department of Justice, and the NW3C announced the creation of the Internet Fraud Complaint Center (IFCC). The new organization was established to provide a vehicle for victims nationwide to report incidents of on-line fraud (in 2002, eBay introduced a "university," where one could go on the Net and take classes that helped a person avoid cyber-fraud).

"The Internet Fraud Complaint Center allows consumers who suspect Internet fraud to share that information with law enforcement quickly and efficiently," Attorney General Janet Reno said at the time the IFCC was introduced. "Our ability to work with private citizens and industry is extremely important to our efforts to fight Internet crime, and the IFCC is a major step forward in that fight."

"The Internet," said then FBI director Louis J. Freeh, "provides a boundless new medium for many traditional frauds investigated by the FBI. That there are real victims suffering significant losses remains unchanged. This center is another positive development as law enforcement responds to yet another facet of cyber-crime."

In early 2001, the IFCC issued its first study on Internet fraud, and the numbers were significant. In its initial six months of operation, the IFCC received 20,014 fraud complaints, and 6,087 of those were referred to law enforcement agencies throughout the nation. California ranked first in Internet fraud victims and criminals, followed by Texas, Florida, Pennsylvania, and New York. The FBI does not have a statistical percentage for the clearance or solution rate, but due to the difficulty of tracing the origin of on-line fraud violation and the overall complexity of this kind of investigation, the clearance rate is currently low.

"E-business is no longer just a buzzword," said Texas State securities commissioner and NW3C board member Denise Voigt Crawford in response to this report. "It's here to stay and we must find ways to help consumers and businesses have confidence in the transaction technology they choose. Part of the commitment to our electronic-commerce community rests in law enforcement's ability to respond quickly to crime problems as they arise. To do that, enforcement professionals at all levels must have training and programs in place to prepare them to meet new challenges."

Later in 2001, the National Cybercrime Training Partnership held a number of focus group meetings and found that "electronic crime is having a profound effect on law enforcement and no agency is escaping it." After conducting a survey of thirty-one state and local law enforcement agencies responsible for training more than eighty-four thousand people to combat Internet crime, the NCTP called for more program coordination, fast-track initiatives implementation, and skills training. In its report, the NCTP listed the ten most critical issues surrounding Internet crime:

1. Raising public awareness of the problem
2. Getting citizens to report on-line crime

3. Uniform training of legal personnel
4. On-site management assistance for electronic-crime units and task forces
5. Updated laws applied at the federal and state levels—to keep pace with electronic crime
6. Cooperation with the high-tech industry
7. Special research and publications to give investigators all the research they need to fight electronic crime
8. More management support for the tools to investigate and prosecute on-line cases
9. More investigative and forensic tools to provide police with expensive up-to-date technology
10. Structuring and training computer crime units so they can best analyze electronic evidence

In May 2001, as a result of the growing sophistication on the part of law enforcement, the FBI, the Department of Justice, and the NW3C announced that criminal charges were being brought against nearly ninety individuals and companies accused of Internet fraud. The massive investigation, called Operation Cyber Loss, was initiated by the IFCC and included charges of on-line auction fraud, systemic nondelivery of merchandise purchased over the Internet, credit/debit card fraud, bank fraud, investment fraud, money laundering, multilevel marketing and Ponzi/Pyramid schemes, and intellectual property rights violations. Altogether these frauds victimized fifty-six thousand people who lost in excess of $117 million.

"Just as neighborhood watch programs keep watch over their neighborhoods and report suspicious activity to law enforcement," said Attorney General Ashcroft, "Internet users now have a 'cyber-community watch program.' When individual citizens, businesses, and consumer agencies work with law enforcement at all levels, we help ensure the safety and security of the Internet."

Government groups weren't the only ones sending out warning signals about the Net. Two Virginia-based private organizations, the National Law Center for Children and Enough Is Enough, provided information to parents, teachers, and local, state, or federal employees about the dangers of child pornography, while supporting legislative efforts to control or get rid of it. Written material produced by Enough Is Enough described child porn as a billion-dollar-a-year industry that was a threat to children "both morally and physically. . . . Any child with a computer can simply 'call up' and . . . 'print out' pictures that are unspeakably pornographic." The literature described in detail how child predators used the Internet to find kids before meeting them in person and molesting them.

"There are more outlets for hard-core pornography in America," it concluded, "than McDonald's restaurants."

(For statistics regarding these Web sites and a list of tips to avoid their dangers, see Appendices A and B starting on page 367.)

<u>Waiting Him Out</u>

XXXIX

John Robinson's preliminary hearing had originally been scheduled for the fall of 2000, but it was postponed twice at the request of his lawyers. After months of delay, the proceedings finally began on the morning of February 5, 2001, in the sober courtroom of Judge John Anderson III. With his Kansas Death Penalty Defense Unit at his side, led by Ron Evans, Robinson prepared to face the first of his accusers in court. Sitting across from the defendant was Paul Morrison and his assistant district attorney, Sara Welch. Because of the hearing, the Johnson County Courthouse had heightened security and everyone who entered the courtroom had been carefully screened. All media people had to get passes and go through a metal detector. Armed deputies were on hand, and most reporters felt that they were being watched closely. This judge wanted them to behave respectfully in his courtroom. The sense that one mistake could derail the entire process for months and months—or get a spectator ejected—pervaded the atmosphere. This was the first case in Kansas in thirty-six years that many people felt could end with an execution, and from the start it was surrounded by gravity.

Some of the victims' relatives had taken up one side of the chamber, while members of Robinson's family were sitting on the other. The scene echoed the one described in *In Cold Blood,* the Truman Capote book detailing the murder of the Clutter family in western Kansas in 1959. Six years later, Dick Hickock, a native of Olathe, along with Perry Smith, had been hanged in Leavenworth.

For five days, witnesses entered the redbrick courthouse in the Johnson County Square, while nearby bell chimes played Christian hymns and other innocent-sounding melodies. The juxtaposition of the graphic testimony and the strains of "How Great Thou Art" or Rodgers and Hammerstein's "If I Loved You" was startling. Many worlds were intersecting here at once, and this lent a surreal quality to the whole event. Lore Remington was the first witness, and her plain appearance stood in striking contrast to the gritty details of her testimony about the world of S&M. This wife and mother from Nova Scotia who looked as average and normal as Robinson shattered all preconceptions about those who take part in the sadomasochistic subculture.

While the journalists furiously took notes in stone quiet, the Robinson family members listened intently but showed no emotion, as if this information was completely foreign to the man they knew. This was the first time that Remington had ever seen Robinson in the flesh, and she tried to avoid his stare. Her voice was absolutely flat as she identified the on-line cowboy picture of Robinson that he'd sent out to so many women in cyberspace, but her demeanor was more forceful when she testified about having warned Suzette about mixing business with pleasure when she went to Kansas for what she thought was a new job. Remington conveyed the impression of someone having second thoughts about her Internet relationships. Courtroom observers couldn't help asking themselves how much her husband and children knew of her double life.

Carol Trouten, an aging blonde with a raspy voice, testified next, and unlike Lore, she could not suppress feelings toward Robinson. Her skin reddened with anger as she tried to make eye contact with Robinson, who turned away from her by scribbling on his legal pad. Suzette's mother said that her daughter was "always on the computer," but Carol admitted that she had no idea of Suzette's involvement in S&M. The prosecutors asked Carol to identify pastel-colored stationery that she thought she was receiving from Suzette. As she left the stand, Carol gave one last, long look of revulsion toward the defendant, who remained impassive. Robinson, dressed in a dark business suit, looked extremely busy throughout the proceedings, just as he had once looked so busy at Santa Barbara Estates, as if he'd now taken on the new role of attorney. He acted as though he were engrossed in a business meeting.

The only witness who took an opportunity to share her feelings about Robinson was Kathy Klinginsmith, Lisa Stasi's sister-in-law. It was to her home that Robinson had come in a snowstorm in January 1985, so he could gather up Lisa and Tiffany and take them away from her relatives for the last time. Kathy told the court that she had been terribly worried about Lisa and the baby that day and she'd wanted to chase after them once Robinson had removed them from her house, but she was "too scared" to make a move. Back then, the defendant had called himself John Osbourne. When Paul Morrison asked Klinginsmith to identify the man who'd used that name in 1985, she stared right at Robinson.

"He looks older," she said, "but he still looks evil."

Following a brief appearance by mobile-home-park maintenance worker Carlos Ibarra, Nancy Robinson was sworn in. With her daughter Christy looking on, the sweet-faced blonde, dressed in a conservative suit, took the stand. After being told by the judge that she did not have to testify against her husband, she went ahead anyway. She did not look at her spouse of thirty-six years and was inscrutable. As she laid out the details of how Robinson had brought home an infant fifteen years earlier and asked her to take care of the baby, she identified Tiffany Stasi from a family photograph. Everyone in the picture, including Don and Helen Robinson and John Robinson, looked extremely pleased with the new addition. When she left the stand, Nancy acted as if she'd never seen her husband before. If she said nothing under oath that directly hurt her husband, she also offered nothing that helped him. She did not provide an alibi for any of the time frames around any of the crimes he was charged with committing. She was cooperative with the prosecution and looked stunned at finding herself on the witness stand. In time, her testimony would evolve.

After testifying, Nancy sat in the gallery and listened as Vickie Neufeld was sworn in and recounted her sexual relationship with the defendant. Nancy, sitting just a few feet behind her husband, watched as the DA brought out the contents from the bag of sex toys that Robinson had taken from Neufeld: rabbit fur, anal vibrators, and riding crops. Nancy revealed nothing of what she was feeling as witnesses unraveled the endless list of things her spouse had done outside her marriage. The grislier the details, the more bland her expression became. The sheer variety of his lovers, as they came into the courtroom and testified, was remarkable. From Alecia Cox, the streetwise African-American woman who had managed to escape from Robinson, to Barbara Sandre, the Canadian who conjured up Tammy Faye Bakker, to the descriptions of the genital rings on Suzette Trouten and the gothic appearance of Izabela Lewicka, it was clear that Robinson's tastes ran the gamut. He had been very busy indeed.

But the most riveting testimony came from Vickie Neufeld and Jeanna Milliron, who had survived beatings by the defendant. Nancy Robinson absorbed the stories of how they had come to Kansas City looking for a relationship and ended up calling the police to file complaints about her husband. Both Neufeld and Milliron were graphic in their recounting of sex with Robinson. That Nancy could listen to all this may have given some hint as to why she had stayed in such a marriage for nearly four decades. Only someone with an extremely high threshold for denial could have endured this spectacle—especially in public. Even veteran courtroom officials were squirming at this testimony. During the breaks, women reporters gathered in the rest rooms and shared their astonishment at Nancy's lack of emotion. Perhaps she was as numb as she looked. The female journalists were surprised at how cavalier some of Robinson's sex partners appeared on the stand. Barbara Sandre, on the other hand, seemed angered and humiliated at how easily she had been duped.

When the courtroom revelations became too intense and embarrassing for some of the legal support personnel, they tittered and blushed and made jokes to ease their discomfort. Olathe had never before been exposed to such a salacious event.

At the end of the week, as a snow and ice storm descended on the metropolitan area, Judge Anderson ruled that Robinson had to stand trial on seven of the eight charges (Milliron's assault charge was thrown out). At first it seemed the trial might get under way later in 2001, but John Robinson had never been predictable and jail hadn't changed that. After numerous delays, the trial was set for January 14, 2002, almost a full year after the preliminary hearing, but this date would not be kept either.

XL

Robinson's next legal move came in the summer of 2001 when he abruptly got rid of his stellar death-penalty team and hired a new lawyer. In mid-July, Robinson fired the three highly qualified attorneys who'd been representing him for the past year and brought in a young and untested Johnson County barrister named Bob Thomas. The thirty-year-old had graduated from the University of Kansas School of Law only a few months earlier and had virtually no experience in the courtroom. Before going to law school, Thomas had been a police officer in the Kansas City suburb of Prairie Village, where Robinson's son-in-law Kyle Shipps was a detective. Thomas had been a friend of Shipps's, but indicated that the two of them had never had a discussion about the Robinson case. If the defendant had been indigent at the time of his arrest, as he'd claimed to be, and if he hadn't made any money from his cell during the past year, then one could only wonder where the money had come from to put Thomas on his payroll.

With this maneuver, Robinson became the first death-penalty defendant in Kansas history to replace his court-appointed lawyers with a privately hired attorney. The American Bar Association enforces strict guidelines for defense lawyers who work on capital cases, but Kansas itself had no such requirements for these attorneys. The ABA guidelines require that at least two qualified lawyers represent each death-penalty defendant and that both of those attorneys have at least five years of criminal defense work and have been the lead counsel in a minimum of nine jury trials. When Robinson brought in Bob Thomas, he'd been the head lawyer in only two cases and had no death-penalty experience. Thomas was an employee of veteran Olathe attorney Carl Cornwell, but the young man was apparently going to represent the defendant by himself, with no help from Cornwall.

The arrival of Thomas into the legal mix threw the case into a quandary—and the strategy behind it seemed fairly obvious. If Robinson was convicted with Thomas representing him, he might later claim on appeal that he'd been denied a fair trial because he'd had inadequate counsel. Judge Anderson now had to decide what to do to avoid such a development, while the lawyers on both sides prepared to offer their opinions on the matter. Only one similar case had ever occurred—a murder charge in Georgia in which a judge appointed an older lawyer to aid a younger one, over the protests of the defendant. The man was found guilty and then appealed on the grounds that the appointment had been illegal, but the Georgia Supreme Court upheld the judge's ruling and the conviction stood.

At a hearing to debate the issue, Paul Morrison suggested that the court appoint another lawyer to assist Thomas, perhaps someone from the Kansas Death Penalty Defense Unit, because it was already so familiar with the case. When Judge Anderson asked the unit's head man, Ron Evans, if this was acceptable, Evans said it was "not a workable situation" as long as Thomas remained the lead defense attorney. Because Robinson had hired his own counsel, Evans pointed out, this also meant that the defendant was not in fact indigent and therefore not eligible for legal representation by a state-financed office. The Kansas Death Penalty Defense Unit, which perhaps felt conned by Robinson into representing him for so many months, would have nothing more to do with the man.

When the judge questioned Thomas about his ability to handle the colossal job in front of him, the attorney said that he planned to bring in four or five support personnel but intended to be the lead lawyer on the case. This information made the DA's office nervous because it smacked of either the possibility of a successful appeal or a mistrial. The last thing that Morrison wanted was to have to try the Robinson case twice. His office now filed written arguments outlining their position that the court had a legal obligation to step in and provide the defendant with a veteran attorney. They cited both Kansas law and the U.S. Supreme Court, stating that they were aware of "no cases where a conviction has been reversed because of over-representation by counsel. We know of many convictions reversed because of under-representation by counsel, however." Under the U.S. Constitution's Sixth Amendment, they said, "the essential aim . . . is to guarantee an effective advocate for each criminal defendant rather than to ensure the defendant will inexorably be represented by the lawyer whom he prefers."

In a strange irony of the law, the prosecution was seeking better legal representation for Robinson than he'd hired.

The prosecutors said that the Robinson case would be "extraordinary in length, complexity and issues. . . . It is absurd to believe that the defendant has the wherewithal to fund effective representation in this case." In papers filed in Johnson County shortly after his arrest, Robinson had listed his income as roughly $1,000 a month, while his wife grossed only about $700 a month (one could only wonder how he'd paid for all the motel bills, phone bills, computers, travel bills for various women, the farm near La Cygne, and all the other expenses that had kept his business fronts and sexual escapades afloat). In referring to Robinson's known income, Morrison and Assistant DA Sara Welch said that they were primarily concerned that a conviction of the defendant would not hold up if he had only one privately hired lawyer because that was all that he could afford. They had "grave concerns about the ability to prevail on appeal if the defendant is convicted and Mr. Thomas is his sole counsel." The right to "select counsel must be carefully balanced against the public's interest in the orderly administration of justice."

A few days later, Judge Anderson concurred with the prosecutors' opinion. After meeting with both Thomas and Robinson, the judge said that he found the latter to be somewhat indigent and therefore qualified to receive legal assistance appointed by the court. For his part, Thomas said that he was looking forward to getting some help. All of this inevitably meant that the trial would be delayed so that new attorneys could enter the case and aid the young lawyer. Despite the many complexities that had arisen, the judge was determined to plow forward as quickly as possible.

"Make no mistake," he said, following his ruling on bringing in more defense counsel, "this is not an invitation to delay this case."

In late July 2001, Judge Anderson did something unusual by reaching across the state line and naming a pair of experienced death-penalty lawyers from Missouri to represent Robinson. Patrick Berrigan and Sean O'Brien now took over the role that had previously been played by the Kansas Death Penalty Defense Unit. Kansas had reinstated the death penalty in 1994, but Missouri's capital punishment law had been in effect since 1970, so the duo were veterans of these legal wars. This ruling satisfied Paul Morrison and the case was back on course. Although the judge had hoped to start the trial on January 14, 2002, Robinson's legal team needed more time to prepare his defense. After taking into account their request for another delay, Judge Anderson set mid-September 2002 for a trial date—and he intended that this one be kept.

So did Morrison. At the end of 2001, when he was asked by the press about his New Year's resolution for the coming twelve months, the DA said that he had only one hard-and-fast resolve for the upcoming year. He wanted to get John Robinson tried, convicted, and prepared to face the death penalty in Johnson County. That would make him a happy man.

This kind of happiness would not come easily. The case had created a legal monstrosity that was equal to the monstrous charges the defendant was facing. In January 2002, Robinson's lawyers conducted a phone survey in Johnson County to determine how the massive coverage of the case had affected the local population. They wanted to show that Olathe and surrounding residents were prejudiced against their client, and because he could not get a fair trial in this county, the court should grant a change of venue. Judge Anderson said he would take this under advisement. In mid-February, when it looked as if Robinson's defense team was finally in place, the defendant lobbed another screwball at the legal system. Bob Thomas now asked to step down from the case because one of his previous clients had been in jail with Robinson and claimed to know hidden details of the case. Marvin Ray, a thirty-four-year-old convicted thief, had been in the Johnson County Adult Detention Center in 2001 and said that he'd received information from Robinson. In the summer of 2001, Ray sent the prosecutors a letter apparently offering to testify against Robinson and contending that he'd helped a man (someone other than Robinson) and a woman transport two female bodies from Topeka to the farm near La Cygne, in exchange for two pounds of crack cocaine. Thomas told the court that because Ray had once been his client, he might have to withhold protected information about him, and this could hamper his ability to represent Robinson.

The judge listened to Thomas carefully but would not let this latest development knock the trial off course. If Thomas wanted to quit the case or if Robinson wanted to fire him because of his involvement with Ray, that was between the two of them. His Honor was ready to get this case in front of a jury, and that was going to happen relatively soon, unless something "extraordinary" occurred. In February, he ruled that the trial would go forward on September 16, 2002, and two weeks later he ruled that there would be no change of venue. Bob Thomas now left the Robinson defense team and Patrick Berrigan and Sean O'Brien took over the case. Initially, because they were death-penalty experts, Berrigan and O'Brien had intended to handle only the sentencing phase of the trial, if Robinson was convicted and facing lethal injection. That plan had ended with Thomas's departure. With the trial date only six months away, the two Missouri attorneys tried to manage the 21,768 pages of documents the DA's office had produced on the case, the forty-seven video-tapes, forty-five audiotapes, twenty CD-ROMs, and other pieces of evidence. It was an overwhelming task, and this was not the only death-penalty case that either of the lawyers was working on. During the spring of 2002, as Berrigan was trying to prepare for the trial, two of his other clients were executed in Missouri.

To make matters even more complicated, some novel legal issues surrounding computer forensics had emerged following Robinson's arrest. After sorting through the defendant's ninety-one thousand computer files, Detective Mike Jacobson had given the Kansas Death Penalty Defense Unit the relevant data on CD-ROMs, with the understanding that the unit would purchase Encase, the software program utilized by law enforcement to conduct forensic exams. In January 2001, the unit was given this data on nineteen CD-ROMs, and the lawyers in Topeka intended to access it through the Encase 2 series of software. But then the unit was dismissed from the case and by the time the data had been transferred over to the new attorneys, the Encase 2 series had been upgraded to Encase 3, making the old software obsolete. To download the Encase 2 program, one needed a password that came from purchasing Encase 3. The upshot of all this was that the defense had not been able to access the computer evidence directly. In April 2002, Jacobson gave the new Robinson lawyers about a thousand pages of hard copy—including e-mails, Web sites, and photos—based on what he'd found on the hard drives. He'd deemed roughly one thousand of the ninety-one thousand files to be pertinent to the case and tried to provide the defense with a road map of his discovery.

With these issues apparently settled, the defense began to battle over forensics. It urged the court to throw out all the evidence that had been gathered from Robinson's rural property, including the two dead women, because Detective Dawn Layman had gone onto Robinson's land and taken pictures in late March 2000 without a search warrant. The outcome of the motions regarding Layman's activities was critical because the Kansas case rested on the bodies in the barrels.

The defense also wanted to toss out the evidence taken from Robinson's rented mailbox, from his Dodge pickup, from his Olathe storage locker, and from his mobile home. They wanted to keep out information that investigators had gathered from talking with Nancy Robinson and her daughter Christy Shipps, months after Robinson's arrest. His lawyers argued that the suspect's relatives should only have been interrogated before formal charges were brought in a capital murder case. The defense also wanted to keep "gruesome photographs" out of the trial and to prevent any predeath pictures of the deceased being shown to the jury. The defense asked the state to provide them with all the records of the numerous e-mail addresses found on Robinson's computer, many of which had S&M handles. They intended to suppress the sadomasochistic devices taken from the defendant's farm, including duct tape, harnesses, and hoists. They wanted the evidence against their client severely limited, but they lost on virtually every one of these motions.

Finally, they argued that Johnson County district judge Larry McClain, who'd signed the search warrants in this case, was prejudiced toward the defendant because he'd been in the Olathe DA's office when they'd prosecuted Robinson for fraud in the 1980s. Robinson's Fourth Amendment right to protection from unreasonable search and seizure, the defense said, had been violated, and the evidence gathered from these warrants should be disregarded. On May 9, Judge Anderson ruled that because Detective Layman had not taken anything from Robinson's property on March 30, 2000, but only snapped pictures of his property, she had not violated his rights. The police had had probable cause to carry out these activities, so Layman did not commit "unlawful trespass."

After more than one hundred motions had been filed and argued in court, Judge Anderson ruled that the evidence gathered against Robinson at every locale could be used at trial. Most of the legal matters seemed to be resolved, and in the spring of 2002, Robinson was finally scheduled to face his jurors in a few short months. He then filed another motion asking that he be allowed to see his family members in "contact visits," something he hadn't been able to do since his arrest more than two years earlier. Ever since then, his relatives had been able to come to the jail during visiting hours and speak to the defendant through a thick and transparent pane of glass, but they'd had no physical contact with him. He now wanted the judge to grant him this right. The prosecutors immediately tried to quash the request, arguing that the defendant had a history of fabricating evidence, and if given the chance, he might try something like that again. The judge sided with the DA's office and no contact visits were allowed.

An uneasy quiet settled over the DA's office as they waited for September. What other legal tactics might the defendant try to employ before late summer? Were any more delays possible? Whatever else they did, all the employees of the Lenexa Police Department and the DA's office had been told and told again not to say anything to the media or anyone else that could jeopardize the start of the trial. The time to talk was when you took the witness stand.

Out in rural Johnson County, in the southern part of this jurisdiction that had not yet been overrun by new construction, the beauties of spring had come to the land. It was covered with freshly cut rows of hay and a delicately colored purple grass called henbit and liver-and-white longhorn cattle grazing in fenced pastures. Hawks flew overhead, landing on wooden posts and constantly searching the ground for prey. Fishermen unpacked their poles and tackle, which had been in storage over the long winter, then drove down to try their luck on the Marais des Cygnes River. When the summer had turned beastly hot in August and early September, and when the webworms had taken hold of the elms in Linn County, spinning their deadly white cocoons and choking the life out of the trees, John Robinson was at last going to trial for being a serial killer. The waiting was over—or was it?

XLI

As the summer waned and jury selection approached, the defense played their biggest strategic card in a year. By now, questionnaires had already been mailed out to the more than a thousand potential jurors in this case (the questionnaires held ninety-four inquiries, including one seeking their views on the death penalty). Stating that they were overwhelmed by the amount of evidence they had to digest and the number of witnesses they still needed to interview—not to mention the entangled computer issues the case had generated—Robinson's lawyers asked for yet another delay. They had, after all, only been in charge of the case for the past several months and had never dealt with anything of this nature. Without more time to prepare, the attorneys wrote in their motion, they could not fulfill their "minimum constitutional obligation" to their defendant. This was not, they argued, just another murder trial or even just another capital murder trial.

"The state of Kansas," they claimed, "has never seen a prosecution of this scale and magnitude."

For months the district attorney's office had been fearful of just this legal maneuver. In response to the defense request, Morrison and Sara Welch now filed their own papers on why the trial should go forward as scheduled. Judge Anderson had to decide if these circumstances were "extraordinary" or "catastrophic" enough to justify another postponement. Or were they just another example of Robinson trying to bend the legal system and everyone involved in it to his will? His lawyers didn't think so.

Besides Berrigan and O'Brien, two other attorneys were now helping to represent Robinson: Jason Billam and Joseph Luby. These four men had in turn hired six legal interns and paralegals to catalog and analyze the evidentiary material, plus the thousands of photographs and hours of videotapes, audiotapes, and CD-ROMs. In asking for another postponement, the defense lawyers wrote that they had devoted 1,474 hours and their support staff an additional 2,812 hours to the case.

"Nevertheless," they contended, "counsel's best guess is that we have reviewed and absorbed less than 25 percent of the material that will be relevant to the trial of this case."

They also claimed that the prosecutors had not provided them with the addresses and phone numbers for about 90 percent of the possible 649 state witnesses. Trial preparation, they wrote, would be just about complete by now if the DA's office had given them "accurate, fully informative lists of witnesses," so they could have interviewed these individuals in a timely manner. According to their position, that had not happened.

"Without such a list, preparation by September 16, 2002, is impossible," their motion said.

This was the most serious challenge Judge Anderson had yet faced. Berrigan and O'Brien were highly competent and respected defense attorneys with excellent reputations throughout the Kansas City area. They were experts in capital cases, which was why the judge had appointed them to this one. If they made a request of this urgency and gravity, it had to be thoroughly considered. On the other side of the legal aisle, the Johnson County DA's office had set aside about two months in the fall of 2002 to present their case. It had told witnesses to be ready to come to Olathe to deliver their testimony. Paul Morrison was in no mood to upset his plans or those of his coworkers. He was dealing with an accused serial killer whose life had been defined by the inability of anyone to set boundaries on his behavior. For almost four decades Robinson had done precisely what he'd wanted to do, and to an astonishing degree he'd gotten away with his activities. Now he was testing the boundaries of American jurisprudence and those who worked inside the Johnson County Courthouse. Now he would learn if he could control this game, as he'd controlled so many others, or was someone else in charge of the situation?

On the afternoon of July 25, the judge listened to the lawyers argue for four hours, carefully weighing both points of view before deciding that the defense team had not been crippled by having had roughly a full year to prepare for the trial. The system had provided Robinson with every opportunity to examine the evidence and talk to potential witnesses. His attorneys were highly qualified and experienced. The case would go forward as scheduled—with no more delays foreseen.

On August 31, two weeks before the start of jury selection, the defense team took its boldest step to date: Robinson's lawyers threatened to quit if the judge did not order another postponement. Claiming they could not adequately represent their client, they insisted that they "cannot and will not" be ready for a September 16 trial; unless they were given another eight months to prepare, they intended to walk. In their motion, Robinson's attorneys

stated that the court had been "insensitive and unresponsive" to their "earnest pleas" for more time. If they had to
begin jury selection on September 16, this would present
them with a terrible legal dilemma, "including whether it
is moral to participate in a trial where counsel's mere presence would only serve to sanitize the execution of John
Robinson."

They had not, they contended, had the opportunity to
conduct independent tests of hair, fingerprints, and DNA
evidence, which they believed included blood and hair
that belonged to someone other than Robinson or those
he'd allegedly killed. Finally, they indicated that the defendant might be showing signs of insanity, as he seemed not
to have a "rational understanding of the evidence and
charges against him." They needed to explore the possibility of mental illness in Robinson, and this would take time
as well. In early September, Dorothy Lewis, a professor of
psychiatry at the New York University School of
Medicine and a clinical professor at the Yale University
Child Study Center, examined Robinson twice. Dr. Lewis
had conducted evaluations of violent adults and juveniles
since 1971, focusing on the interaction of psychiatric disorders, neurologic dysfunction, and environmental stres-
sors as the cause of recurring violent behaviors. She was
also the director of the Dissociative Disorders Clinic at
Bellevue Hospital in New York City.

After speaking with Robinson and some members of
his immediate family, she also reviewed the available
information on his mental and medical history.

In a motion filed by the defense and written by Jason
Billam and Joseph Luby, they said, "Dr. Lewis indicates
that Mr. Robinson has a history of severe physical and
emotional abuse throughout childhood, resulting in

episodic dissociative states. History obtained independently of Mr. Robinson reflects that as many as four generations of family members may have suffered from such psychiatric illness similar to his. Dr. Lewis suspects that Mr. Robinson may suffer from bipolar mood disorder with dissociative features, although substantial additional testing and investigation is necessary to reach a final conclusion."

Based on Dr. Lewis's diagnosis, this motion said, "We have stumbled across several possible indicia of mental disease, including dissociation, emotional liability, and depression. Mr. Robinson lacks a rational understanding of the evidence and charges against him and has been unable to assist in his defense in any meaningful way. Medical records reflect that in 1987 Mr. Robinson suffered a stroke that left him temporarily disabled. MRI films made in connection with that stroke reveal abnormalities in the basal ganglia of Mr. Robinson's brain." (This diagnosis did not address the issue that Robinson was suspected of killing at least two, if not more, women prior to the stroke.)

Because of all these factors, Berrigan and O'Brien went even further in their August 31 motion for a continuance. They suggested that when they'd been appointed by the court to help the defendant's inexperienced defense team, back in the summer of 2001, they'd been misled.

"Had we known at that time how events would subsequently unfold," the attorneys said when asking for more preparation time, "the court would have received a firm, resolute and resounding NO! in response to its request."

With this motion, the defense had thrown down a legal gauntlet. Fundamental questions of due process had been raised. Had the defendant been treated fairly or hadn't he? Had the prosecutors acted appropriately toward the defense? Had Robinson's lawyers had enough time to prepare their case? Or was this just a stalling tactic? No one knew how any of this would be resolved, and all of it was happening at several minutes past the eleventh hour. Witnesses were making plans to come to the Olathe courthouse and testify. Robinson may have been mentally impaired, as his defense implied, but he appeared to be using whatever brainpower he had to slow down the process that could end in his conviction and execution.

Perhaps buried inside his lawyers' contention that the defense was not ready for jury selection was Robinson's view of himself as a victim. He was the one being dealt with unfairly, after the state of Kansas had provided him with highly qualified death-penalty counsel for a year at no cost. He was the one who wasn't ready for trial after another year had passed and the court had given him two more experienced lawyers to argue his case. He was the one who could not confront what lay ahead in the courtroom, where a procession of witnesses were going to take the stand, swear an oath to tell the truth, and lay out what Robinson had done over the past fifteen to twenty years. He was about to be exposed to the world and, more important, to twelve jurors.

On the afternoon of September 5, eleven days before jury selection would begin, Judge Anderson ruled that there would be no delay and ordered Robinson's lawyers to stay put. The case had teetered on the brink of chaos, but now it rumbled forward once again.

"We will have our trial on September 16," Judge Anderson said in his ruling, and he meant it.

★   ★   ★

Five days before the proceedings were to get under way at the Olathe courthouse, the defense lawyers filed yet another motion, stating that all of the roughly one thousand prospective jurors should be disqualified because they were already prejudiced against their client. The judge should recognize this and start the process over, sending out another thousand questionnaires to another thousand people. Months earlier, Judge Anderson had ruled against shifting the venue of the trial, even though it had generated enormous local publicity. He wasn't a man who lightly changed his rulings. On September 12, he patiently listened to the defense argument before making his final decision. The trial was set to begin and nothing was going to stop it. This coming Monday morning, the first one hundred or so of the potential jurors would be questioned by both sides, so everyone had better be prepared.

On September 16, nearly 850 days after Robinson's arrest, jury selection commenced. The largest criminal investigation in Johnson County history was about to be used in the biggest criminal prosecution ever undertaken in Kansas. Never before had one thousand jurors been called for prospective duty. Never before had Olathe—or the state—seen anything of this legal magnitude.

"The extraordinary allegations in this case," wrote the defense lawyers in one of their motions, "are unprecedented in Kansas history in the nature of the charges, the technical nature of the evidence, the span of time covered in the allegations, the extent of media coverage, and the volume of evidence generated by multiple federal, state and local jurisdictions that committed massive and unprecedented resources in the investigation of this case."

The prosecutors had quietly waited for this moment for more than twenty-seven months.

Barrels of Evidence

XLII

It had been one of the hottest and driest Kansas summers on record. By late September crops stood burnt in the fields, trees were dying alongside the roads, and cattle had been sent to market early for lack of food to fatten them up. Temperatures were still crowding a hundred degrees each day and the drought had broken open crevices in the earth. No relief was forecast. One morning, as prospective jurors rode to the Olathe courthouse for questioning, they could have tuned in a story on National Public Radio stating that in 2000 one in five Americans between the ages of twelve and seventeen had had a bad sexual encounter on the Internet. There were estimates that as many as fifty thousand people logged on to the Net on any given day looking to make illicit contact with a child or trying to sell pornographic images of youngsters.

After the potential jurors entered Judge Anderson's courtroom, they were questioned rigorously by both sides and told what to expect if they were selected. They heard about sadomasochism and other sexual games being played both on-line and off. They were asked if they could listen impartially to testimony about graphic sex and violence. Some said they could not and were dismissed. A few hinted that doing this might make them sick, but they were willing to try.

Jury selection was supposed to take five days. Those five stretched into ten and then into fifteen. The trial would have been daunting enough for most jurors if it had only centered on S&M, but the two capital charges made it much more demanding. Many prospective jurors were uncomfortable with having to decide life or death questions. Some could not put aside their feelings about this issue, and they were sent home. Over those fifteen days, nearly five hundred men and women were brought into the courtroom in small groups, but less than one out of three people made the first cut. Later on, several expressed great relief that they had not had to serve on this jury.

During the selection process, Patrick Berrigan, a big-shouldered Irishman with a mass of brown hair and a friendly gleam in his eye, showed himself to be intelligent and charming. He bantered easily with everyone and seemed humbled by the task in front of him. He moved gracefully through a near impossible job. It would have been hard to imagine Robinson ending up with better counsel. On the other side of the courtroom, Paul Morrison and Sara Welch were all business and seemed to embody inexhaustible determination and patience. They stared out from their table with the absolute focus of soldiers fighting in a trench. They'd come this far and nothing would deter them now. Morrison had hoped to call his first witness on September 23 and then September 30, but both schedules were pushed back. Finally, on Friday, October 4, twelve jurors (seven women and five men, all of them white) and five alternates were chosen.

Just before this happened and the trial was set to open the following Monday morning, Sean O'Brien made another plea for a delay:

"We shouldn't be trying this case with this panel in this county at this time. Frankly, Your Honor, we're not ready to go."

The judge disagreed. He too had come this far with this cast of characters and legal issues, and he was committed to forging ahead.

Throughout the jury selection, Robinson had sat quietly beside his lawyers, looking something like a ghost. He was extremely pale, wore a hearing aid, and had lost weight and more of his hair. He looked much older than he had two years earlier. From his blustery persona he had been reduced to a subdued, shrunken figure who looked remarkably small and harmless in his tie and dark business suit. He never made eye contact with anyone except certain female witnesses and members of his family. His skin seemed to get paler as the trial wore on. Like everyone else in the courtroom he may have been cold. Judge Anderson had set the thermostat low to keep everybody awake and alert. He knew it would be a long haul.

If security had been tight for the preliminary hearing, it was tighter now. One could not read a newspaper in the hall leading to the courtroom for fear that a headlined story about the case might prejudice someone involved in the trial. Two armed guards stood outside the courtroom and would not allow anyone inside unless there was a break. Three more armed guards were inside at all times watching Robinson and monitoring other activities in the courtroom. The lawyers were under such a strict gag order that they could not even talk about their educational backgrounds with reporters. The judge, who had a flat, forceful voice and manner, was absolutely determined to keep shenanigans out of the trial. He almost succeeded.

★ ★ ★

On Monday, October 7, Paul Morrison presented his opening remarks in a surprisingly understated fashion. He did not go in for histrionics, and even this case would not push him in that direction. He spoke for only a few minutes, soberly laying out the charges against Robinson and quietly contending that Robinson had killed women for fifteen years. He lured them and murdered them, for money or bloodlust. All seven charges in this case were part of a long-standing common scheme or course of conduct that should result in a capital murder conviction.

In his presentation, Sean O'Brien went into far more detail, describing how his client was a serial philanderer who'd been unfaithful to his wife for decades. The attorney acknowledged that these things had hurt the Robinson family and that Nancy surveilled her husband while he was having an affair. O'Brien had a soft voice and gentle demeanor. He wore a graying beard and a thoughtful expression. He seemed interested in ideas and in searching for the intellectual or psychological truth behind John Robinson, which is an unusual thing in an attorney. Like Berrigan, O'Brien was also an excellent choice to defend the accused.

He tried to counter Morrison's argument by suggesting not so much that his client was innocent as that the various charges were significantly different. They were not part of a common scheme or course of conduct, and should therefore not lead to a capital conviction. O'Brien's opening remarks set the tone for the entire defense. They raised the possibility that others might have been involved in some of the crimes (how could one middle-aged man who was not in good shape have moved those barrels by himself?). O'Brien brought up a fingerprint found on a roll of duct tape in Robinson's farm trailer—it did not belong to the defendant—and mentioned other DNA that could not be connected to him. From the beginning, O'Brien seemed to be walking a delicate legal tightrope: he didn't appear to be asking the jury for an acquittal as much as he was preparing them not to take Robinson's life.

The lawyer went into considerable detail about the BDSM lifestyle and spoke of the importance of fantasy in this subculture. He clearly did not want to tarnish the memory of any of the victims but raised the possibility that those delving into sexual games on or off the Internet were potentially courting danger. Both women and men were responsible for their actions in this realm. He pointed out that Izabela Lewicka had moved to Kansas City of her own free will to learn to be a dominatrix, and Suzette Trouten had surfed Gorean chat rooms looking for partners. Hadn't Suzette come to Olathe after placing an ad on the Internet looking for a BDSM master and Robinson had answered it? Hadn't Vickie Neufeld also consented to her relationship with the defendant? O'Brien went further, suggesting that social scientists believe that people who enjoy BDSM were sexually abused as children and associate love and affection with pain and bondage.

But the lawyer kept returning to Robinson's wife, as he would throughout the trial. Just as she'd stood beside her husband during all of his troubles and taken loyalty to new levels, she would now be his main line of defense.

"Nancy Robinson," O'Brien said, "has remained faithful to John and she will say that his main fault is his affairs. She will say that they had a normal and frequent sex life. She calls him a dreamer and he'd get euphoric about a new business opportunity. He'd carry these ideas too far and too fast. Nancy will criticize his philandering.

She'd follow him around and gather evidence. . . . She found videos and hotel receipts at storage lockers and would kick him out of the house and would demand the affairs end. The kids would beg her to bring him back. She now says that John loves her and she loves him and he loves his children. He never missed a volleyball or soccer match and was very actively involved in his children's lives."

The first witness was Carol Trouten, who created the same impression as Nancy Robinson had at the preliminary hearing but for a different reason. She looked and sounded numb, especially when talking about her deceased daughter. Resignation permeated her voice and eyes. She'd been married to the same man three different times, had raised five children, and appeared to be someone who'd seen a great deal of life, yet nothing had prepared her for what she was doing now. Unlike Nancy, she wasn't trying to save someone's life but to understand the death of her youngest girl. She also did not seem to be the sort of person who would take much comfort in helping the state of Kansas execute the defendant.

Carol was soon followed by Lore Remington, who was anything but numb. She was obviously angry and for at least several reasons. One was that because of the drawn-out jury selection, she'd had to stay in Kansas City for a number of days waiting for the trial to begin. Second, until one day earlier, she'd not been aware that the police had taped a phone conversation she'd had with Robinson on May 25, 2000. When the prosecutors now played the tape in the courtroom, as she sat on the witness stand and lowered her head, Robinson went into detail about Lore placing electrodes on her rectum for sexual stimulation as part of her training as a submissive. He gave her other orders, and as she listened to them, she visibly stiffened with embarrassment.

She'd clearly not expected these details to be revealed in open court, in front of a roomful of strangers and reporters. She acted genuinely hurt at having her secrets exposed to the world. Like many others in the BDSM realm, she'd enjoyed a fantasy life in cyberspace, an escape from her daily existence as a wife and mother. Robinson had shattered the fantasy for her just as he had for Nancy and his children. He was no more faithful to the BDSM rules than he was to the rules of conventional marriage. Until now, for people like Lore, that realm of S&M had retained its own kind of honor or innocence, but Robinson had violated the customs and taken away the innocence of sexual role-playing; you could see the effects of this on Lore's face. She was enraged at having to be on the stand.

The only thing that made her mood worse was that she did not finish testifying the first day of the trial and was supposed to stay over another night in Kansas City. To the young woman from Nova Scotia, this was intolerable. At the end of court that Monday afternoon, the judge asked her if she would be returning to the stand the following day. She defiantly said no—she was going back to Canada. The judge ordered the armed guards near Robinson to arrest Lore, and he set her bail at $25,000. The guards rushed the Canadian, grabbed her, and hustled her away. She spent the night across the street in the same jail that had been housing Robinson since June 2000. An evening behind bars did not improve her attitude. She seemed just as angry the next morning when she showed up in court and even more anxious to go home. After going back to Canada, she sent the Johnson County legal system an e-mail saying she hated them all.

One final thing had upset Lore on the stand. During her testimony, the prosecution had tried to introduce some e-mails that she'd sent to Suzette on the last known day of Suzette's life. This evidence set off a hugely complex, dragged-out debate between the prosecutors and the defense over what is an original e-mail document and what is a second- or third-generation duplicate. Can apparent originals be tampered with on-line by cutting or pasting in new information? Had that happened in this case? Should e-mails be treated as real evidence in a murder trial or as virtual evidence that can't be relied upon?

The debate had been triggered because of a time discrepancy in one e-mail between when it had been sent and when it had been received, and this led the trial into a legal quagmire almost before it could get started. Throughout the first and second day of testimony, the lawyers constantly stopped the process to run up to the bench to argue these issues. They hotly discussed all this while standing just a few feet away from the jury. The judge was so concerned that jurors would hear the discussions and be influenced by them that he ordered a boom box brought into the courtroom to play music during the bench conferences. When nobody could decide what music to listen to, Judge Anderson told the jurors just to tune in some static to drown out the talk. They did and court was filled with a low, annoying buzz.

At the end of two days of sparring over e-mail, the judge had become exasperated with how the Internet was affecting the trial.

"This is a new area of the law," he said. "The law lags behind technology quite a ways. . . . Technology creates evidentiary problems faster than the law can come up with evidentiary solutions. . . . Some of these issues are being treated in more novel fashion than they deserve."

He was tired of the arguing over what is a first-generation e-mail and what is not. Perhaps because of this, the prosecution did not do much more in this area. Following Robinson's arrest, the ninety-one thousand computer files that Mike Jacobson had so painstakingly sorted through and reduced to one thousand relevant files for the case saw almost no play in the courtroom.

Nearly every day a different group of high school students showed up to listen to testimony. They'd been sent there by their teachers to learn more about how the American government, and the legal system in particular, functioned during a criminal trial, but they were probably absorbing more about sexual behavior. From the dominant-submissive advice that Robinson had given Lore Remington on the phone to the accounts of witnesses meeting others for S&M games in Gorean chat rooms, the trial's underlying theme was how the Internet had connected people all over the nation and the world who were looking for ways to hook up with a new sex partner. The Net had opened up a fantasy world to millions.

Fittingly, the first trial of someone accused of being a cyber serial killer was taking place in a modest Midwestern setting and was filled with the testimony of modest-looking people. One could not have guessed the erotic lives of these witnesses by glancing at them or known how deep the need for escape ran inside them. Individuals were never quite what they seemed to be; they were often much more than one imagined. High school students don't often picture the prospect of grandmothers (like Jean Glines) having phone sex with alleged murderers (like John Robinson). The trial was, in some ways, about sex among unglamorous people and how the Internet had unleashed so many pent-up possibilities. The case evoked all the questions and mysteries about human desire and the human longing for connection.

On the trial's third day, a local radio personality named Randy Miller sent one of his minions out to the courthouse to give away T-shirts. They were emblazoned with the words "John E. Robinson Trial 2002 Roll Out The Barrels." In smaller letters, the shirts read, "Of Evidence." The incident outraged the defense team, which asked for a change of venue. Judge Anderson denied their request, but was agitated over the matter. From the bench, this gray-haired, stern-looking man, who projected complete humorlessness, acknowledged that if he said what he really felt about the T-shirts, that would "not be a good thing."

XLIII

The state called 110 witnesses, including Izabela
Lewicka's parents, Don Robinson, Kathy Klinginsmith, Barbara Sandre, Alecia Cox, and Vickie Neufeld.
After testifying, Don Robinson surprised everyone by
walking over to the defense table and shaking his older
brother's hand. Kathy Klinginsmith had no doubt been
coached by the prosecution since her outspoken appearance at the preliminary hearing. On this occasion, she did
not say that Robinson looked evil (the kind of characteri-
zation that can cause a mistrial). While Kathy testified,
members of Carl Stasi's family looked on from the gallery,
including a teenage cousin of Tiffany/Heather. The cousin
bore a haunting resemblance to both Lisa and her daughter, who had by now grown up and become a teenager herself. Some people in court could not take their eyes off the
cousin; it was as if one of the dead women had shown up
at the trial of her murderer.

On the stand, Barbara Sandre looked mortified at having been dragged into this mess, Alecia Cox retained the
confident swagger she'd previously displayed in court,
and Vickie Neufeld seemed quite shaky. She was not
pleased when defense attorney Jason Billam brought up
that after she'd returned to Texas following her violent
engagements with Robinson in April 2000, she'd sent

him a positive-sounding e-mail about their time together. The complexities of adult sexuality had surfaced again. Quoting from her e-mail, Billam read, "These fantasies were pure joy and more fun than anything I've ever encountered."

After listening to her testify, the judge told the prosecution that he wanted to throw out the sexual battery charge that Neufeld had brought against Robinson. She was not concerned for her physical safety when visiting the defendant in Kansas City, the judge suggested, but worried that if she didn't go along with his sex games, he would not help her find a job. After some minor resistance from the DA, Judge Anderson dropped the charge. This meant that both of the original sex assault counts—brought by Jeanna Milliron and Neufeld—had now been tossed aside. Without saying as much, the judge had made it clear that if adults came together to participate in BDSM relationships, they needed strong evidence to accuse their sex partner of committing a crime.

The most intriguing prosecution witness was Nancy Robinson, who arrived in court well dressed and freshly coiffed. She wore a handsome cream-colored suit with a blue blouse, her blond hair sweeping around her cheek in a youthful curve. Despite her best efforts to make a good appearance, her mouth looked defeated and she walked with a slump. On the stand, she appeared to be working hard to maintain control of herself and not to show anger toward Paul Morrison. The DA remained cool. Morrison was relentlessly folksy, dropping his *g*'s from words like *talking* or *laughing,* but underneath his friendly manner lay a forceful prosecutor. When someone under oath did something unexpected and made him livid, as Nancy Robinson would while testifying, his down-home demeanor would suddenly vanish.

From time to time, Robinson's youngest daughter, Christy, showed up in the courtroom as a spectator. She stared at her father with a fierce protectiveness and conveyed her love for the man. She gave one a glimpse into his home life, but not nearly as much as his wife did. Nancy made the Robinson household real as no one else could have. She described the three computers that sat side by side in the office of their Olathe residence. She'd used one of them to trace the roots of her family tree, and another was for her grandchildren to play games on. The third was the machine Robinson had logged on to in the mornings after Nancy had gone to work; this computer had guided him through cyberspace in his endless quest for more and more women. It had taken him into some of the darker recesses of the Internet and led to several of his affairs in local motels. But those affairs, Nancy pointed out, took place in the daytime. Regardless of what he did when the sun was up, she told the jury, "My husband was always home in the evening." (Robinson was, as Morrison once told the *Kansas City Star,* an "8 to 5 serial killer.")

During the trial, I couldn't help looking at Nancy Robinson as a victim who was verbally, emotionally, and psychologically browbeaten. I believe that she was dominated and controlled by her husband in every aspect of her life. She became dependent on him and as the years went by her self-esteem was affected. Her goal was to keep the family together with the hope that as her husband grew older, he would lose interest in other women. Unfortunately, Robinson and people like him do not change their interests; their need to take advantage of and harm others does not lessen. They will stop only if they are caught or die.

Under cross-examination by O'Brien, Nancy lightly ventured into Robinson's family background, as if she were laying the groundwork for more psychological testimony to come. What she now told the court caused her to pause and start crying.

"His relationship with his mother was not very good," she said. "His mother was very cold. There really wasn't a relationship between him and his mother."

Nancy underlined the animosity between Robinson and his mother by saying that her husband didn't even want to see his parents after the birth of his first child.

O'Brien questioned her in depth about March 1, 2000, when the DA believed that Suzette Trouten had been killed at the farm. Phone records had established that someone had made a call from the farm at 11:43 that morning. The prosecutors had used this phone record to conclude that Robinson had finished with the killing and was about to return to Kansas City to pick up Suzette's dogs, check her out of the Guest House Suites, and put some of her possessions into storage. By October 2002, the authorities had spoken to Nancy a couple of times and had queried her under oath during the preliminary hearing twenty months earlier. During none of her prior discussions with the prosecution had she mentioned where her husband had been over the noon hour of March 1, 2000, but now she seemed to remember much more.

She told the court that at around 11:30 A.M. on the first, she'd noticed John driving by her office in his pickup to go get one of his grandchildren at school. When she went home for lunch that day, both her husband and her daughter Christy were there. Nancy also said that when she came home from work that evening, John had cooked dinner for her.

Her testimony stopped Morrison cold, and now it was his turn to try to keep his emotions in check. On his redirect examination of the witness, he questioned why she'd never before brought up seeing her husband with his grandchild around noon on March 1, 2000. How could she have suddenly remembered that today? Nancy was unflappable. She deflected Morrison's inquiry and stood by what she had just said—just as she'd stood by her husband since the early 1960s. Morrison looked incredulous. His scalp had turned pink but he decided not to push her any harder.

It was the defining moment of the trial. It was also the defining moment of the thirty-eight-year marriage of John and Nancy Robinson. If a determined group of women— Carol Trouten, Lore Remington, and Tammy Taylor— had come together to work with the police to get Robinson arrested, the women in his family had now banded together to try to save his life. No matter what he'd done, Nancy tried to convey, his virtues as a father and husband had to count for something. While testifying, she indicated that she'd considered divorce back when her kids were small, but she'd never taken that option because her children loved their father and "wanted him back." In more recent years, she'd thought about leaving him again, but she "never went through with a divorce because of our grand-daughter." What she'd learned about her husband since his arrest had apparently not diminished her feelings for him. She told the jurors that she "always loved him but I don't understand this."

Murders often produce an odd chemistry. It was impos-sible to say what John Robinson would have done or how his criminal career would have developed if his wife and children had left him back in the 1960s or 1970s. But it was possible to believe that his domestic stability and the love of his family had anchored him in such a way that he could be relatively normal at home and a monster in other places. It was possible to believe that he could go out and do horrendous things knowing that he could always return to those who perceived him as a basically good and productive man. It was as if he had to leave the house to express his violence so he could come back and be peaceful inside the home. Then the rage and violence would build up all over again, perhaps from trying to be a good husband and father. He was like a lot of men who don't fit that comfortably into domesticity; his solution was not to leave the marriage but to kill. The two things—the outer world where he unleashed his rage and the inner world where he tried to be loving to others—were somehow kept in balance for many, many years. Each one fed the other until he was caught.

Perhaps the most frightening thing about Robinson was that everything people said about him was true. He may have been a good father and grandfather and an asset in the community with his involvement in civic affairs. He genuinely seemed to like children. He was a decent provider and his four kids had all turned out well. When they came forward after his arrest and said they did not know the person they were reading about on the front page of the *Kansas City Star,* they were likely telling the truth. If the crimes in the paper were horrifying, there was something equally horrifying about living this closely to someone for decades and never peeking through his facade. The man who was on trial for beating Suzette Trouten to death with a blunt instrument one March morning had gone home that day and made a nice dinner for his wife. He was considered an excellent baby-sitter for his grandchildren.

What was more terrifying than how deeply our own minds could fool us?

Nancy was not present for the trial's most lurid part. On Monday morning, October 14, the prosecution presented the video of Robinson and Suzette having sex in the motel room, which had been seized during a search of his Olathe storage locker. The thirty-nine-minute film was not shown until after the prosecution and the defense had argued heatedly in front of the judge without the jury present. Ironically, Morrison and Welch only wanted the jurors to see six minutes of the tape. The defense countered by saying that the edited version was misleading and biased, showing their client in a highly negative light; if the jurors were going to see any of it, they should see all of it. After ruling in the defense's favor, the judge announced that anyone under the age of eighteen had to leave the courtroom. The jurors were brought in, the lights were dimmed, and a screen was lowered right in front of the jury box and the defense table.

The tape began with a radio playing in the background in the motel room and a naked Suzette lying on a bed and penetrating herself with a buzzing dildo. The businesslike atmosphere of the courtroom had immediately shifted. It was as if everyone had been thrown into the middle of an XXX-rated theater. As the sex and the chatter unfolded in front of reporters, legal personnel, spectators, and one nun (there to support the death-penalty defendant), people had different reactions. The judge and all of the attorneys looked down, acting as if they were trying to take notes, but that's hard to do in the dark. The journalists craned their necks to see everything on the screen. An elderly couple in the gallery stared at the screen with stunned expressions, and some jurors had covered their eyes. Even with eyes covered, one could still hear the echo of the buzzing dildo throughout the courtroom and the demeaning violence of Robinson's words directed at Suzette, as he called her a "bitch" and a "slut" and a "whore." As for the defendant, he now came alive with what seemed to be pleasure for the first and only time during the six weeks of jury selection and testimony. He leaned over in his chair as far as he could to get a better look at the action, and he appeared quite pleased with his performance.

Thirty-nine minutes is a very long time. Halfway through the tape, people were looking at their watches and doing other things to avoid the porn film. It was extremely strange to see the defendant prancing around nude, just a few feet from the jurors' faces. When the tape approached its conclusion and the golf balls emerged from Suzette, this only added to the shock permeating the room. What made the scene even more surreal was that as the video neared its end and the sex finally stopped, everyone saw a fragment of *Willy Wonka and the Chocolate Factory* pop up on the screen. Nothing could have underscored Robinson's double life, as doting grandfather and sexual predator, any better. When the tape was at last over and the court took a recess, several women gathered in the rest room and reviewed what they'd just seen. A couple said they could only attribute the stamina of Robinson, who was fifty-six when the video was shot, to Viagra.

The next civilian witness was the deeply religious Retia Grant, one of Robinson's neighbors at his farm. She was a great relief from the tensions and strain that had accumulated in the courtroom during the film, and she brought with her some much needed comic relief. In detail, she described how, in the fall of 1999, she'd inadvertently come up on Robinson in his barn when he was digging two trenches. She talked about how she'd startled him that day and the obscenities he'd aimed at her because of this. Retia was moving along fine through her testimony until Sara Welch asked her to repeat for the jurors the expletives Robinson had used after she'd surprised him.

This was more than the devout Retia could do. She didn't use that kind of language anytime or anywhere and she could only convey such thoughts by saying "blankety-blank." She did this for the jury until Welch, who was not at all prissy, insisted that the witness be more explicit. When Retia still balked, Welch explained to her that this was the one and only time in her life it was not only all right to use bad language, it was necessary.

Clasping her hands in front of her as though she were starting to pray, the petite brunette looked up at the heavens and in her best Midwestern twang said, "Sweet Jesus, forgive me!"

The whole courtroom erupted into laughter and even the defendant got a chuckle.

Then Retia cut loose with the F-word.

All levity ended when the prosecutors introduced pictures and videos of Suzette and Izabela being removed from the barrels found on Robinson's farm, as well as some autopsy photos. Once again, these images were strongly challenged by the defense team. Not only did they find them highly prejudicial, they did not want the jurors to have the option of revisiting them during their upcoming deliberations. Morrison countered this argument by simply saying, "Judge, as grisly as this may seem, this case is about dead women in barrels." Judge Anderson concurred and allowed in some of the images, as well as others of Lewicka lying nude on green-and-maroon-patterned sheets in an apartment Robinson had rented for her.

The trial had already featured several disturbing moments, but nothing could quite match what the jurors were about to see. In the color video, it was jarring enough to watch the lids being removed from the barrels, but then came a direct view of the purplish, decomposing bodies. It was now clear why the lawyers, during the drawn-out jury selection, had gone to such lengths to make sure that the people they picked had strong constitutions. Being on any jury is hard work; being on this one could have brought on recurring nightmares.

The autopsy photos were even more unsettling. The courtroom was dark and absolutely silent as still photos were shown of the two women after they'd been removed from the barrels and laid out on plastic sheets. Their bodies were yellowish and shapeless, their faces featureless, and they looked more like alien life-forms than human beings. A close-up showed Suzette's head partially covered by a blindfold, and other photos showed both women's peeled-back scalps, revealing the fatal wounds. The pictures reinforced the true brutality of how they'd died and the force needed to inflict such damage. During the display of the video and the photos, Robinson had no reaction at all. He too seemed totally numb.

The various images of Suzette presented to the jury were the most haunting of all. The juxtaposition of her nude body and lively, gregarious personality—as seen on the porn video—and her dead, shrunken figure lying on the plastic sheeting was alarming. The life force that had been so present in her one instant and gone forever the next conjured up the value and the fragility of every human being. In both the video and the autopsy photos, she was wearing the same nipple rings connected by the same butterfly pendant. Her life and her death could be felt by anyone witnessing these images. The prosecution had five other murder victims to focus on, but they built the bulk of their case around Suzette. Her story was more recent than any of the other victims', and it was perhaps more poignant. In twenty-seven years, the one and only time she had left her mother and her home to wander out into the world on her own, she never came back.

Studying her pictures, the jury looked pale and grim.

XLIV

Morrison's next legal maneuver was to roll the eighty-five-gallon yellow barrels into the courtroom on metal pallets and position them a few feet away from the defendant. This strategy was effective because the barrels stood in such sharp contrast to the subdued mauve colors of the courtroom and the dark suits of the lawyers. You could not stop looking at them, and the DA would leave them there for part of the duration of his case. In private, the two-hundred-pound Morrison had climbed into one of the barrels and had a female assistant roll him around in order to prove that a single individual could move a full barrel. Something about the yellow barrels standing naked in open court hour after hour could not be forgotten. They made a fantastic story extremely real.

Day after day, Morrison brought in a parade of criminologists and other expert witnesses to testify about the evidence recovered from Robinson's home, his farm, and his storage lockers. They'd found his DNA on many of the pastel envelopes that had been sealed and mailed out to various relatives of the dead. They'd counted up the amount of money he'd taken from several of the victims over the years: he'd cashed alimony checks from Beverly Bonner worth about $14,000 and Social Security checks from Sheila and Debbie Faith worth about $80,000. The experts talked about how Izabela's blood had been found on duct tape at the farm and on the walls of the apartment she'd occupied at Edgebrook. Suzette's blood was positively identified on the wallboard in the farm trailer. Traces of violence had been left behind at each of the locations and were now presented to the jury.

After offering nearly three weeks of testimony, the state rested. For the past few days, the courtroom had been abuzz with what to expect from the defense. Would they bring Robinson's children or at least his most loyal daughter, Christy, to the stand and have her talk about her father's goodness? Would they bring Nancy back to bolster what she'd already said about her husband? Would Dr. Dorothy Lewis, the Yale psychiatrist who'd examined Robinson in September, be sworn in and speak to the jurors about child abuse in the defendant's background and how this had led to mental illness? Or would Robinson's lawyers save some of these witnesses in case their client was convicted on the capital charges and needed them to testify in the death-penalty phase of the trial? Would they then be used to ask the jury to spare his life?

In the end, the defense put up less of a fight than many people had expected, and after presenting only three insignificant witnesses, they abruptly rested. Maybe they'd decided to save their energy for the appeals process that would automatically follow a death-penalty conviction. Or maybe they'd felt, as they'd been saying for months, that they simply hadn't had time to prepare for a trial this massive or to examine the mental health of their client in depth. Near the end of presenting his case, O'Brien again sounded this theme.

"We haven't had adequate opportunity," the lawyer told the judge, "to develop these issues."

Then O'Brien added, "The jury will know nothing about how crazy this man is. He has been on suicide watch since the beginning of the trial."

Once more Judge Anderson held firm, saying that Robinson had had plenty of time to get ready for trial. It had been his decision to change lawyers twice since his arrest, and he was the one responsible for all the delays.

Hearing this, O'Brien sat down and looked genuinely distraught. Like Berrigan and the other defense attorneys, he'd conducted himself well in tough circumstances throughout the long trial. He'd gently tried to raise doubts in the jurors' minds and introduced them to the S&M subculture with sensitivity and discretion. He'd been polite, soft-spoken, and thoughtful with all the witnesses, even when they were severely damaging his case. He'd consistently acted as if he cared not only for the defendant's family members, but for the defendant himself. On one occasion at the defense table, when Robinson's suit collar had been ruffled, O'Brien leaned over and straightened it out, patting his client on the back.

It was standing room only in the courtroom for the closing arguments, and some people had to be turned away at the door. The gallery was jammed with journalists, spectators, Johnson County courthouse employees, law enforcement personnel, plus relatives of the victims and the man on trial. The barrels had been brought back into court and put up front, by the judge, where everyone could see them.

Morrison began by saying that it was hard to come up with terms to describe a man like John Robinson, but one that did fit him was "sinister."

"Sinister," the DA said, moving toward the big yellow

barrels, "in that he's JR, J. Osbourne, or others, always luring vulnerable people. Sinister, in that we've got rotting
bodies in the barrels."

As he said this last word, Morrison reached over and
lightly tapped the lid of one barrel. The hollow sound
echoed throughout the room and hung eerily in the air.

"Sinister," he went on, "in that he took a baby from
her mother, and sinister in that Sheila and Debbie Faith,
in her wheelchair, were murdered and put into barrels.
You wonder, did Debbie watch her mother get murdered?"

As he spoke, Carol Trouten, her ex-husband, Harry, and
their daughter Dawn sat behind the prosecution table.
On the other side of the gallery, Nancy Robinson's two
daughters, Christy and Kim, sat on either side of her.
They stared straight ahead and Christy kept her arm
around her mother.

Morrison began talking about Suzette and how in her
diary she'd mentioned a fantasy of being blindfolded and
serving her master.

"She's a master's dream," the DA said. "You saw the
tape. . . . If you want to put that tape in—it's in evidence—
close your eyes and just listen [to Robinson say], 'Who
owns you, bitch? Who owns you? You give your life to your
master,' as she sucks his penis. She was valueless to him."

Nancy listened and did not flinch. Christy gave her
mother a hug.

"Suzette wanted a twenty-four/seven master-slave
relationship," Morrison said, "but it's hard to do that and
to pretend to be a husband and grandfather. So what did
he do? Killed her and put her in a barrel."

The DA tapped the lid again and let the empty sound
echo around the room. "Like a piece of valueless trash."

The Trouten family absorbed the words and looked on the verge of tears.

Robinson, Morrison continued, had not only made a phone call from his farm at 11:43 A.M. on March 1, 2000, but that call had been to his wife. This remark was personal and directed right at Nancy: the DA had not forgiven what she'd said during her testimony.

Morrison shifted away from Suzette and said that Izabela Lewicka had been killed after Robinson had taken up with his new girlfriend, Barbara Sandre.

"Lewicka died," the prosecutor said, "so his new girl-friend could have new furniture. This is a guy who puts his signature on one of his victim's paintings. She was in a bar-rel for about nine months." He tapped the lid again and let it echo.

"We'll prove this case not only beyond a reasonable doubt, but beyond any doubt."

Sitting in the gallery this morning was a woman who'd dated Robinson a few years earlier. She had the same name as a famous person and claimed to be writing a book about the defendant. His lawyers had wanted to keep her out of the courtroom, but eventually she'd got-ten in. She was heavyset and had a reddish tint to her hair. She was friendly and periodically spoke to the reporters present, saying that Robinson had been a lot of fun to go out with because he gave you so much attention.

"He gave you all the attention you wanted," she said.

When they were dating, she'd believed that he was not married because he carried with him divorce papers to prove that he was single. She'd wanted to pursue their relationship, but after a while she'd realized that he was lying to her about a number of things, and the lying had driven her away. She now sat in court each day and stared at the back of Robinson's balding head, studying him and taking a lot of notes. She wore an expression of deep curiosity, as if she'd seen or learned something from him that she didn't really want to know about people. Once, when she was asked if she'd ever considered Robinson insane, she instantly replied, "No. Not insane, but evil. The lies were evil."

One early evening after the trial had recessed and the sun was going down, she left the courthouse wrapped tightly in her overcoat, leaning into the cold wind, her reddish hair blowing as she made her way steadily up the sidewalk. Her refusal to swallow the lies may have been the only thing that had kept her from being interred in a barrel.

Sean O'Brien made the closing statement for the defense, and his argument was as probing and gentle and intelligent as everything else he'd done in the courtroom. He tried to undermine the prosecution's notion that all the crimes in this case were connected by a common scheme or course of conduct, pointing out that they had occurred over many years and in very different circumstances. He said that a lot of unanswered questions remained about the evidence, and that other people may have been involved in the murders, and not all of the killings were premeditated, and for these reasons the crimes were not necessarily connected to one another.

"If there is reason to doubt this," he said, "you must find the defendant is not guilty of capital murder. If even one of you has a reasonable doubt that this is capital murder, then you go to first-degree murder. . . . If you find him guilty of first-degree murder, the sentence goes to the judge and you all go home."

He seemed to be asking less for an acquittal than for mercy from the jurors, and for them not to execute the defendant. And as he continued to speak, he revealed just how educational defending John Robinson had been for him and how much he'd learned about the Internet changing people's lives. This veteran defense lawyer had never seen anything quite like this trial before, and O'Brien, more than anyone else in the courtroom, gave voice to the thoughts that had permeated the entire proceeding.

"One obstacle in this case that makes it difficult for us," he told the jury, "is that it's rooted very deeply in fantasy. I didn't know that this existed in the world until I was appointed to this case. We've all stepped through the looking glass together. . . .

"Common sense is only of limited value in this case. Common sense never told me that men and women surf the Internet looking for these relationships . . . and that people go to distant cities to have sex with people they only met on the Internet. Common sense never told me that people derive sexual pleasure from pain. Or that people like John Robinson and Lore Remington have BDSM relationships by day and go home to families at night. . . .

"Is there any doubt in our mind that we are talking about damaged people? What happens that brings people together in these activities? Dr. Neufeld might try to convince you that this is a perfectly normal thing between consenting adults. There are people in the world who need the fantasy to make sense of what's in their lives."

Then he quoted perhaps the most famous words ever written by Henry David Thoreau—"The mass of men lead lives of quiet desperation." The comment was oddly appropriate because the case had been filled with average people hunting for a little something extra from life, something that took them away from their isolation or desperation and gave them a certain hope. They'd wanted to be attached to something larger than themselves, and the Net had been the doorway.

Near the end of his speech, O'Brien reiterated things that had come up before—that no hair or DNA of Robinson's had been found on the barrels and that a palm print on the plastic covering one of the barrels remained unidentified. He suggested that in the future some of these lingering questions might be answered and it would make the jurors "look at this case in a different light. . . . How much kinder will you be to yourself if you make a mistake and err on the side of the angels? It would be easy in a case like this to take something other than the high road. We ask only for a verdict that is just and true."

Morrison got to speak last and he quickly attacked O'Brien's use of the Thoreau quotation.

"These lofty words," he said, "don't have much to do with extramarital affairs, BDSM, torture, and death, do they?"

Then he tapped the barrel a fourth time and let the hollow sound echo again.

"There is *no evidence*," he said, "that anyone else had anything to do with these women in their last days."

The force of this last sentence had caused his face to darken.

The one common thread in all these crimes, he told the jury, was John Robinson and that all of the women had come to him looking for something more, whether it was travel, money, a job, or a relationship. The only thing that evolved over time was the nature of his sexual involvement with some of them and the technology he used to lure them to Kansas City.

"In John Robinson's world," Morrison said, "when he's done with you, he throws you away. These are trash barrels for John Robinson and tombs for his victims."

He tapped the lid slowly now, seven times in a row, and let the taps spread out through the room.

"Can you think of a better, faster way of killing someone than a couple of blows to the head? Only Sheila Faith had a defensive wound."

All of those checks from Beverly Bonner and the Faiths, he said, lined Robinson's pockets while they sat dead in the barrels for at least half a decade.

"The misery this defendant has inflicted all those years is beyond human comprehension," he said. "This is your opportunity to hold the defendant accountable for his actions."

He stared right at the jurors and his folksy manner was gone.

"I hope you do."

XLV

Following the closing arguments, some members of the viewing public lingered outside the courthouse in the square, as they often do when a murder trial is about to conclude. They wanted to hang on for a little while longer to the special feeling of community these events create. The case had brought a feeling of movement and excitement to the heart of Olathe and to the coffee shop that sat catercorner across the street. All day long people chatted in the shop and watched the lawyers coming and going and the TV trucks that circled the courthouse, broadcasting fresh reports on the trial at noon and then again in the evening. All day long police sirens and train whistles bounced back and forth across the square. The coffee drinkers provided a running commentary on everything that happened in the courtroom, from the sex toys to the motel video to the arrival of the yellow barrels. The trial was the most riveting thing that had happened here in recent memory, and by the last week of October it was almost finished.

The hundred-degree days that had lain on eastern Kansas at the start of jury selection had given way to damp and foggy forty-degree weather. The leaves on the oaks and maples in the square had turned red and orange and purple, before falling and collecting in the gutters. They blew across the courtyard and rattled on the ground. The fountain in the center of the square, holding the sculpture of the two pioneer children, had been turned off for the winter and would soon be drained. The wooden benches surrounding it were empty, and the gazebo, which had seen picnics and barbecues at the time of Robinson's arrest in June 2000, was all but abandoned now, except for a few smokers trying to escape the bitter wind.

On Tuesday, October 29, after deliberating for eleven hours, the jurors found Robinson guilty of all six charges. His daughter Christy had come to the courtroom for the verdict, and when her father was led in that afternoon to face the judge and jury, she looked at him and mouthed the words "I love you." When the verdict came down, he showed no emotion, but Christy began crying and quickly left the courthouse, covering her head with her coat. Kathy Klinginsmith and Betty Stasi, who was Lisa Stasi's mother-in-law, were also there, and they too began weeping. Carol Trouten had "no comment" on the verdict and did not seem much relieved by what the jurors had done, but resigned to what lay ahead.

After giving the jury a day off, the judge began the sentencing phase of the trial. Would Robinson become the first man to be executed in Kansas in the past several decades, or would he receive life in prison? Before this phase could begin, Sean O'Brien asked the judge to delay this part of the trial so that more psychological testing could be done on the defendant, but again the judge had said no.

The state called no witnesses but the defense was expected to be quite aggressive in arguing for the jurors to keep Robinson alive. Nancy Robinson was their key witness and she gallantly made her last appearance on the stand in Judge Anderson's courtroom. It was her job, finally, and no one else's, to save her husband from the grave. She called the thought of him being put to death by the state "devastating, absolutely devastating." She said that her family members "have listened to the facts presented in court but they grew up with someone else"—not with the man who'd been convicted of these terrible crimes. Sometimes denial is the only option left, and it is not just denial about another but also about oneself. What kind of a person would she be, after all, if her husband had really done all these things over all these years and she hadn't even noticed? How do you live with that self-image?

She talked about Robinson's four children and seven grandchildren, describing how "he was everything" for these youngsters. She mentioned that soon after his arrest, one of his granddaughters had visited him in jail and seen him wearing the standard prison garb, an orange jumpsuit. She'd run up to her grandfather and given him a big hug.

"Papa," the child had told him that day, "orange is not your color."

Hearing these words spoken in court by his wife, Robinson lowered his head and cried publicly for the only time since his incarceration.

In his twenty years as a prosecutor, Paul Morrison had never asked a jury to put someone to death, until now. He and his office, which was only a handful of steps down the hallway from Judge Anderson's courtroom, were determined to see Robinson not just convicted, but executed. That meant finishing the business at hand and taking on the defendant's wife one more time. Morrison did not seem to relish this task, but it had to be done.

While cross-examining Nancy, he asked her if she had any reasons to leave her husband now—after hearing about all of his affairs with women both living and dead. This question did something that his others hadn't been able to do and broke through her politeness and self-control.

"I don't know," she fired back at him, her eyes flaring with anger. "I don't know."

"It's not," the DA said, "a great description of a family man, is it?"

"It's not a great description of a great husband," she conceded.

Instead of pushing harder and trying to get her to show more of her emotions to the jury, the DA decided to back off.

On Friday, November 1, the two sides made their closing arguments for the sentencing phase. Morrison raised the possibility that if Robinson was allowed to live, he might get hold of computers in prison and start playing his cyber-games with women all over again. The defense said that would not happen and contended that he would not be a threat to anyone behind bars. Taking his life, Berrigan told the jury, would bring "grief and loss" to his family.

Morrison spoke of how Robinson had been moved to tears only once during the trial, when Nancy had recounted her granddaughter visiting him in jail.

"He did not cry for Suzette Trouten," the DA said. "He did not cry for Izabela Lewicka. He cried for himself. That says it all. He doesn't care about anybody but himself."

Berrigan asked the jury for compassion for his client: "I'm not telling you that John Robinson is deserving of mercy. We don't give mercy to people who deserve it. We choose to give mercy to people who do not deserve it. . . . In granting it, we're almost godlike. We don't have to kill this man."

Morrison was up against a worthy opponent and death-penalty expert in Berrigan, and perhaps that caused him to reach farther down into the emotional well than he ever had before. He told the jurors that Robinson had denied the victims the "tender mercies" of life. He'd taken away their right to hear the sound of rain coming down on a rooftop or to enjoy a fresh cup of coffee in the morning or to watch a sunrise or simply to sit and talk with people they loved. Yet now John Robinson was asking them, the jury, to grant him the tender mercies of his own life inside of prison for as long as he would live.

Capital punishment, Morrison concluded, was only for the most severe crimes and the worst criminals.

"If not him," he said, looking at the defendant, "who?"

The jurors left the courtroom and deliberated for about three hours on Friday evening but were unable to make a unanimous decision. They took a brief vote before retiring to their hotel rooms for the night: eight were for the death penalty while four were uncertain. The next morning they went back to work at 9 A.M. and within a few minutes all twelve had voted to execute Robinson. After taking this vote, they spent a few moments in silence to think about what they'd just done. A male juror had brought with him from his hotel room a Gideon Bible. When the silence was broken, he began talking about how various scriptural passages had helped him conclude that it was all right for Robinson to die. Other jurors listened to what he was saying, and word of his unexpected comments quickly filtered back to the judge. His Honor was about to come as close to panicking during a trial as this sober Kansas gentleman ever did.

The news now reached the lawyers on both sides.

Morrison tried to dismiss the Bible incident as a harmless error, but inside he was deeply concerned. He knew that this one act by a lone juror could derail the entire prosecution and void the conviction. To his extreme dismay, the defense immediately asked for a mistrial. The judge had to make one more difficult ruling.

During the next five hours, Judge Anderson individually questioned each juror about the biblical passages in question, saying that they could play no role whatsoever in the deliberations. He was painstakingly assured and reassured by every juror that the passages had not affected anyone's decision. At 3 P.M. the judge sent the jury back into the deliberation room with a final instruction to disregard the Bible. Thirty minutes later they came back and said they'd once more reached a unanimous decision: John Robinson was to be put to death.

For his sentencing, the defendant stood but again showed no reaction to the final verdict. Suzette's sister Dawn Trouten had come to the courthouse that afternoon because she'd wanted to see the look on Robinson's face if he received death.

"I'm sorry he deserves to die," she later told the *Kansas City Star.* "A death sentence is what we were hoping and praying for . . . if there had to be a purpose to my little sister's life, it's that she stopped this man from hurting another soul."

Her remarks carried an underlying irony and truth: the very women Robinson had wanted to control had ended up controlling him—even from the barrels. Ultimately, the power of women over him was greater than his ability to destroy them. He'd been conquered by those he'd sought to crush.

EPILOGUE

The appeals process following a death-penalty conviction could go on for years. Now that the Kansas trial was over, Robinson was also scheduled to go on trial in Cass County, Missouri, in the spring of 2003 for the murders of Beverly Bonner and the Faiths. Eventually, he would likely be transferred to a prison in Lansing, Kansas, near Leavenworth, to await execution. His stay in the Olathe jail across from the courthouse had cost taxpayers about $80,000. Since 2000, he'd been represented by a total of eight lawyers at a cost of around $500,000. The total expense of prosecuting him in Kansas was estimated by the *Olathe Daily News* to be about a million dollars.

Once he'd been transported to Lansing, he would spend twenty-three hours a day in an eight-by-ten-foot cell. For an hour each day he would be moved into a ten-by-twenty-foot yard with a pull-up bar and a basketball hoop. If all of his appeals failed, he would be allowed a last meal from the prison kitchen or given as much as $15 worth of food from a local restaurant. Then Robinson, who as a promising youngster had once sung for the queen of England and been kissed by Judy Garland at the Palladium, would be led into his last room. There his body, wrists, and ankles would be strapped to a gurney and two IV catheters would be inserted into his veins. As many as thirteen witnesses could watch as sodium pentothal entered his bloodstream first and put him to sleep. Pancuronium bromide would then stop his breathing and potassium chloride would stop his heart. He would become the twenty-fifth man executed in the history of Kansas.

★   ★   ★

About a month after the death-penalty verdict, a few jurors indicated to the *Kansas City Star* that they hadn't had much difficulty in recommending Robinson for execution. It might have made a difference, they said, if one or more of the defendant's children had come into the courtroom during the sentencing phase and asked them to spare their father's life, but that hadn't happened. During their first set of deliberations, a couple of jurors had taken the opportunity to examine the evidence more closely and to handle the yellow barrels for themselves. They'd wanted to see how much the barrels weighed and if one person could move them by himself, even if it contained a body. The jurors were satisfied that one man could do this alone. The jurors also talked about how hard it had been for them to watch the video of Suzette Trouten and Robinson in the motel room; even with their eyes closed, the sounds and words were still terribly disturbing. The group that had sat in judgment of Robinson had bonded during this ordeal, and with their work as a jury done and the holidays approaching, they'd made plans to get together outside the courtroom.

By now autumn had descended on eastern Kansas. The damp fog had given way to cold, driving rains that knocked the last leaves off the branches and turned the fields into standing bodies of water and mud. The rain came down in sheets and made the land seem grayer and more open all the way to the horizon. Winter was coming fast. The naked limbs of the elms down by La Cygne had dropped their big cocoons holding the webworms—the maggotlike creatures were at last gone for the year and would not return until next summer. Everything in the countryside that had not yet died was about to. The snows would soon fall and cover the rolling landscape with a blanket of white.

APPENDIX A

Back in the late 1980s, Donna Rice gained national notoriety and unwanted fame when the notorious photo of her sitting in then presidential candidate Gary Hart's lap was flashed around the world. The scandal eventually died down and Rice went on to marry someone else and change her name to Donna Rice Hughes. With the emergence of the Internet, she became one of the leading crusaders in the fight against child pornography. She regularly appeared on TV and spoke passionately about the problem, she wrote at length about it, and she created a Web site called protectkids.com. She became an expert on cyber-behavior and put together statistics on the subject, accumulated from many different sources. The numbers and the sources, which are available on her Web site, reveal the effect of the Net on many American households. Some of the findings include:

- On-line pornography was the first consistently successful e-commerce product.
- In excess of forty thousand individual URLs contain child pornography, pedophilia, and pro-pedophilia content.
- According to Nielsen//NetRatings, 17.5 million surfers visited porn sites from their homes in January 2000, a 40 percent increase compared with four months earlier.
- Thirty percent of all unsolicited e-mails contain pornographic information.
- Web surfers spent $970 million on access to

adult-content sites in 1998 and this number is expected to rise to more than $3 billion by 2003, according to the research firm Datamonitor.

- Cyber-porn—including videos and accessories ordered on-line—accounted for 8 percent of 1999's $18 billion e-commerce sales.
- Fifty-three percent of teens have encountered offensive Web sites that offer pornography, hate, or violence. Of these, ninety-one percent unintentionally found the offensive sites while searching the Web.
- Sixty-two percent of parents of teenagers are unaware that their children have accessed objectionable Web sites
- Pornographers disguise their sites by using "stealth" sites. These can use common brand names such as Disney, Barbie, and ESPN and are designed to entrap children.
- The bulk of teenagers' on-line use occurs at home, immediately after school, when working parents are not at home.
- Students are most at risk for cyber-sex compulsions due to several factors: greater access to computers, more private leisure time, and increasing sexual awareness and experimentation. Those teaching computer classes need to be aware of this vulnerability and institute prevention strategies.
- Sixty percent of all Web site visits are sexual in nature.
- Sex is the number one searched-for topic on the Internet.
- Twenty-five million Americans visit cyber-sex

sites one to ten hours per week; 4.7 million Americans visit these sites more than eleven hours per week.

- Of all born-again Christian adults in the United States, 17.8 percent have visited sexually oriented Web sites.
- Sixty-three percent of men attending Men, Romance & Integrity seminars admit to struggling with porn in the past year. Two-thirds are in church leadership and 10 percent are pastors.

APPENDIX B

Here are my tips for helping adults and kids avoid the dangers of on-line predators. For adults they include:

1. Do not give out personal information about yourself or anyone else on-line.
2. Become more computer literate and Internet savvy. It's important for those who want to explore in cyberspace to educate themselves about Net lingo and rules of conduct—the so-called Netiquette.
3. Certain words and symbols mean very specific things in cyberspace and have strong sexual connotations. Stalkers can identify the innocent and the naive (or "newbies") by their lack of Net sophistication and will regard them as prey.
4. Avoid a physical description of yourself in your on-line profile. When going into a chat room, you should choose a genderless screen name. Don't flirt on-line unless you're prepared for the consequences.
5. If a situation becomes hostile, log off or surf elsewhere. Don't confront the offender yourself, as this only escalates the problem.
6. Save any offending messages and report them to your service provider. Report any attacks or threats to police.
7. If you agree to meet someone off-line that you've met on-line, take along a friend and always meet in a public place.

8. When making on-line purchases, make sure a Web site has a stated privacy policy about not giving out your e-mail address or personal information to other companies or individuals.

9. Be appropriately skeptical of virtually everything that you read on-line. Make certain the Web site or organization you're interacting with is legitimate.

10. No e-mail is private unless it's encrypted. Never put anything on an e-mail that you wouldn't put on a postcard.

11. Block personal messages from people you don't know.

12. Participating in a chat room greatly increases your chances of receiving unsolicited pornography. Without the filtering technology to prevent this, it will come in regularly.

Here are some tips adults can share with children:

1. Never give out personal information (such as name, age, home address, phone number, school, town, password, schedule, or your picture) or fill out questionnaires or any forms on-line.

2. Never meet in person with anyone you have met on-line without mom and/or dad present.

3. Do not enter a chat room without mom and/or dad's presence or supervision. Some "kids" you meet in chat rooms may not really be kids but adults with bad intentions. Remember—people on-line may be very different from who you think they are.

4. Be suspicious of anyone who tries to turn you against your parents, teachers, or friends. They may have a hidden agenda.

5. Never respond to or send e-mail or instant messages to new people you've met on-line. Talk to your parents first so that they can check out the situation. Never engage in an on-line conversation that makes you feel uncomfortable; log off and tell your parents. If you get such a message, DO NOT respond. Sending a response only encourages the person. Instead, show it to your parents and let them handle it.

6. Use Control-H while browsing the Web to see a list of Web sites that have been accessed by your computer in the last few weeks. This can help you determine if your child is visiting any dangerous sites.

7. Install filtering software like CYBERsitter, CyberPatrol, or Net Nanny. The software costs about $50 and acts as a digital chaperon, blocking any inappropriate content. These programs work by checking which sites your child visits against a list of disapproved sites, compiled by the makers of the software.

8. Install software that will actually record images of every Web site that your child visits. The software won't stop them from accessing sites, but it will let you know if you have a problem. For truly concerned parents (or employers), you can now buy Investigator, which allows you to track every mouse click made by your child when on-line. It reads secret passwords, records everything that has been deleted, cata-

logs Web sites that have been visited, shows credit card usage on the Internet, and can even tell you what your child purchased. At present, it is the most sophisticated software yet created to spy on those in cyberspace.

9. Be a part of your children's on-line lives as well as their off-line ones. Talk to your children about what sites they visit, whom they communicate with, and who are on their buddy lists. No software will ever be a substitute for being an active parent.

ACKNOWLEDGMENTS
FROM JOHN DOUGLAS

I wish to thank my long time editor Lisa Drew for her support in writing this book. Additionally, her assistant, Erin Curler, has made the publication process run smoothly. Also, a nod to my agent, Jay Acton, who helps keep me on the straight and narrow.

ACKNOWLEDGMENTS
FROM STEPHEN SINGULAR

My wife, Joyce, was instrumental in the whole process of putting this book together. Before we had a contract with Scribner, Joyce attended legal proceedings in Kansas City for the case, she did research about the Internet, she conducted interviews with people, she was in attendance at parts of the trial, and she helped shape certain areas of the manuscript that were tied to very complicated forensic testimony. She was an important part of transferring that testimony into clear and readable sections of the book. Her help was especially critical near the end of this long process—at crunch time. I would also like to thank our editor, Lisa Drew; my agent, Reid Boates; Gerald Hay of the *Olathe Daily News*; and Sarah Hitt of the Lyndon (Kansas) Public Library.

INDEX

POCKET STAR BOOKS
PROUDLY PRESENTS

MINDHUNTER

JOHN DOUGLAS AND MARK OLSHAKER

Now available in paperback
from Pocket Star Books

Turn the page for a preview of
Mindhunter. . . .

1

Inside the Mind
of a Killer

Put yourself in the position of the hunter.

That's what I have to do. Think of one of those nature films: a lion on the Serengeti plain in Africa. He sees this huge herd of antelope at a watering hole. But somehow—we can see it in his eyes—the lion locks on a single one out of those thousands of animals. He's trained himself to sense weakness, vulnerability, something different in one antelope out of the herd that makes it the most likely victim.

It's the same with certain people. If I'm one of them, then I'm on the hunt daily, looking for my victim, looking for my victim of opportunity. Let's say I'm at a shopping mall where there are thousands of people. So I go into the video arcade, and as I look over the fifty or so children playing there, I've got to be a hunter, I've got to be a profiler, I've got to be able to profile that potential prey. I've got to figure out which of those fifty children is the vulnerable one, which one is the likely victim. I have to look at the way the child is dressed. I have to train myself to pick up the nonverbal clues the child is putting out. And I have to do this all in a split second, so I have to be very, very good at it. Then, once I decide, once I make my move, I've got to know how I am going to get this child out of the mall quietly and without creating any fuss or suspicion when his or her parents are probably two stores down. I can't afford to make any mistakes.

It's the thrill of the hunt that gets these guys going. If you could get a galvanic skin response reading on one of them as he focuses in on his potential victim, I think you'd get the same reaction as from that lion in the wilderness. And it doesn't matter whether we're talking about the ones who hunt children, who hunt young women, or the elderly or prostitutes or any other definable group—or the ones who don't seem to have any particular preferred victim. In some ways, they're all the same.

But it is the ways they are different, and the clues that they leave to their individual personalities, that have led us to a new weapon in the interpretation of certain types of violent crimes, and the hunting, apprehension, and prosecution of their perpetrators. I've spent most of my professional career as an FBI special agent trying to develop that weapon, and that's what this book is about. In the case of every horrible crime since the beginning of civilization, there is always that searing, fundamental question: what kind of person could have done such a thing? The type of profiling and crime-scene analysis we do at the FBI's Investigative Support Unit attempts to answer that question.

Behavior reflects personality.

It isn't always easy, and it's never pleasant, putting yourself in these guys' shoes—or inside their minds. But that's what my people and I have to do. We have to try to feel what it was like for each one.

Everything we see at a crime scene tells us something about the unknown subject—or UNSUB, in police jargon—who committed the crime. By studying as many crimes as we could, and through talking to the experts—the perpetrators themselves—we have learned to interpret those clues in much the same way a doctor evaluates various symptoms to diagnose a particular disease or condition. And just as a doctor can begin forming a diagnosis after recognizing several aspects of a disease presentation he or she has seen before, we can make various conclusions when we see patterns start to emerge.

One time in the early 1980s when I was actively interviewing incarcerated killers for our in-depth study, I was sitting in a circle of violent offenders in the ancient, stone, gothic Maryland State Penitentiary in Baltimore. Each man was an interesting case in his own right—a cop killer, a child killer, drug dealers, and enforcers—but I was most concerned with interviewing a rapist-murderer about his modus operandi, so I asked the other prisoners if they knew of one at the prison I might be able to talk to.

"Yeah, there's Charlie Davis," one of the inmates says, but the rest agree it's unlikely he'll talk to a fed. Someone goes to find him in the prison yard. To everyone's surprise, Davis does come over and join the circle, probably as much out of curiosity or boredom as any other reason. One thing we had going for us in the study is that prisoners have a lot of time on their hands and not much to do with it.

Normally, when we conduct prison interviews—and this has been true right from the beginning—we try to know as much as we can about the subject in advance. We go over the police files and crime-scene photos, autopsy protocols, trial transcripts; anything that might shed light on motives or personality. It's also the surest way to make certain the subject isn't playing self-serving or self-amusing games with you and is giving it to you straight. But in this case, obviously, I hadn't done any preparation, so I admit it and try to use it to my advantage.

Davis was a huge, hulking guy, about six foot five, in his early thirties, clean-shaven, and well groomed. I start out by saying, "You have me at a disadvantage, Charlie. I don't know what you did."

"I killed five people," he replies.

I ask him to describe the crime scenes and what he did with his victims. Now, it turns out, Davis had been a part-time ambulance driver. So what he'd do was strangle the woman, place her body by the side of a highway in his driving territory, make an anonymous call, then respond to the call and pick up the body. No one knew, when he was putting the victim on the stretcher, that the killer was right there among them. This degree of control and orchestration was what really turned him on and gave him his biggest thrill. Anything like this that I could learn about technique would always prove extremely valuable.

The strangling told me he was a spur-of-the-moment killer, that the primary thing on his mind had been rape.

I say to him, "You're a real police buff. You'd love to be a cop yourself, to be in a position of power instead of some menial job far below your abilities." He laughs, says his father had been a police lieutenant.

I ask him to describe his MO: he would follow a good-looking young woman, see her pull into the parking lot of a restaurant, let's say. Through his father's police contacts, he'd be able to run a license-plate check on the car. Then, when he had the owner's name, he'd call the restaurant and have her paged and told she'd left her lights on. When she came outside, he'd abduct her—push her into his car or hers, handcuff her, then drive off.

He describes each of the five kills in order, almost as if he's reminiscing. When he gets to the last one, he mentions that he covered her over in the front seat of the car, a detail he remembers for the first time.

At that point in the conversation, I turn things further around. I say, "Charlie, let me tell you something about yourself: You had relationship problems with women. You were having financial problems when you did your first kill. You were in your late twenties and you knew your abilities were way above your job, so everything in your life was frustrating and out of control."

He just sort of nods. So far, so good. I haven't said anything terribly hard to predict or guess at.

"You were drinking heavily," I continue. "You owed money. You were having fights with the woman you lived with. [He hadn't told me he lived with anyone, but I felt pretty certain he did.] And on the nights when things were the worst, you'd go out on the hunt. You wouldn't go after your old lady, so you had to dish it out to someone else."

I can see Davis's body language gradually changing, opening up. So, going with the scant information I have, I go on, "But this last victim was a much more gentle kill. She was different from the others. You let her get dressed again after you raped her. You covered up her head. You didn't do that with the previous four. Unlike the others, you didn't feel good about this one."

When they start listening closely, you know you're onto something. I learned this from the prison interviews and was able to use it over and over in interrogation situations. I see I have his complete attention here. "She told you something that made you feel bad about killing her, but you killed her anyway."

Suddenly, he becomes red as a beet. He seems in a trance-like state, and I can see that in his mind, he's back at the scene. Hesitantly, he tells me the woman had said her husband was having serious health problems and that she was worried about him; he was sick and maybe dying. This may have been a ruse on her part, it may not have been—I don't have any way of knowing. But clearly, it had affected Davis.

"But I hadn't disguised myself. She knew who I was, so I had to kill her."

I pause a few moments, then say, "You took something from her, didn't you?"

He nods again, then admits he went into her wallet. He took out a photograph of her with her husband and child at Christmas and kept it.

I'd never met this guy before, but I'm starting to get a firm image of him, so I say, "You went to the grave site, Charlie, didn't you?" He becomes flushed, which also confirms for me he followed the press on the case so he'd know where his victim was buried. "You went because you didn't feel good about this particular murder. And you brought something with you to the cemetery and you put it right there on that grave."

The other prisoners are completely silent, listening with rapt attention. They've never seen Davis like this. I repeat, "You brought something to that grave. What did you bring, Charlie? You brought that picture, didn't you?" He just nods again and hangs his head.

This wasn't quite the witchcraft or pulling the rabbit out of the hat it might have seemed to the other prisoners. Obviously, I was guessing, but the guesses were based on a lot of background and research and experience my associates and I had logged by that time and continue to gather. For example, we'd learned that the old cliché about killers visiting the graves of their victims was often true, but not necessarily for the reasons we'd originally thought.

Behavior reflects personality.

One of the reasons our work is even necessary has to do with the changing nature of violent crime itself. We all know about the drug-related murders that plague most of our cities and the gun crimes that have become an everyday occurrence as well as a national disgrace. Yet it used to be that most crime, particularly most violent crime, happened between people who in some way knew each other.

We're not seeing that as much any longer. As recently as the 1960s, the solution rate to homicide in this country was well over 90 percent. We're not seeing that any longer, either. Now, despite impressive advances in science and technology, despite the advent of the computer age, despite many more police officers with far better and more sophisticated training and resources, the murder rate has been going up and the solution rate has been going down. More and more crimes are being committed by and against "strangers," and in many cases we have no motive to work with, at least no obvious or "logical" motive.

Traditionally, most murders and violent crimes were relatively easy for law enforcement officials to comprehend. They resulted from critically exaggerated manifestations of feelings we all experience: anger, greed, jealousy, profit, revenge. Once this emotional problem was taken care of, the crime or crime spree would end. Someone would be dead, but that was that and the police generally knew who and what they were looking for.

But a new type of violent criminal has surfaced in recent years—the serial offender, who often doesn't stop until he is caught or killed, who learns by experience and who tends to get better and better at what he does, constantly perfecting his scenario from one crime to the next. I say "surfaced" because, to some degree, he was probably with us all along, going back long before 1880s London and Jack the Ripper, generally considered the first modern serial killer. And I say "he" because, for reasons we'll get into a little later, virtually all real serial killers are male.

Serial murder may, in fact, be a much older phenomenon than we realize. The stories and legends that have filtered down about witches and werewolves and vampires may have been a way of explaining outrages so hideous that no one in the small and close-knit towns of Europe and early America could comprehend the perversities we now take for granted. Monsters had to be supernatural creatures. They couldn't be just like us.

Serial killers and rapists also tend to be the most bewildering, personally disturbing, and most difficult to catch of all violent criminals. This is, in part, because they tend to be motivated by far more complex factors than the basic ones I've just enumerated. This, in turn, makes their patterns more confusing and distances them from such other normal feelings as compassion, guilt, or remorse.

Sometimes, the only way to catch them is to learn how to think like they do.

Lest anyone think I will be giving away any closely guarded investigative secrets that could provide a "how-to" to would-be offenders, let me reassure you on that point right now. What I will be relating is how we developed the behavioral approach to criminal-personality profiling, crime analysis, and prosecutorial strategy, but I couldn't make this a how-to course even if I wanted to. For one thing, it takes as much as two years for us to train the already experienced, highly accomplished agents selected to come into my unit. For another, no matter how much the criminal thinks he knows, the more he does to try to evade detection or throw us off the track, the more behavioral clues he's going to give us to work with.

As Sir Arthur Conan Doyle had Sherlock Holmes say many decades ago, "Singularity is almost invariably a clue. The more featureless and commonplace a crime is, the more difficult it is to bring it home." In other words, the more behavior we have, the more complete the profile and analysis we can give to the local police. The better the profile the local police have to work with, the more they can slice down the potential suspect population and concentrate on finding the real guy.

Which brings me to the other disclaimer about our work. In the Investigative Support Unit, which is part of the FBI's National Center for the Analysis of Violent Crime at Quantico, we don't catch criminals. Let me repeat that: *we do not catch criminals*. Local police catch criminals, and considering the incredible pressures they're under, most of them do a pretty damn good job of it. What we try to do is *assist* local police in focusing their investigations, then suggest some proactive techniques that might help draw a criminal out. Once they catch him—and again, I emphasize *they*, not *we*— we will try to formulate a strategy to help the prosecutor bring out the defendant's true personality during the trial.

We're able to do this because of our research and our specialized experience. While a local midwestern police department faced with a serial-murder investigation might be seeing these horrors for the first time, my unit has probably handled hundreds, if not thousands, of similar crimes. I always tell my agents, "If you want to understand the artist, you have to look at the painting." We've looked at many "paintings" over the years and talked extensively to the most "accomplished" "artists."

We began methodically developing the work of the FBI's Behavioral Science Unit and what later came to be the Investigative Support Unit, in the late 1970s and early 1980s. And though most of the books that dramatize and glorify what we do, such as Tom Harris's memorable *The Silence of the Lambs*, are somewhat fanciful and prone to dramatic license, our antecedents actually do go back to crime fiction more than crime fact. C. August Dupin, the amateur detective hero of Edgar Allan Poe's 1841 classic "The Murders in the Rue Morgue," may have been history's first behavioral profiler. This story may also represent the first use of a proactive technique by the profiler to flush out an unknown subject and vindicate an innocent man imprisoned for the killings.

Like the men and women in my unit a hundred and fifty years later, Poe understood the value of profiling when forensic evidence alone isn't enough to solve a particularly brutal and seemingly motiveless crime. "Deprived of ordinary resources," he wrote, "the analyst throws himself into the spirit of his opponent, identifies himself therewith, and not infrequently sees thus, at a glance, the sole methods by which he may seduce into error or hurry into miscalculation."

There's also another small similarity worth mentioning. Monsieur Dupin preferred to work alone in his room with the windows closed and the curtains drawn tight against the sunlight and the intrusion of the outside world. My colleagues and I have had no such choice in the matter. Our offices at the FBI Academy in Quantico are several stories underground, in a windowless space originally designed to serve as the secure headquarters for federal law enforcement authorities in the event of national emergency. We sometimes call ourselves the National *Cellar* for the Analysis of Violent Crime. At sixty feet below ground, we say we're ten times deeper than dead people.

The English novelist Wilkie Collins took up the profiling mantle in such pioneering works as *The Woman in White* (based on an actual case) and *The Moonstone*. But it was Sir Arthur Conan Doyle's immortal creation, Sherlock Holmes, who brought out this form of criminal investigative analysis for all the world to see in the shadowy gaslit world of Victorian London. The highest compliment any of us can be paid, it seems, is to be compared to this fictional character. I took it as a real honor some years back when, while I was working a murder case in Missouri, a headline in the *St. Louis Globe-Democrat* referred to me as the "FBI's Modern Sherlock Holmes."

It's interesting to note that at the same time Holmes was working his intricate and baffling cases, the real-life Jack the Ripper was killing prostitutes in London's East End. So completely have these two men on opposite sides of the law, and opposite sides of the boundary between reality and imagination, taken hold of the public consciousness that several "modern" Sherlock Holmes stories, written by Conan Doyle admirers, have thrown the detective into the unsolved Whitechapel murders.

Back in 1988, I was asked to analyze the Ripper murders for a nationally broadcast television program. I'll relate my conclusions about this most famous UNSUB in history later in this book.

It wasn't until more than a century after Poe's "Rue Morgue" and a half century after Sherlock Holmes that behavioral profiling moved off the pages of literature and into real life. By the mid-1950s, New York City was being rocked by the explosions of the "Mad Bomber," known to be responsible for more than thirty bombings over a fifteen-year period. He hit such public landmarks as Grand Central and Pennsylvania Stations and Radio City Music Hall. As a child in Brooklyn at the time, I remember this case very well.

At wit's end, the police in 1957 called in a Greenwich Village psychiatrist named Dr. James A. Brussel, who studied photographs of the bomb scenes and carefully analyzed the bomber's taunting letters to newspapers. He came to a number of detailed conclusions from the overall behavioral patterns he perceived, including the facts that the perpetrator was a paranoiac who hated his father, obsessively loved his mother, and lived in a city in Connecticut. At the end of his written profile, Brussel instructed the police:

> Look for a heavy man. Middle-aged. Foreign born. Roman Catholic. Single. Lives with a brother or sister. When you find him, chances are he'll be wearing a double-breasted suit. Buttoned.

From references in some of the letters, it seemed a good bet that the bomber was a disgruntled current or former employee of Consolidated Edison, the city's power company. Matching up the profile to this target population, police came up with the name of George Metesky, who had worked for Con Ed in the 1940s before the bombings began. When they went up to Waterbury, Connecticut, one evening to arrest the heavy, single, middle-aged, foreign-born Roman Catholic, the only variation in the profile was that he lived not with one brother or sister but with two maiden sisters. After a police officer directed him to get dressed for the trip to the station, he emerged from his bedroom several minutes later wearing a double-breasted suit—buttoned.

Illuminating how he reached his uncannily accurate conclusions, Dr. Brussel explained that a psychiatrist normally examines an individual and then tries to make some reasonable predictions about how that person might react to some specific situation. In constructing his profile, Brussel stated, he reversed the process, trying to predict an individual from the evidence of his deeds.

Looking back on the Mad Bomber case from our perspective of nearly forty years, it actually seems a rather simple one to crack. But at the time, it was a real landmark in the development of what came to be called behavioral science in criminal investigation, and Dr. Brussel, who later worked with the Boston Police Department on the Boston Strangler case, was a true trailblazer in the field.

Though it is often referred to as *deduction,* what the fictional Dupin and Holmes, and real-life Brussel and those of us who followed, were doing was actually more *inductive*— that is, observing particular elements of a crime and drawing larger conclusions from them. When I came to Quantico in 1977, instructors in the Behavioral Science Unit, such as the pioneering Howard Teten, were starting to apply Dr. Brussel's ideas to cases brought to them in their National Academy classes by police professionals. But at the time, this was all anecdotal and had never been backed up by hard research. That was the state of things when I came into the story.

I've talked about how important it is for us to be able to step into the shoes and mind of the unknown killer. Through our research and experience, we've found it is equally important—as painful and harrowing as it might be—to be able to put ourselves in the place of the victim. Only when we have a firm idea of how the particular victim would have reacted to the horrible things that were happening to her or him can we truly understand the behavior and reactions of the perpetrator.

To know the offender, you have to look at the crime.

In the early 1980s, a disturbing case came to me from the police department of a small town in rural Georgia. A pretty fourteen-year-old girl, a majorette at the local junior high school, had been abducted from the school bus stop about a hundred yards from her house. Her partially clothed body was discovered some days later in a wooded lover's-lane area about ten miles away. She had been sexually molested, and the cause of death was blunt-force trauma to the head. A large, blood-encrusted rock was lying nearby.

Before I could deliver my analysis, I had to know as much about this young girl as I could. I found out that though very cute and pretty, she was a fourteen-year-old who looked fourteen, not twenty-one as some teens do. Everyone who knew her assured me she was not promiscuous or a flirt, was not in any way involved with drugs or alcohol, and that she was warm and friendly to anyone who approached her. Autopsy analysis indicated she had been a virgin when raped.

This was all vital information to me, because it led me to understand how she would have reacted during and after the abduction and, therefore, how the offender would have reacted to her in the particular situation in which they found themselves. From this, I concluded that the murder had not been a *planned* outcome, but was a panicked reaction due to the surprise (based on the attacker's warped and delusional fantasy system) that the young girl did not welcome him with open arms. This, in turn, led me closer to the personality of the killer, and my profile led the police to focus on a suspect in a rape case from the year before in a nearby larger town. Understanding the victim also helped me construct a strategy for the police to use in interrogating this challenging suspect, who, as I predicted he would, had already passed a lie-detector test. I will discuss this fascinating and heartbreaking case in detail later on. But for now, suffice it to say that the individual ended up confessing both to the murder and the earlier rape. He was convicted and sentenced and, as of this writing, is on Georgia's death row.

When we teach the elements of criminal-personality profiling and crime-scene analysis to FBI agents or law enforcement professionals attending the National Academy, we try to get them to think of the entire story of the crime. My colleague Roy Hazelwood, who taught the basic profiling course for several years before retiring from the Bureau in 1993, used to divide the analysis into three distinct questions and phases—what, why, and who:

What took place? This includes everything that might be behaviorally significant about the crime.

Why did it happen the way it did? Why, for example, was there mutilation after death? Why was nothing of value taken? Why was there no forced entry? What are the reasons for every behaviorally significant factor in the crime?

And this, then, leads to:

Who would have committed this crime for these reasons?

That is the task we set for ourselves.

Visit
❖ **Pocket Books** ❖
online at

....

www.SimonSays.com

....

Keep up on the latest new
releases from your favorite
authors, as well as author
appearances, news, chats,
special offers and more.

SIMON & SCHUSTER
A VIACOM COMPANY
www.SimonSays.com

Pocket
Books